Books should be returned on or before the
last date stamped below.

D0519214

The
DEMIGODS

ALSO BY JEAN LACOUTURE

EGYPT IN TRANSITION (with Simonne Lacouture)

VIETNAM: BETWEEN TWO TRUCES

DE GAULLE

HO CHI MINH: A POLITICAL BIOGRAPHY

The
DEMIGODS:
Charismatic Leadership in
the Third World

Jean Lacouture

Translated from the French by Patricia Wolf

Secker & Warburg · London

First published in England 1971 by
Martin Secker & Warburg Limited
14 Carlisle Street, London W1V 6NN

Copyright © 1970 by Alfred A. Knopf, Inc.

Originally published in France as Quatre Hommes et leurs peuples
© 1969 by Editions du Seuil

SBN 436 24051 3

Reproduced and printed in Great Britain by
Redwood Press Limited
Trowbridge & London

In speaking, a prophet causes a green fruit to ripen in his mouth.
　　　　　　　　—*From the Ritual of the Athapaskes*

CHRISTOPHE: *I have wanted to extract the mystery of these peoples on the move.*

HUGONIN: *The people go at their own pace, Your Majesty, their own secret pace.*

CHRISTOPHE: *Blast it! The others have made it bit by bit in centuries. How are we to save ourselves at all unless we do it in great strokes of years, long inhalations of years?*
　　　　　　　　—AIMÉ CÉSAIRE, *Le Roi Christophe*

Those chosen to stand for the multitude, though they lead it, must pretend to be led by it: it is bound to demand myths. For doling out myths and images, who is better equipped than a dictator in whose unique person, that of a demigod risen from itself, the sovereign multitude can deem itself wholly reabsorbed?
　　　　　　　　—JACQUES MARITAIN, *Le Pouvoir*

Acknowledgments

The first part of this book was written between January and June 1966 at Harvard University's Center for Mid-Eastern Studies, which I attended through the gracious invitation of Professor Lockhard, who had just replaced Professor Gibb.

Through the efforts of my friend Leon Carl Brown, now a professor at Princeton, I was invited to work in the setting of that prestigious university. Without this encouragement it is unlikely that I, a journalist, would ever have entertained the idea of embarking on a semiacademic study such as this.

I am grateful for this opportunity to express my thanks for the hospitality of Professor Brown and his colleagues at the Center for Mid-Eastern Studies, which is now under the chairmanship of Professor David Landes. Professor Brown guided my initial research work and gave me helpful criticism in reading the beginning of my manuscript.

Also, I would like to thank Professors Rupert Emerson, Nadav Safran, Stanley Hoffmann, Stuart Hughes, Barrington Moore, Jr., and a number of other scholars at Harvard, M.I.T., Boston University and Brandeis for their assistance.

It was Professor Jacques Berque, of the Collège de France, who guided my work in Paris and who, on November 20, 1969, reported this thesis for a doctorate in Sociology to a committee of the Sorbonne headed by Professor Georges Balandier and assisted by Professor Maurice Duverger.

I am grateful to all of them.

—J.L.

Contents

III   *BELIEF AND RITUAL*

I

A Mid-Century
Pandemic

Concentration and
Incarnation

———◦∞◦———

*"The leader is not solely the decision maker, the
initiator. . . . He is much more: he is the incarnation of the group, its mirror, its spokesman in the
mysterious domain of power."*

—JACQUES ELLUL

While the industrial West was incarnating its vast enterprises
in "heroes" summoned in time of crisis and popularized by the
sprawling communications network it employs, while the
socialist world was unfurling giant banner-portraits of its
leaders above the heads of the working class (thus sowing the
seeds of a perversion Marx had not foreseen, and which came
to be called the "cult of personality") all during this time
"new" nations came bobbing to the surface of history.

Instead of encouraging the malleable, faceless, unsophisti
cated multitudes to oppose any such theatrical display of power,
the new nations carried it even further. They arrayed their
own demigods to confront the masters of the capitalist world
and the prophets of socialism. The personification of power,
so characteristic of our times and especially of the decade 1955–
65, has spread like a jungle in the Southern Hemisphere. So it
is tempting to infer that if power has created personification
in the West and in numerous socialist states, personification
has built power in what we call the Third World.

Though this brief surge of vigorous authority began to
subside in or about 1965 owing to the close of a particular
stage of decolonization, the appearance of new states and the

resurgence of national identities in no way detract from its significance in the field of political research.

Our study derives to some degree from what Max Weber called "the sociology of knowledge."[1] Judging from the public behavior of emerging nations, it would seem that although the study of history in its "troughs" can be rewarding, as Georges Lefebvre maintains, at the same time, we should not neglect to learn from the "crests." By your heroes shall you be known . . . We have also chosen a number of borderline cases that illustrate the political and social evolution of countries whose apparatus of myth and symbol has been renewed.

The kind of power we are examining has been established recently in certain types of states: those either newly founded, or restored from ruin, or awakened from the lethargy of colonialism. At the same time, we will be referring to nations that are said to be both older and more modern—older because of the imposition of internal and external constraints, more modern owing to completed processes of social integration and political diversification. This will allow us to deal briefly with interrelated situations.

In established societies the concept of power is woven so closely into the social fabric that we find it hard to isolate. Bertrand Russell,[2] among others, has tried: for him, power is the key factor in the social sciences, its role comparable to that of energy in the physical sciences, to sexuality in Freud's system, and to economic motivations in that of Marx. But he sees its shapes and deformities rather than its essence.

Power is best understood in relation to its absence, which is why it is especially interesting to examine the first signs of its existence in new nations. Its scope and nature emerge

---

[1] Jean-Claude Passeron has made an intensive analysis of this from another point of view (Paris: PUF; 1968).
[2] *Power* (New York: W. W. Norton; 1969), p. 90.

against the "clean slate" left in the wake of outswept colonialism. In these surroundings, power is shown to be the means
employed by the majority to control the minority: the monopoly of public violence. Like all monopolies, it can be challenged, but tends to expand. Like all violence, it has its own
season, but will recur; it is both ephemeral and permanent.[3]

Violence, which Marcuse describes as self-repressed and
self-censured, is ordinarily no more perceptible to a whole
society than combustion is to the driver of an automobile; but
the violent birth pangs of a nation are readily felt, like the
explosion occurring with the first turn of a motor crank.

Yet in what name is violence committed? Or rather, in what
name is it tolerated, accepted, acclaimed? The ability to command a group, to shape its existence and determine its behavior, is among the most curious of social phenomena. In
wartime extreme danger dictates the need for protection and
hierarchy; command goes unquestioned. But civil obedience
is more enigmatic. Rousseau considered this problem, and compared the exercise of power to Archimedes's gesture as he sat
on the riverbank and calmly motioned a large ship to approach.
Surprisingly, we are seldom aware of the strangeness of the
situation until the legitimacy of power is at stake.

So it was in France in May 1958, and again in May 1968,
when the machinery of government was "coasting," that the
levers disengaged and the official monopoly of public violence
had vanished. In May 1958, who was using it in Pflimlin's
name or de Gaulle's? And who the following year, in the name
of the General or of the vast, unorganized throng in the

---

[3] Richard MacKeon: "Most languages have a single word for these four
concepts: power, authority, force, violence," in Chevallier, et al; Le Pouvoir
(Paris: PUF; 1956–7).

Also, Maurice Duverger notes (De la Dictature. Paris: Julliard; 1961,
pp. 23–4) that the original meaning of the word *tyrant* was simply *master*
or *chief*.

streets? In both cases it was by recourse to an authority quite different from classic power that de Gaulle played upon the reflexes of a mass avid for leadership.

This is exactly the situation or type of situation we want to examine, that of nations involved in an initial process of social affirmation that progresses from the crystalization of factual power to the establishment of government, from the foundation of sovereignty to the recognition of legitimacy. This evolution, which required centuries in the West, took only a few years in lands with no tradition of political legality. Yet, judging from the remarks leveled at the heads of new states, it would seem that this process should have required only a few months.

At the same time, the stages in the consolidation of power are a subject of controversy for such authors as Max Weber and Bertrand de Jouvenel. Weber traces a graph of history running from the emergence of a "charismatic," or prophetic, leader whose authority over his disciples (and eventually over the people) derives from a "gift of grace," all the way to the establishment of a bureaucracy resulting from the routinization of prophetic inspiration and the building of tradition—which is the root and the rationalization of power, and which institutionalizes its founder's and the bureaucrats' achievement. For Jouvenel, power is generated by war, magic, or senility, and has an aura of unapproachable majesty that constitutes its divine right; but insatiable ambition drives it to prey upon social order and to make excessive use of popular sovereignty.[4]

---

[4] Georges Davy has observed that "the existence of societies will always be threatened by extreme danger. . . . This paves the way for certain individuals to reveal themselves as uniquely fitted to handle the threat by taking triumphant command. When lives depend on them, does this not proclaim and consecrate their calling to power? How could these saviors not see their chieftaincy as divinely endorsed and themselves as the embodiment of a group soul?" (Chevallier, et al, *Le Pouvoir*, p. 2.)

Both of these writers are describing the evolution of secular institutions. The developments we have to deal with occur at the rate of press communiqués. From the sounding of an emotional call-to-arms to the establishment of some form of governmental structure and the founding of institutions, progress is faster than one of Alexander the Great's campaigns or the completion of a Soviet economic plan. Though power may assume extraordinary shapes in the modern world, we should bear in mind that the burden of colonization and the rapidity of decolonization have imposed even more extraordinary conditions on new nations.

For this reason, we will have frequent cause to quote men whose responsibilities keep them more directly in contact with realities. Two such leaders, Hassan II of Morocco and Sékou Touré of Guinea, are not "case histories" in this book, but their actions and beliefs are significant in several ways.

Hassan II has said: "I am obliged to personify power as strongly as possible, for people do not obey a program or plan. They obey men, a team of men, and it is all for the best if that team is embodied in a chief and symbolized by one face, one voice, one personality."[5] And the President of Guinea, whose credo has more of a Marxist flavor, has remarked: "Of course, history is not made by men. It is made by peoples. But each people requires a man."[6]

The emergence of a leader can be the decisive factor in the chain of events linking the formation of power to recognized sovereignty. Henri Laugier maintains that two major imperatives confront new nations: *being,* which implies recognition of a national identity, consciousness of belonging to a community and sharing a common culture and common aspirations; and *having,* which means mobilizing resources and organizing development in order to break away from poverty.

[5] Statement made to the author in April 1962.
[6] From an address made in Tunis on March 30, 1964.

Both of these presuppose the exercise of authority. In his introductory course at the Collège de France in December 1968, Jacques Berque offered another duality to the peoples of the Third World: *being* (identity) and *doing* (modernizing efficiency). That new approach probably does not change the outlook so far as power is concerned. In any event, on the level of *being,* as on the levels of *having* and *doing,* authority can be exerted more effectively if embodied in a symbolic figure, a creator of collective identity and mobilizer of energies.

We are told that the rise of a hero promotes the growth of national consciousness and gives momentum to the struggles for economic development. But should this type of power, which is essential in the beginning, endure and become institutionalized? For what purpose, and in what ways?

Is it not true that the means employed to achieve group identification, cohesion, and development around and through one symbolic and pivotal figure can alter the end product? Is it not possible for the hero-catalyst-pioneer, the symbol of collective identity, to become an end in himself, a cult object, the instrument of a regression to inviolable rule? And doesn't the self-appointed messenger of modernization run the risk of being the instrument of a return to the primitive?

That is the subject of this study, which is divided into three parts: the first covers a general examination of the personification of power in the mid-twentieth century in emergent states; the second, a more detailed study of four "case histories" from the annals of the Middle East, Northwest Africa, Black Africa, and Asia; the third section attempts to draw political conclusions.

My use of the deductive method will be criticized, but perhaps the reader will understand that it is an unconscious reflex of journalism, which tends to synthesize on the humblest, most specific level.

. . .

Whether in Western countries, in the Socialist universe, or in the nations of the Third World, the personification of power assumes two different forms, which may combine or diverge, and which we will formulate as follows: *operational concentration* and *mythical incarnation*.

Operational concentration is the process whereby the leader, or a group of governing officials, assembles and controls the entire apparatus of the state, which Jouvenel calls the "machine-chamber." The phenomenon is as old as power itself, which by its very nature tends to be absolute. In this area, excess rather than equilibrium is natural.

In the small cities of ancient and medieval times, the tendencies to absolutism were sometimes checked by the existence of military, financial, or religious aristocracies; even in the seventeenth century, Bellarmin could use church teachings as his authority for braking royal power. Then came Bossuet and Rousseau: in the name of divine right, or that of popular sovereignty, the state took sole possession of everything and placed it in the hands of the sovereign, whether king or nation.

This formidable polarization has not been weakened either by advanced techniques of industrial production[7] or by the territorial expansion of states. In the name of national unity, modern methods of extending and consolidating power are used to minimize centrifugal forces, and turn a threat into an

---

[7] Lenin, defining "the immediate tasks of Soviet power" in the April 28, 1918, issue of *Izvestia*, stressed this point: "We must face the fact that every large mechanized industry, the acknowledged source and foundation of socialist production, demands a *united effort*, unfailing and absolute, on the part of tens of thousands of people in order to regulate the work of hundreds of thousands. Technically, economically and historically, this necessity is self-evident, and anyone who has given serious thought to socialism has recognized that it is one of its conditions."

incitement. The giantism of states, which threatens to dilute authority, has provided a new pretext for accentuating concentration.

Rousseau was categorical: democracy is suitable only for small republics, such as the Geneva or Corsica of his dreams. The greater the area of rule, the greater is the drive to intensify power. Peter the Great was more autocratic than the Elector of Saxony, and Richard Nixon is more so than John Quincy Adams. For a directive from Moscow to be obeyed in Kazan, the person issuing it must have a singular credibility—his voice and gestures must stir the air around him if they are to carry great distances. By lopping off heads in Paris, Saint-Just commanded obedience along the Meuse.

What we call mythical incarnation is of another nature, regardless of whether power is concentrated or not. It operates when a figure reaches the stage, more or less consciously, of symbolizing power, when a political program assumes a face and a name. Of course, this results from the rapid diffusion of audio-visual communications. Thus, the face of George Orwell's "Big Brother" in *1984*, imposed by the "telescreen," is the inescapable and obsessive image of the state. But one can reverse the idea and ask whether such an image is not the product of mass demand rather than of a bid for power.

Beginning with the situation analyzed by David Riesman in *The Lonely Crowd*, Jacques Ellul maintains (in *Propaganda*) that the public has a basic need to be propagandized. At a major conference on "the personalization of power"[8] Ellul presented his thesis this way:

> Man in mass society has the feeling of being inferior, so he summons the hero and transfers to him all the things he would like to do himself but cannot. . . . This is why

[8] Held in Dijon in 1962 under the joint chairmanship of Léo Hamon, Mabileau, and Eisenmann, it resulted in the publication of *Personalisation du pouvoir*, 1964.

the analysis of leadership as a function of command is notoriously inadequate. . . . The leader cannot be solely the decision maker, the initiator, the one who stands apart to impose authority. He is much more: he is the embodiment of the group, its mirror, its mediator in the mysterious domain of power.

The two processes described above are aptly summed up in two types of leaders found in the Arab-Moslem world: the *zaïm* and the *raïs*.

Jacques Berque defines the *zaïm* as "the individual whose person and actions signify the most basic, yet the most profound, reality: the sociological conditions that surround him within his own country." Personification, significance, authenticity—we are dealing with mythical incarnation, a process that is especially well-adapted to Arab societies, in which imagination, mysticism, and thirst for symbols play an essential role.

But another type of man is emerging as an alternative (the shift from Ben Bella to Boumediène): the *raïs*, the French *patron*, the American *boss*, the one who gets things done, who *realizes* them (the Latin word *res* and *reification* are related). He is the one responsible for operational concentration, the mirror image and complement of the premier. In many respects, he may resemble the *zaïm*. In Bourguiba, a *zaïm* who became a *raïs*, and in Nasser, a *raïs* turned *zaïm*, it is sometimes difficult to separate the two types of quality, prestige, and significance. That is why narrow definitions will be avoided in this study, which is focused upon theatricalization and the mythical aspects of power.

The two phenomena—concentration and incarnation—can appear simultaneously, as in the person of Charles de Gaulle. But they can also be successive: Stalin laid the groundwork for the concentration of power over a period of more than ten years (1924–35) before he consciously incarnated it. After the fall of Nikita Khrushchev, concentration remained, but not incarnation. Eisenhower clearly personified a power that he scarcely used, and even allowed to deconcentrate. And while personification is taking place, as in the figure of Naguib, concentration may be operating in other hands—those of Nasser. (Ultimately, Nasser will synthesize concentration and incarnation.[9])

Just as operational concentration can be achieved without recourse to an extraordinary personality, by careful exercise of bureaucratic control, by slow and persistent one-party action, by the methods of "democratic centralism," for example, so the cult of the leader can occur without concentration (Mendès-France, Fouad Chehab)—and even without power: this last situation, typically postcolonial, was that of Patrice Lumumba, a classic example of the phenomenon of projection (identification without real hold on any mechanism of power). Aimé Césaire's play *A Season in the Congo* is a psychodrama of the leader without a State.

But the mockery here is merely apparent: when searching for its identity, a people needs a face and a voice more than it needs a policeman. The risk is that in its pursuit of symbols and of rallying-signs it will find only alibis for its confusion.

---

[9]The reaction of Cairo's crowd or masses, on October 1 1970, day of solemn and frantic funeral of the *raïs*, threw a light on the strange and deep relationship existing between the leader, incarnating power and the people.

The seizure of the body by the mob and some sophisticated slogans showed how identification is bilateral, how the possessing hero is possessed, how the mandate of the people is his own property—and can be taken back by the people in a fantastic ceremony of recuperation.

That kind of power belongs to the world of psychoanalysis as well as the universe of politics, ethics and religion. There was something great there, together with something perverse. What could be Nasser's reaction, as leader of a developing society, attending Nasser's funeral?

Charisma, Leadership, Authority

―――――❧❧❧―――――

"Whom do you take yourselves for, departmental deputies, to speak as you do? The people do not know you, they know only me."
— NAPOLEON,
exhorting the legislative assembly on January 1, 1814

Personification in the form of incarnation is our subject here. The bureaucratic phenomenon will not be neglected completely, but the accent will be on what Arthur Schlesinger has called "heroic leadership," with particular attention to group psychology and the dramatization of politics.

Although we shall not completely ban all references to the "modern" political world, our focus is upon the new nations, which, having provoked the ebb tide of colonialism, are re sponsible for "dispossessing the possessors of the globe"; which have ceased to be the objects of history and have become its subjects; but remain in a state of "anomie,"[1] of a "crisis of belief."[2]

Because they still ask to be "founded," they cry out for a founding father; because they emerge from societies disoriented by colonialism and ill-fitted to handle the responsibilities of statehood or the problems of arbitrarily imposed boundaries; because they are struggling to recover long-hidden cultures, groping for their true heritage and new vocation in

[1] Alain Touraine, *Le Mouvement de mai ou le communisme utopique* (Paris: Éd. du Seuil; 1968).

[2] Maurice Duverger, *De la dictature* (Paris: Julliard; 1961), p. 43.

the world—they look for a guide. Because of the gnawing fear of "neocolonialism" (the by-product of colonialism after its laws are abolished and its policemen expelled), they are obsessed by the idea that foreign powers are forever conspiring with a fifth column. For all these reasons, the new nations consider it absolutely essential to choose tested, truly "national" leaders to represent their anxious peoples in confrontations with outsiders.

Thus, the leader is at once a destroyer of colonialist alienation and a defender against neocolonial penetration. But occasionally he serves as a glorious shield for hidden operations or as an alibi for citizens' collective refusal to shoulder their own responsibilities. In that case, the leader will have helped only to camouflage the reality of neocolonialism or of collective resignation, and the personification will seem nothing more than a childish disease of power.

Let us now try to define briefly two basic concepts: *charisma* and *modernization,* one the means, the other the goal.

The question of charisma will often arise here in connection with one or another leader. We hold to the view (which Max Weber borrowed from Rudolf Sohn[3]) that charisma is an essential ingredient of power in the situations under study. In contrast to such authors as Carl Friedrich[4] and Clement Moore,[5] we will not limit use of the term to denote powers inspired or molded by religious faith. This is the reason for Friedrich's denial that Hitler possessed charisma,[6] although in our view Hitler provides one of the most impressive ex-

---

[3] *Kirchenrecht,* Volume I (Munich: 1923), pp. 26–8.

[4] *Man and his Government* (New York: McGraw-Hill; 1963), pp. 89–108.

[5] *Tunisia since Independence* (Berkeley: University of California Press; 1965), p. 46.

[6] In an article, "The Pathology of Politics" (*Political Quarterly;* January–March 1966), Friedrich examines the concept of *manna*—the crime of opposing the leader's sacred power. He nevertheless applies the concept to Hitler, recalling the purely mystical nature of the *Hitlergruss,* the oath of allegiance to the swastika and to the Führer.

amples of it, and why Moore prefers not to use the word in speaking of Bourguiba, owing to the Tunisian leader's avowed laicism.

Despite the constant abuse of the word *charisma,* we shall use it here essentially in the sense it held for Weber: "an extraordinary duality," "a gift of grace," "a charm" that elevates the individual above ordinary men, confers "exceptional powers" on him, and confirms him "as a leader."[7]

To be sure, a less esoteric and more explicit expression would be preferable: prophetic, inspiring, surrealistic. But Max Weber's concept, like the phenomenon itself, contains elements of the irrational, of magic and mystery, that justify the term he chose. So we shall use it, fully aware of its religious undertones, until we come to deal with someone like Bourguiba, whose political concepts are—in appearance—strongly secular. As we shall see, the Tunisian leader builds his power on rational bases, but does not shy away completely from prophethood, the *mahdism* evident in a Ben Bella.

It is not our intention to "correct" Max Weber, even less to improve upon him, but in the area of charisma, which he formulated so brilliantly, there is room for stronger emphasis on four premises that he mentions, but which are more clearly developed by such others as Rudolf Otto and W. E. Mülhmann: relationship, milieu, movement, and finality.

As Mülhmann has expressed it:

> When we speak of charisma as a quality, obviously we are talking neither about real or innate gifts nor about demonstrable traits of psychology or character: what is involved is the impact exerted upon environment, the

[7] *The Theory of Social and Economic Organization* (New York: Glencoe Free Press; 1957). The examples of charisma mentioned by Weber range from the Persian shaman (often an epileptic) to the founder of the Mormons, including the condottiere, the gang leader, and the hot-headed Achilles. All of them mortals.

"effect" of behavior. Charisma is, to a great extent, a sociological, not a personal, duality. In the same way, ideas of charismatic type and milieu must be understood sociologically. Charismatic qualities are in the realm of belief: they are the radiations of a personality in the beliefs of others.[8]

Like power, charisma is not a property, it is a relationship: of an individual to others, of an individual to his environment. In an established society, what would pass for a frenzied agitator would in another milieu represent a prophet or an empire-founder. Think of Marat under the Second Empire, Hitler in the Germany of 1880, and, in contrast, Blanqui in the spring of 1968 in Paris.

Referring to the Berkeley explosion of April 1966, the American sociologist Daniel Lev maintained that "there is no such thing as charismatic power, [there are] only charismatic situations." This is what Narayan, the Indian Socialist leader, meant when he said that "it is not so much the hero who shapes the times as the times that shape the hero."

Hence the interest in charismatic ideas about environment and climate. Rudolf Otto wrote that "some periods of history abound in demons." Referring to the birth of Christianity, he explained that the influence of spirit-possessed men was an essential factor in the mood of that period, given that "foreign domination is expressed symbolically by the notion of being possessed by spirits alien to the tribe"; such was the case of the Jews after the decisive failure of the Maccabees' revolt and the consolidation of the Roman protectorate. "This combination of circumstances is favorable for demons," and hence for the message "of a charismatic exorciser."[9]

[8] *Messianismes revolutionnaires du Tiers-Monde* (Paris: Gallimard; 1968), p. 186.
[9] Rudolf Otto, quoted by Mülhmann.

Thus Otto links the situation and milieu of colonization and decolonization to what Mülhmann describes as "symbolic hyperdetermination," "constant alertness for signs," "a mood of active inner excitement sustained by a whole vocabulary of love and brotherhood," "a paranoiac investment of the group."[1]

Along the same lines, but with a psychoanalytic slant,[2] Erik Erikson offered some useful guidelines at the time of the conference on leadership in Tuxedo. Notably, he held that the masses can be "starved for charisma" when certain conditions exist: fear—in the case of the Jewish communities during the Middle Ages, for example; anxiety, experienced by those caught in an "identity vacuum"; and existential dislocation.

According to Erikson, the charismatic leader is one who offers a people protection, identity, or ritual. Seen in that light, charisma is somewhat functional, a view that seems to us somewhat trivial. Is it possible to trace a royal road of charismatic power between the semimetaphysical demands of Carl Friedrich and that other concept of a good shepherd—or sickroom attendant?

There can certainly be no charisma without finality. There is nothing final about mere protection or revolutionary change that seems to end where it started. Charismatic leadership is dynamic by definition and normative in destination. The charismatic dimension of power can be understood by comparing it to the poetic dimension of a writer: the discovery of a relationship among words which gives them a particular energy, a dynamism of their own.

---

1 Mülhmann, p. 186.

2 Erikson's study of Gandhi is entitled "The Leader as a Child" (*The American Scholar*, Autumn 1968). He defines the true leader as one "who offers the people solutions he has not been able to find for himself"; hence, a frustrated individual.

The debate over the meaning of charisma is related to the distinctions among leadership, power, and authority. Sharing the view of Maritain, who draws a firm line between *potestas* and *auctoritas* (a tyrant uses one, Socrates the other, Marcus Aurelius both), Robert Bierstedt says:

A leader can only request, an authority can require . . . Leadership depends upon the personal qualities of the leader in the situation in which he leads. In the case of authority . . . the subordinate must obey the command even when he is unacquainted with the person who issues it. In a leadership relation, the person is basic; in an authority relation, the person is merely a symbol.[3]

In most of the cases examined here, the situation of leadership and that of authority will often mingle. Bierstedt based his argument on established societies in which the leader was accidental. In the situations considered here, the transition from leadership to authority is often undiscernable. In any event, the role of the person will remain, or will tend to be basic. But the suppleness and fluidity of the concept of charisma and of the forms that it takes rule out any serious conflict between the practice of leadership, which it establishes, and the existence of authority, which it heralds.

All of these arguments about ideas of charisma, authority, and leadership recur, in any case, in our chosen field of discussion: that of emergent nations summoned to themselves by showmen of behavior.[4]

[3] Bierstedt quotes from Reinhardt Bendix, *Max Weber, an Intellectual Portrait* (New York: Doubleday Anchor; 1960), p. 298.

[4] "Charismatic power flourishes most freely today in the new nations that have loosed themselves from colonial bondage." Ann-Ruth and Dorothy Willner, in *Annals of the American Academy of Political and Social Science* (March 1965), p. 77.

TRUE AND FALSE CHARISMAS

Charismatic power has its critics and its limits even in the opinion sectors and areas most readily inclined to give it credence. Popular feelings, political organizations, intellectual elites, feudal and private interests can band together against it. The strength of its resistance is an indicator, but not the only one, of its validity.

True and false charisma cannot always be distinguished immediately on the basis of duration or success. Hadj Messali in Algeria, the Tunisian Sheikh Taalbi, like Rachid Ali El-Kilani in Iraq and Ruben Um Nyobe in Cameroon, were endowed with this sort of prestige but never really or durably transformed it into political energy. The power structure was not in their favor. Also, what interests us is charisma put to the test once it has been "routinized" in the form of power. But that is just when it is most difficult to measure. While it is the initiator of power, which in some way it sparks, it flares up so rapidly, feeding on governmental controls and restraints, that one is at a loss to judge whether the "hero's" natural ability or the vigilance of his pretorians does most to maintain this type of leadership.

When the consolidation of charisma within the State apparatus has not been completed, as in the case of Lumumba and (to a lesser degree) Ben Bella, one is tempted to blame the naïveté of its possessor rather than its own precarious nature. In the world in which they must act, the leaders of the Third World certainly cannot put their entire trust on popular support, which provides spurs, not armor. The overthrow of Lumumba does not prove that he lost his "gift of grace" or his magnetism, but rather that the responsibilities with which the mob invested him called for weapons other than those that exalt a people.

Perhaps the genuineness of charisma can be measured by its ability to close the gap between the broad aims of the founder of the State and the limited means at his disposal. The fact that a merchant of the Hejaz, exiled by his fellow Meccans, could in a few years unite the Arab world without any "instruments" other than prophecy, negotiation, and an aptitude for fighting exemplifies the binding force of charisma among the faithful.

When a high Persian dignitary, retired from active political life, pays serious attention to nationalist demands and, solely through his own words and convictions, is able to bring the oil interests to heel; when the resigning vice-president of a provisional government returns home and can rally the majority of the political elite and of the masses and, after campaigning for less than two months, become sole "boss" of Algeria— these are signs of extraordinary stature in men. Such events cannot be explained either by the rush of bazaar merchants to embrace Mossadegh or by the intervention of the ALN (National Liberation Army) in support of Ben Bella. Like the poetic gift, charismatic power consists of making something out of nothing.

Even Carlyle, who was Weber's precursor in this field, wanted his hero to be a poet. Without this gift, only rational and muscular forces and brute strength (economic or military) are in play, and they are not on the side of aspiring nations. The charisma of a Sukarno or a Nkrumah is no more discernible (or, at least, no more definable) than the poetic gift of Nerval or of Keats. Just as a poet transforms the associations among words, so the charismatic leader upsets the relationships of power. It is when the "natural" balance has been restored between the end and means, between real strengths and idealistic longings for emancipation, that charisma shows its limitations.

In 1951 the twisted and pathetic fervor of Mossadegh toppled Iran's power structure. But he hesitated to challenge imperialism, so he lost his gift of grace and sank to the strangest kind of political death. The aim of achieving for his country the preeminence it enjoyed during the Pan-African conference of Addis Ababa in April 1963 inspired Ben Bella with the gift of multiplying Algerian power as if it were the biblical loaves. But a year later at the Congress of the FLN (National Liberation Front) he failed to make his views prevail both as to secularization of power and to the purging of the party, and his settling for victory through new dosages of influence was bitter evidence of a cruel loss of charisma. Thus, all the pressures the leader could bring to bear on his party no longer had the desired effect and could not move it toward even a relatively modest goal.

In examining the validity and scope of charisma, we should not overlook the role of eloquence, particularly in the Arab world, where the prophet's words have a profound influence that is accented by the harsh beauty of the language. Yet, surprisingly, Pascal's maxim is still valid: true eloquence has no use for "eloquence." It is apparent that the leader's sorcery and power to influence do not grow in proportion to his mastery of language, and that the charm of an admirable speaker like Nkrumah evaporated in inverse ratio to his development as an orator. This happened also to Ben Bella, who within two years became an accomplished speaker but a leader listened to less. Nasser and Bourguiba are different: both of them managed to preserve in their mastery and trickery some element of prophetic simplicity, which has saved them and has kept some of the original freshness in their summonings.

Despite Carlyle's wish that his poet-hero be a silent one—a British hero—there is no true charisma without eloquence.

Even Naguib, a poor speaker, was eloquent in his way. And though he had no real means of communicating with the masses, Boumediène seemed determined for a long time to exercise power without charismatic enlargement of it. But eloquence alone cannot provide the charismatic dimension, even in Islam. In Syria, Akram Hourani, despite his Arabic vehemence and the fiery rancor of his speeches, could not develop it; nor could Allal El-Fassi in Morocco (except briefly under the French protectorate, from 1936 to 1937).

Charisma is creative, but founds nothing. It provides the keys to power, which then remains to be developed. To the energy that charismatic power confers, duration must be added. But this duration is itself uncertain if charisma is not "routinized" so as to become the base institutionalization, if it remains nothing more than the protraction of an emotional shock exchanged between an individual and the crowd.

SKETCH FOR A TYPOLOGY OF LEADERS

It is tempting to sketch a typical founder of "legitimacies." In the process, we are led to discover a number of archetypes from which, in turn, various categories of leaders can be determined.

Whether or not he is charismatic, whether he has reached the stage of ritualization or has remained at that of a creative inspiration, the leader has been invested with a task of primary importance, owing to his talent, to history, or to a particular type of condition. The people expect him to answer the questions asked by the collectivity: from the maker of rain or of laws, it is always the same hope, if not the same personage or the same power.

There are—among others—categories of leaders: those personified by power[5] and those who personify it. The first is a product of history, and the extent of his authority depends greatly on the success of his administration, greatly on his propaganda techniques and his popular influence. The second is primarily a personality, a "genius," a will power. He is invested with that "gift of grace" of which Max Weber speaks. He gravitates naturally to power or, better, to the incarnation of power. Authority is part of his nature: he rarely doubts its legitimacy. He believes in making history and not in submitting to it—even if his political culture has been influenced by Marxism.

But beyond this general classification there are numerous types of leaders, five of which will be mentioned here:

(A) *The destined leader.* Artificial as such a "calling" may seem, it is evident in men such as Bourguiba and Nkrumah and to a lesser degree in Sukarno and Ben Bella. The mere appearance of such a leader can change the entire outlook. Of course, the political leader does not produce something out of nothing. But he makes a royal road out of a favorable situation —such as a collective thirst for justice (he becomes a judge) or for national identity—and has an answer for everything.

Destiny, or his own mistakes, can bring his downfall. But not for a moment does he doubt his calling or the necessity and legitimacy of his function. He persists beyond the sanction of events. He believes in himself and even more strongly in the indissolubility of the ties that bind him to the people.

(B) *The leader chosen by history.* At first, he is shaped more by events than by his convictions. He needs a concrete signal to believe himself entrusted with a mission. He waits for

5 During a conversation with the author on February 8, 1968, Edgar Faure offered a rounded definition of personification of power: the "empowering of an individual' (for example, Truman). Perhaps he was also thinking of Pompidou.

history to judge him first, and only after it does will he come onstage and allow it to invest and personify him. He will play this part to the hilt and occasionally will outdo the spontaneous leader in this type of self-validating strategy.

Nasser seems to be of that sort, a cautious prophet chosen at the *n*th hour and who would have preferred to be a *raïs* rather than a *zaïm*, to play the cards rather than merely deal them. But once he became a symbol, how quickly he made up for the period of hesitation!

(C) *The void-filling leader.* He comes to prominence only on the heels of an event and does not build upon it. Summoned to fill a void, like the Indian leader Shastri, or because of a very confused situation, like the Lebanese Chehab, he slips aside or disappears when personification threatens to consecrate him.

(D) *The nonexistent leader.* Why mention him if he does not exist? Because the dawning history of the Third World is full of these false prophets, false not for what they say or do—as happens with the large majority—but because they have no faith even in themselves and their mission. A man such as Quadrose in Brazil or Aref in Iraq falls apart in the excitement and destroys himself in the struggle, whether he gives up like the Brazilian or hangs on until death like the colonel from Baghdad.

This is a strange species of men, corresponding, in the Populist era, to Wittelsbachs during the time of European monarchism. They deserve only halfhearted attention, but in an era of meteoric personalities it is important to keep these "flying saucers of power" in mind.

(E) *The antileader.* Summoned by events, by a vacuum, by indignation, or by a group that thrusts him forward as its spokesman or spearhead, this type of leader refuses to be incarnated and mythified. Instead of displaying himself, he governs behind closed blinds. Houari Boumediène is such a man.

This type of man may well have a drive for personal power. What sets him apart and makes him interesting is precisely the fact that he is the opposite of the summoned and incarnated leader whose exercise of power is our theme. Is the antileader's dedication as profound and sincere as the leader's? Can he forever refuse the crown that others eagerly grasp for? We have seen antileaders allow themselves to be transformed into idols: who could appear less interested in the deification Stalin "underwent" than the militant Georgian, Dzugashvili? Which will be first to answer the call of the demigod makers, grim-faced Ahidjo of Cameroon or the wily Tanzanian, Nyéréré?

One of the leader's basic characteristics is his consciousness of his high office and his acceptance (tacit, at least) of personification.[6] But can he be a real *zaïm* or charismatic leader when he permits no statues to honor him, accepts no crown, and disavows all symbols?

Perhaps we must make an exception for someone like Castro, who condemns *caudillism* and refuses any promotion ("Although I won a war, I still hold the rank of commander!"[7]) or any title but prime minister ("Here, there are no statues of anyone!"[8]).

In this respect, Castro is of course very different from Nkrumah, Sukarno, Bourguiba, Tito, or even Sihanouk, whose names are household words and serve to baptize their cities. But is he so different from Nasser or Ben Bella? After all, he is the *"lider maximo."*

In the emergent nations, the "modernization" of society is the accepted goal justifying, or serving as a pretext for, the

---

[6] In the beginning, he can submit, almost passively, to personification. To his enemies, who (until January 30, 1933), dubbed him "Hitler *trommler,*" the Führer retorted: "Yes, I am a drum, the drum on which all the misery of Germany resounds!"

[7] Speech made on January 8, 1968.

[8] Speech in Havana, March 13, 1966.

incarnation of power. In any case, leaders claim this to be the objective in order to gain support for it "in periods of transition." It is, again, a term we will have to define.

The basic significance of "modernization" has been explained by Samuel P. Huntington:

> Political modernization involves: (1) the rationalization of authority, the replacement of a large number of traditional, religious, familial and ethnic political authorities by a single, secular, national political authority; (2) the differentiation of new political functions and the development of specialized structures (legal, administrative, military) to perform these functions; (3) increased participation in politics by social groups throughout society, and the development of new political institutions —such as political parties and interest associations—to organize this participation.[9]

A state, political functions, popular participation—the policy of modernization thus tends to destroy tribalism and feudalism, to distribute public responsibilities and to induce the masses to take an active role. It is evident that the trends and practices we are examining are more closely related to the objective outlined in (1), the centralization of authority, than to (2) and (3).

The personification of power, in its two forms, is directed toward modernizing society, but, as we shall see, it is not always the instrument by which it is achieved. For although "heroic leadership" tends to become law-creating, thus confirming Georges Burdeau's definition, "Power is the law of the future,"[1] it can twist itself into rather odd shapes in order to

---

[9] "Political Modernization: America vs Europe," in *World Politics* (April 1966).

[1] *Le Pouvoir politique et l'État* (Paris: Librairie générale de droit et de jurisprudence; 1942).

replace legal authority. From then on, the exercise of legal power becomes the objective, and whoever wields it—and symbolizes it—will see it crushed when he himself is crushed. This type of power, a lifetime investment, is characteristic of poorly integrated societies and does not really insure popular participation.

Our theme has been limited in order to avoid possible confusion with other questions that, though related, are not tributary to the mainstream of the discussion, namely, those dealing with the single party, the role of the army in new states, and "Caesarism."

Dynamic leadership, which tends to create a cult of the leader, and the single-party system are often linked: from the Soviet Union's Communist Party of the 1930's to Nkrumah's Convention People's Party of the 1960's, the single party has often launched a superman (not to mention Mao Tse-tung). But the two phenomena can be separated: for example, in the USSR after 1953 and again after 1964, in Algeria after 1965, and (in another sense) in Morocco, where the exaggerated personification of monarchic authority goes hand in hand with formal pluralism.

It seems all the more inaccurate to relate the development of the single party to the personification of power because the mythification of a leader is often not so much the product of concentration or monopoly of political power as it is the psychological reward offered to a people denied democratic participation by the single-party structure. "Your rights? Why, the hero symbolizes them and exercises them." Thus, the leader can be the messenger of antidemocratic values.

As for the profusion of military regimes in the Third World, it is more the result of the second stage in the historic process of self-determination, which Max Weber described, than of the first, i.e., the structuring of charismatic power rather than its establishment.[2]

The logic of this report to "soldiery" has been emphasized by Georges Balandier:

> . . . Tyranny, abuse, scandal, and corruption have justified attacks on power: weak loyalty to modern political institutions, further accentuated by the fact that the single-party system eliminates all confrontation. The officer corps then becomes a transitional political class, unexposed to the discredit heaped upon the middle class in recently formed nations, and is supported by the young who want to provoke social changes. In the words of one African student, the army is "the only available force."[3]

The military establishment appears less likely to produce a hero (the army of the Directory hatched Bonaparte) than to breed a bureaucracy. It does happen that this type of homogeneous community sends forth a Perón or a Nasser. But the high priesthood of this bureaucracy, reflecting the cultural semienlightenment of the petty bourgeoisie (and its technical advance even more), can often manage to preserve its anonymity, the ghostly gray of military dress in Turkey, Brazil, and Nigeria.

An interesting remark was made on this subject to Raymond Aron during the conference on "heroic leadership" held in Berlin in 1960. When he asked a Brazilian university student why Latin American revolutions were made by the military, the reply was: "Because our officers are equivalent to your intellectuals." In those countries, the army would assume power based upon "residual legitimacy," similar to the young Japanese officers in 1930, whose background was rural, nation-

[2] See Léo Hamon's analysis of this subject in *La Personalisation de pouvoir* (Dijon: PUF; 1964).

[3] In *Le Monde diplomatique* (April 1966).

alistic, vaguely socialist, antiparliamentary, and "antipluto-cratic" (tendencies that, incidentally, were to take them far). In Japan, however, it is the caste system that turned a man like Tojo into a modern shogun. There, where no tradition of personal command and victory exists, the military staff, with its petty-bourgeois attitudes, is able to retain a solid and fairly anonymous position. This was the case in the Sudan between 1956 and 1965, in the Central African Republic, and in South Vietnam from 1954 to 1969. Perhaps, too, in Libya?

The military regime provides an alternative to charismatic leadership rather than a springboard for it. Egypt's example certainly should not be underestimated. But this "military society" is so firmly attached to the older nationalist tradition (as Anouar Abdel-Malek has shown[4]) and the *raïs* has managed to keep at such a respectful distance from the bureaucracy that spawned him that even in this instance the distinction holds between a military regime and personified power.

As for Caesarism, we will mention it at the proper time. However, the situation it represents is rather different from those we are examining, which relate quite specifically to the creation or reemergence of nations in the twentieth century.

Antonio Gramsci's definition is more or less binding: "Cac-sarism is the product of a situation wherein opposing forces reach a balance in some sudden and violent manner . . . such that the struggle can end only in mutual destruction."

A stalemate, a crisis in the affairs of long-established social groups, that has little to do with our principal theme. It recalls Louis-Napoleon, a product of the balance between the party of reaction and the party of progress, or Mussolini between the commandos of Fiume and the Turin commune—but not the Nasser of 1952, rising from the ruins of flaming Cairo, or Bourguiba, who came to power atop the debris of the pro-

[4] *Egypt: Military Society* (New York: Random House; 1968).

tectorate he was instrumental in abolishing, or Nkrumah, wrenching the Gold Coast from foreign domination in order to found Ghana. Caesarism comes of excessive equilibrium. The personification we are studying is the product of an emerging imbalance.

Personalization or personification? The first expression is more widely used. But we might note that still a third word has been employed by Georges Burdeau in his *Traité de Science Politique*. He speaks of the "individualization" of power,[5] which he considers the "pre-statehood form of power," adding that this form may recur "in case organized power shows signs of failure."

In the collection of articles published under the title *La Personalisation du pouvoir,* Jean Dupuy makes a distinction between "individualization" and "personification." And in that same volume Albert Mabileau relates personalization to concentration, keeping the concept of personification for what Edgar Morin calls "star promotion."

So now we have "personalization," "individualization," "start promotion," and "personification." The semantic debate would be rather pointless if it did not have a bearing on the choice we have made. What is significant is the process whereby a figure puts on or receives a mask that is the rallying-sign of leadership for a group in search of its identity, its political status, and its historic function.

Also, the exercise of personal power is of less interest to us here than the means, conscious or unconscious, by which power is incarnated in an individual: power in the making, not power attained.

Guided by Mabileau's suggestions as to language,[6] we prefer to use the word *personification,* not out of a concern for

[5] Conclusions drawn from the 1962 Dijon conference.

[6] In *La Revue française de Science politique* (March 1960) he had already published an important article on this subject.

originality, but because the terms evokes most clearly both the process of taking control and the theatrical setting. The Latin word *persona* referred to a mask for the stage. And in speaking of an actor, we say that he personifies Richard III, not that he personalizes him.

Personalization seems to cover more broadly the whole web of operations we have been discussing. *Personification* more aptly qualifies and pinpoints in terms of psychology, drama, and technique the system leading from the acquisition of power to the individual interpretation of it, to the "stage setting" for the hero, to the preparation of the crowd through propaganda, to the weaving of the myth, to the incarnation of the individual, and to the gradual merging of the sign-given group with the sign-giving demigod.

Showmen of
Behavior

*"There should be a glint of magic in the per-
formance. If the actor evokes and radiates it, by
incarnating this person he will do what Churchill himself did: awaken the imagination of a vast
audience and focus it upon a single figure."*
—ROLF HOCHHUTH, *Soldiers*

As old as the exercise of power is—and the ancient Greek
rulers were law incarnate—the personification of power has
acquired new energy in the mid-twentieth century. Maurice
Duverger calls it *pandemia*[1] to account for its universality.
There are many reasons for its growth, and they are too
familiar to warrant repetition.

We should note, however, that this ballooning of authority
is owed in great part to the national and international conflicts that have raged for the past fifty years, causing not
only governments and nations but also classes and entire
civilizations to confront one another. It appears that, as a
general rule, the intensity of power is proportional to the
danger at hand. The greater the danger, the greater the degree
of authority that tends to be imposed and to make itself

[1] *De la Dictature* (Paris: Juillard; 1961), p. 25. Further on (p. 157),
the author remarks that the wasting away of power occurs most notably "when
underdeveloped societies awaken and enter a growth phase. The necessary
development of investments results in a further drop in already very low
normal production, demanding sacrifices from the people which only an
authoritarian regime can impose. . . . The first efforts at modernization break
down autochthons exposed to diseases from the outside world."

prophetic. It can also be seen that whereas power expands readily, it diminishes very reluctantly. That it builds up constantly is one of Bertrand de Jouvenel's fundamental observations.

Technological development also contributes to concentration (except in the area of nuclear weapons, the use of which, after all, negates the idea of shared responsibilities). For who has a greater sense of his own isolation than the top man at the moment when he has to "press the button"? And in facing this very situation, we find that the crises of today arise so suddenly that consultation becomes difficult, the nucleus of decision making extremely narrowed.

Similarly, government intervention in capitalistic economies has grown, following the example of socialist collectives, particularly in the area of mass media and propaganda techniques. The plan is getting a name and the political campaign a face. The distance between leader and people is narrowing; intermediaries and spokesmen are fading into the background; "politics," the art of unceasing compromise, is on the wane. "From you to me," General de Gaulle said to the French people.[2]

Within the boundaries of the Third World, we shall continue to isolate the reasons for the concentration of authority and the incarnation of myth before looking for their results, and shall define their limits and offer some suggestions as to what may prevent them from becoming harmful.

In his book The Savage Mind[3] Claude Lévi-Strauss compares "cold societies" (those seated on the sidelines of history) with "warm societies" (those activated by it). He finds that they share at least one characteristic. whether they employ

[2] This is not the place to inject questions of personality, but in an interview on Swiss television on February 13, 1969, Georges Pompidou stated quite clearly that he favored the personification of power, which he linked to expanding techniques of communication.

[3] (Chicago: University of Chicago Press; 1966).

borrowed institutions in an attempt "to block the adverse effects of history on their stability and progress," or whether they "adopt the future as the motor of their development," each places its faith in the leader, who is the guarantor of continuity for one, the spark of action for the other: the two faces of leadership's function.

There are many differences between these societies, but one seems to stand out: in tribal communities, where the chief acts as protector, what Bertrand Russell calls the "power impulse" can emanate from either the leader or the led. Frazer gives a striking example provided by the King of Etatin (Nigeria):

> The village forced me to become chief. They hung the great juju around my neck. . . . I am the eldest male. With the aid of our ceremonies, I bring game to the hunter, I make the harvest plentiful, I make the rain fall. . . . But if I ever left these village walls, I would cease to exist. . . .[4]

But "counterpower" exists even in hereditary societies. In his *Anthropologie politique*,[5] Georges Balandier gives several examples of this, stressing force of a religious origin. In Ruanda, for instance, a "mythical" king, Imandwa, challenged the political chief's authority, seeking to limit it or at least make it more tolerable, and offering to replace the public spirit with "a better type of spirit" (Luc de Heusch).

In the same book, Balandier contrasts the two complementary principles underlying political life for the Tiv people in Nigeria, a balance between *tsav,* a special aptitude for command, and *swem,* the capacity to live in harmony with nature.

---

[4] *The Magical Origin of Kings* (New York: Barnes and Noble; 1968).
[5] (Paris: PUF; 1967), 143–5.

So we must not assume that absolute power is a universal law. Hereditary societies have their "democracies," too, and the art of politics in the most backward communities has often consisted in striking a balance of power, either by "halting power with power," according to the principles of *l'Esprit des Lois,* or by limiting the term and powers of the ruling body. In his *Structures sociales du Haut-Atlas,* Jacques Berque described some excellent systems of checks and balances developed by the Moroccan mountain people with little help from Montesquieu.[6]

Evans-Pritchard also has observed: "The tribal system is one of balanced opposition. Authority is distributed at each point in the tribal structure, and political direction is limited to situations in which the tribe, or a segment of it, acts collectively."[7] This unstructured distribution of authority, whether based on a division into *cofs* or *leffs* (extended family groups), according to Robert Montagne, or on territorial and economic rights, such as Jacques Berque noted, can extend far beyond the mere tribal circle: Ibn Khaldun demonstrated how periodically the tribes found methods to destroy dynastic power in order to check the authoritarian tendencies of monarchy in the Maghreb. In general, as Ernest Gellner[8] has pointed out, the Maghreb has produced some remarkable systems for maintaining the balance of power.

Even in the North African setting, there is no single system of tribal authority. The chief can be all-powerful, as the *caïd* of the Rehamnas once was in the Marrakech region, or can merely serve a decorative purpose, like the *amenokal* of the Hoggar. But what is most striking is the fact that in the

---

6 *Structures sociales du Haut-Atlas* (Paris: PUF; 1955).

7 *The Sanusi of Cyrenaica* (London: Oxford University Press; 1949), p. 59.

8 "Tribalism and Social Change in North Africa," *The Listener,* (London, July 1964).

changeover to postcolonial society, these very diverse traditions almost invariably favor the development of personalized power.

It might be said that if a tribe has a legacy of dynamic leadership, that leadership can be expected to inject itself into the new state; and that if the tradition is one of anarchy, the tribe will become integrated only through a difficult process keyed to a symbol of authority and concentration: the chief of a centralized government. Thus, we can say that to incorporate such a tribe into the nation entails violence of some kind—either internal or traditional or external and new.

In nations where there is scarcely any evidence of a tribal system—for example, Egypt and Tunisia—relatively complex institutions designed to limit power had existed before the advent of colonization. Almost simultaneously in the nineteenth century, the two countries developed the framework of modern government. In Egypt there was the advisory Assembly of 1866, in Tunisia the "Constitution" of 1861. But perhaps even more important than these modern fixtures appended to societies unprepared to accommodate them (it is notable that the revolt of 1864 in Tunisia was directed in part against the Constitution by the people of the "bled") were the corporations and trade associations, which at least in the urban areas possessed a commercial system and a social structure that were threats to sovereign power.

Here again, tradition does very little to limit power. And just as the tribal framework is either a good instrument of authority leading to concentration or is too weak to undertake a serious "housecleaning," the middle-class aristocracies, which might have projected their social influence into the political domain (as they did rather successfully in Europe—in the seventeenth century in England, the eighteenth century in France, the nineteenth century in Germany), were recruits in the service of postcolonial power, though their sympathies had wavered under colonialism.

The leader of postcolonial emancipation is not likely to be beguiled by the call of ancient traditions. References to village-level democracy or to the rule of trade and business associations excite the imagination of sociologists and historians rather than of leaders. In the beginning, the latter see their role as highly creative: they are the first of a breed. And if occasionally they give the word *revolution* its original meaning of a return to the past, and an interpretation based on the idea of recovery rather than discovery, they have no intention of restoring a heritage of inhibitions. Even in rare cases in which precolonial groups possessed no system of authority and tradition could have encouraged separatism and "counterpower," sovereign leadership has emerged from decolonization like a glaring truth.

We also have to consider another concept that is firmly anchored in numerous tradition-bound societies. In China, for example, "law did not protect the individual from the state, as in the European tradition (habeas corpus), but the state from the individual."[9] This holds out great prospects to the authoritarian leader—who, in this case, proved himself a good historian.

Discontinuity is one of the essential characteristics of the societies in question. One could even say that the "new nations" can be identified not only by their economic underdevelopment, their cultural indecision, the inadequacy of their resources (technicians, equipment, funds, trade relations) to meet immediate needs, but especially by what the Argentine sociologist Gino Germani calls "the simultaneity of the non-contempo-

[9] John Fairbank, "How To Deal with China" (*The New York Review of Books*, February 17, 1966).

rary" the coexistence in one nation of cultural areas belonging to different periods of history: modern and feudal sectors.

It takes exceptional methods to unite the *zlass* horsemen, the Tunisian intellectuals, the trade unionists of the UGTA, and the Tuareg shepherds. But along comes a mediator between the educated and the illiterate who claims to have more influence than the unions and the universities put together. Cohesion is to be the answer to discontinuity.

In this respect, we should not underestimate the rupture inflicted by decolonization. It is true that colonialism improved precolonial conditions to some degree. But although colonization penetrated only certain social strata, notably the urban superstructures, its collapse shook the entire community, changed the existing relationships, and disenfranchised one group while it promoted another. The entire network of relationships, and therefore customs, was transformed.

Bertrand De Jouvenel drew this conclusion:

> Social and moral discord favor the growth of absolute power: social instability, lax conduct, lawlessness, signs of bewildered and disordered lives. . . . Disoriented people enter a new life without finding any principles of behavior to guide their new selves. . . . In every era, groups have had, and will always have, their leaders, their standard makers. Social stability has to be imposed, with rules of conduct established at every level . . .[1]

In judging the behavior of their leaders, we often forget that the problems facing these new nations are not solely economic and political in nature, but also are problems of civilization itself. What must be achieved is the integration of needs and aspirations rooted in different centuries, of the handful of moribund traditions persistent despite the settlers

[1] *On Power* (Boston: Beacon Press; n. d.)

and the uncertain longings now animating the rural masses. Frantz Fanon made his own attempt to synthesize these two sectors of the new nations, describing with great admiration the pioneering spirit that he credited to the peasant world. But the amalgam of the two, apparently forged at the time of the revolt, disintegrated during the reconstruction.

The peasantry is not inherently resistant to the revolution, but it nonetheless is at a great disadvantage all the same in comparison to the urban regions. No matter how comradely its attitude was toward the insurgents, or how purposefully it supported them in action in Cuba and in Algeria, its efforts were never self-generated. Not surprisingly, Fanon took issue with the personification of founding power, but his criticism, although valid in many respects, is not entirely convincing because it is based on a deep misunderstanding. For the author of *The Wretched of the Earth* does not recognize the primary importance of religion: a factor that is a mainstay of conservatism in the countryside and encourages authoritarianism in leadership.

Religious saturation of the uneducated masses usually aids the development of authority in the postcolonial period, whether or not the clergy takes a resistive role against colonialism (as in the Algerian *Oulema* and Congolese *kibanguism*) or facilitates "colonizability"—the spirit of resignation (Maraboutism in the Maghreb, the powerful grip of the Flemish clergy in the Congo). Islam and Christianity in its African dress are social, perhaps even "total," religions, for they guide the behavior as well as the spiritual life of people, both individually and in groups. The policing function of the clergy in all its aspects has left the stamp of authoritarianism as well as of religion on these communities.

Whether it is the witch doctor of the Yoruba or the *alem* of Kairouan, a system of authority is superimposed on political power: a self-perpetuating, clerical tradition of command, subjecting the masses to organized, rigid control. In post-colonial regimes it is extremely rare for Church and State to come into conflict, whereas that struggle is one of the basic chapters in Europe's history.

People molded by religious constraints who once in their history heard a prophet's call are better prepared to respond to an illuminist leader's exhortations, the overwhelming nature of which sometimes seems to guarantee "credibility." For if he had no "gift of grace," how could he thrust himself forward so boldly? Nkrumah proclaimed himself a redeemer; reverence is a quality highly prized among the Fanti people, who live by the Bible and the prophets. The irony will be seen only afterward, when wrath descends.

Is the advent of modernization bound to sow conflict between political and religious leaders? The answer is uncertain, for in its present stage, religion is doing such a good job of strengthening political authority (even in Tunisia) that it is paving the way for its own deterioration. The leader may not have to confront it, for the battle is half won. He will make himself the clergy's protector—unless he turns out to be Ataturk.

In Europe the main resistance to absolutism came from the Church, or, at least from the time of Abelard to Bellarmim, was led by the intelligentsia with the tacit approval of the Church, which promoted the idea of equality more or less openly. No such force exists in the Third World, even in Bourguiba's Tunisia, where Islamism does no more than offer a timid challenge to secular powers (this is indeed a transfer of authority).

Gamal Abdel Nasser's situation is different. The ups and downs of political struggle determine his actions more than a compulsion to bring the Moslem Brotherhood to its knees, yet he finds ways to placate officialdom, as well as the faculties of El Azhar University and the muftis, who are more inclined

to humor him in turn because he opposes the powerful Brotherhood they fear and envy. After all, as the Egyptian leader once
told a delegation of Coptic priests, you cannot deal with Islam
in Cairo the way you can in Tunis. In the event he might
want to pull a "Bourguibism" in this domain, Nasser would
run into trouble, for Egypt is in the heartland of Islam, and he
recognizes certain responsibilities as a result.

Although their positions are quite different (we will return to this point), both men know how to use religion and
religious principles to consolidate or extend their power. The
state is not growing at the expense of religion: it is turning it
to good account along with the mass respect for it. From the
standpoint of power, it is easier and more profitable to Islamize
modernism (including the "necessary" concentration of
power) than to modernize Islam.

And it is no minor feat of the new leaders to put religion
to use as a moderating influence on democracy. In the name of
Islamic *ijma,* which expresses the need for consultation and
agreement in advance of any decision making, the leader will
merely sound out the opinions of close advisers, feeling perfectly free to disregard them, or will organize a referendum—
an approval-gaining device that has been widely successful.
Thus, the spirit of a relatively democratic tradition reinforces
the exercise of personal power. Should there be any objections,
he can always find a panel of legal experts ready to discover
(or to draw up) written evidence justifying him.

Even before the new power is implanted, and as a result of
the struggle for independence, conditions exist which do little
to encourage lasting freedom. To begin with, we can say that
the conflict was bound to produce a "hero" (more or less
genuine), but one who has become a symbol for the under-
ground and the guerrillas. For example, despite the goal of
equality which Algerian nationalism promoted over the long
years of crisis, the predictable outcome of the struggle was Ben

Bella's rise to power, though he played a role no more significant (until August 1962) than certain others. But the colonialists vilified him, and this gave him an aura of sainthood.

While strife produces heroes, it also opens up severe internal conflicts. Even though the leader knows that his claim to
authority is justified and based on past performance, he har-
bors an extremely suspicious attitude fostered by years of
outlawry and imprisonment. One would think that the grim
experience of revolutionary violence would have a cleansing
effect in the domain of power. But the relations between former battle-comrades are often more strained than those between individuals who attain power by conventional paths.
The contrasting situations in Algeria and Morocco illustrate
this.

Whether or not colonialism has succeeded in arousing ideological or ethnic conflicts among the spearheads of revolution,
every stage of decolonization is marked by individual and
group struggles that affect the shape of power. Without the
haunting threat of "Youssefism,"[2] would Bourguiba's power
carry as much weight? Or would Kwame Nkrumah's dictatorship have turned into a caricature without the obsessive presence of the pioneering Dr. Danquah, who was prematurely
taken from the scene? Defense reflexes and bitter memories
fire the passion for unity in these republics, which came into
being after a stormy period of decolonization.

Illiteracy contributes to the personification of power in these
nations. For an uneducated person, it is easier to understand
a man than a program. Illiterate communities revere the
spoken word, hence the power of oratory. And education does
not change the situation overnight. In an early stage, the opposite holds true. The leader has a chance to develop and "ele-
vate" his position. He resembles the type of educator Rousseau

---

[2] Salah Ben Youssef, with whom Bourguiba shared power for a time.

had in mind which is suited to his outgoing temperament. Thus we find Nasser, Bourguiba, and Nyéréré beating a path from school to school and offering the artless crowds some fascinating interpretations of world politics and their own reforms in the guise of parables or of dramatic sketches complete with mime, or playing the role of St. George felling the dragon.

At the same time, the great man's pronouncements are the classics that schoolchildren study, and the latest speeches of the *raïs,* or Supreme Warrior, are used for dictation. The sacred texts of the Prophet must be consulted, too, wherein the student will discover enough contemporary parallels to make his reverence for religious leaders reflect upon the political chief. Thus, submission builds up, and because education and learning have not yet created a society of citizens, an illiterate mass constitutes a semicaptive audience.

In addition, a society deprived of a modern language is particularly susceptible to the type of propaganda spread by an authoritarian regime through radio and television as well as certain simplistic newspapers that are published to support its program. The more intellectually retarded a community is, the greater the influence exerted on it by the simplification of power.

"Western-style" democracy has lost whatever prestige it had for the Third World: this decline, which is an important factor in strengthening the power of new leaders, has a number of causes, of which we will mention three.

The first is the interrelation of colonial expansion and "bourgeois" democracy which Marxism propounds; could the political freedom developed in Great Britain and France since the mid-nineteenth century be conceivable without coexistent colonial exploitation? Did the colonized subproletariat pay for the European proletariats' right to struggle and to become middle-class? This is the heart of the argument put forward by Sultan Galiev, Frantz Fanon, and Palm Dutt. All of them agree that there is a correlation between a given political structure and a given economic system. It is not surprising that those who want to change the economic form "throw out the baby along with the bath water."

Apart from the link between European liberty and colonial alienation, there is a historic relation between democracy and imperialist enterprise. The parliamentary type of governments in London and Paris at the end of the nineteenth century were the ones that campaigned most relentlessly and successfully for overseas expansion; elected representatives of free peoples consistently sustained that policy. And it was under the strict control of duly elected parliaments that the Indian people and the Algerians saw colonialism imposed on them. Zaghloul and Nehru were not disheartened, but many leaders such as Chandra Bose and Nasser found these ambiguities sufficient cause to condemn parliamentary liberalism.

The third and perhaps most important reason for the discrediting of "classic democracy" in the new nations is the relative failure of experimental parliamentary government. In a study of "the alteration of liberal democracy in Asia," Vietnamese jurist Tran Van Minh maintains that, with respect to a number of Southwest Asian regimes (Thailand, Indonesia, Pakistan):

> . . . on the surface, we find the normal institutions that are basic to liberal democracy. But . . . these organs tend to have a different significance and purpose. . . . From instruments designed to limit and control power, they have developed into a means of reinforcing power. Once agencies of popular participation in power, they have become a kind of democratic security for a more or less oligarchic government.

Hence the extinction or withdrawal of the system.

But in other situations dynamism, not immobility, crushes parliamentary government. A plural-party system becomes a multiparty system, control turns into persecution and competition into guerrilla tactics—at which point the promoter of law and order enters the scene. The best example is provided by General Ne Win in Burma: he managed two coups d'état in two years, the first, in 1962, to protect the constitution, the second, in 1964, to abolish it. Between times there had been a regime in which the parties obstructed the government's efforts to install a socialist system.

Studying the decadence of the Egyptian parliamentary system, Adel Amer writes: "The whole trouble lies in the wrong adaptation of a foreign-made system of government to a country that was in no way prepared for it."[3] Like his Vietnamese colleague, Amer is criticizing primarily the inappropriateness of institutions and their inadaptability to the particular social milieu. These objections come from competent jurists and are well founded. But the founders of new governments apply them, often less justifiably, as general indictments of classic democracy in underdeveloped nations—and as another argument for centralized power.

Has the condemnation of the cult of personality formulated in the Socialist states (although until now it has affected only the posthumous cult of Stalin, not the daily practice of this cult in countries boasting the most doctrinaire Socialism, such as China, Albania, and North Vietnam) been able to check the extension of personification in those nations that pay homage to socialist principles? It is a curious fact that the concept of the leader, of leadership and its possible perversions, has a minor place in the whole span of Lenin's writing (only twenty-three references to it have been found in the

[3] *La Faillite du système constitutionnel égyptien* (Paris: Doctoral dissertation; 1955), p. 341.

thirty volumes of his complete works). It is remarkable that
a revolutionary so preoccupied with the concept and exercise
of power gave so little space to a problem that was to prove
fundamental.

In fact, Lenin presents the question almost always in relation to the Party, described as the vanguard of the proletariat:
"In all periods, in all countries, a given class is guided by its
most cultivated representatives. It cannot be otherwise in the
Russian workers' movement."[4] And, in another place, denounc-
ing the "working-class aristocracy" created in England at the
end of the nineteenth century and calling for all-out struggle
against these "opportunistic leaders," he warned: "But to
conclude from this that the dictatorship of the people is generally in conflict with the dictatorship of the leaders is a ridiculous absurdity, absolute nonsense."[5] Further on, he criticized
the "ridiculous condemnation of leaders" by the German leftists.[6]

In an editorial in *Izvestia* in April 1918, he maintained that
"there is no contradiction between Soviet democracy and the
return to personal dictatorial power." And in the speech he
made in March 1919 in tribute to Sverdlov, Lenin paid homage
"to the leaders who best incarnated this heretofore unknown
characteristic of revolutions, the organization of the masses."
And he went on: "History has long demonstrated for us that
in the course of the struggle, great revolutions bring forward
great men and foster abilities that until then seemed impossible."

Perhaps a story related by Trotsky best illustrates the basic
importance that Lenin and he attributed to their role. During
a work session together Trotsky asked Lenin, "If they shoot

[4] *A Propos a Profession of Faith* (N.p., 1899).
[5] *Left-Wing Communism: An Infantile Disorder* (San Francisco: China
Books and Periodicals; 1965).
[6] Ibid.

us, what will become of the revolution?" Lenin thought a moment, smiled, and replied, "Maybe they won't shoot us after all."[7]

It is apparent in all these statements that the leader is always mentioned in a collective sense, in references to the word "incarnation" and the relation between "great revolutions" and "great men." It is also evident that the founder of the Soviet system refused to pave the way for the cult of the hero, confining himself to the concept of the vanguard, however reduced to its simplest terms. The leader is not isolated from the group: he is ahead of it but linked to it. He represents an acute state of the collective revolutionary spirit, but is not a prophet launching his appeal from the mountaintop.

After the damage done by the Stalinist system had been assessed, the Chinese Communist Party began to attack the cult of personality more vehemently. An editorial published in 1963 in the Party's official daily and ascribed at the time to Mao himself put the problem thus:

> The cult of personality is a vicious inheritance that comes down to us from the farthest reaches of history. Rooted not only in the exploiting classes but in the small producers as well, . . . this force of habit can influence many government officials and has not spared even a leader like Stalin. The cult of personality is the reflection of a social phenomenon in the minds of men.[8]

But we can assume that the leaders of the Third World, who justly admire the achievements of the Chinese Revolution, have detected behind such a warning an implicit condemnation of the bond between a European system of influence and the power that maintains it.

---

[7] Quoted by Merleau-Ponty in *Humanism and Terror* (Boston: Beacon Press; 1969), p. 94.

[8] "On the Stalin Question," in *Renmin Rinsao* (September 13, 1963).

In Search of a
Collective Identity

*"People's concern for social values depends upon
the transformation of their primitive hostilities
into an attachment, which is at bottom an identification. . . ."*

—SIGMUND FREUD
*Group Psychology and
Analysis of the Ego*

A people struggling for independence against colonial power
has few resources—it is consistently outclassed. The only way
it can offset its weakness is by strong leadership, sometimes
spontaneous, embodied in one man or in a small group. This
cult of the leader is apparently so effective that it arose in the
already highly developed society, neither illiterate nor impoverished, that fought the American War of Independence.
Such cultivated men as Franklin and Hamilton sought to personify the struggle in the person of George Washington.[1]

Freed from a lie, a decolonized people renews the search
for a truth. It is in search of an identity. This involves the
concept of "nativism" (a better choice than "messiahship"),
which Ralph Linton defined as a society's attempt to "revitalize
or to perpetuate certain determined facets of its culture."[2]
W. E. Mülhmann seems to go farther on the right track, describing nativism as a

[1] Seymour Martin Lipset, *The First New Nation* (New York: Basic Books;
1963), pp. 18–23.
[2] *Nativistic Movements* (N.p., n. d.), p. 230.

. . . process of collective action motivated by the desire
to receive a sense of group consciousness that has been
overcome by the invasion of a superior foreign culture—
thanks to the massive evidence of a native cultural contribution. . . . Nativism is wedded to the conscious rejection of an alien culture . . . symbolizing foreign
tutelage. . . . The role of leadership must be evalu-
ated. . . . There is a constantly shifting struggle for
recognition on the part of chiefs, subordinates, apostles,
and disciples. . . . It is important to note that gifted and
ambitious personalities reflect other cultures as well as
their own.[3]

In this process (or "movement," a fundamental concept of
Mülhmann) the people identify spontaneously and enthu-
siastically with a visible and prestigious human being, who in
turn infuses each of them with his glamour and his glory. He
is their highest common denominator, at once the evidence of
their individual and collective existence and a certitude of their
cultural identity and political unity; he is you and I when you
and I have a relationship, a common purpose.

The leader is both focus and measuring standard for the
group; through him the individual and collective desires for
identity are fulfilled. In the fall of 1962, when Algeria was
in upheaval, Ben Bella's appearance on television and on the
rostrum symbolized Algeria's existence, just as Lumumba's
appearance in Leopoldville symbolized the Congo's two years
earlier.

And so this cultural hero and standard-bearer sees himself
marked for an extraordinary mission. Why not? For he is not
just a king-maker or a king, but the genius of a new people.
Such an overwhelming personality might swallow up the na-

---

[3] *Messianismes révolutionnaires du Tiers-Monde* (Paris: Gallimard; 1968.
Originally published as *Chiliasmus et Nativismus*.).

tional identity, his own creation, and be repudiated by the people. But it is also possible that the impact of his image would be transferred to his descandents, as in the case of Indira Gandhi.

It may be surprising that the demand for self-esteem creates such problems for the tropical powers; it appears that the citizens of new states tend to abandon their rights all too quickly and bow down before their leaders. But we must remember that the postcolonial legacy of alienation accounts for the appraisal of situations in terms of foreign powers rather than in the framework of purely national relations. Once an alien power has ceased to be the master, it persists as an obsession, a focus of reference; so it was with England in India after 1947, and with France in Morocco after 1956.

To the extent that a decolonized people sees its image as a reflection of its former ruler, the growth of a key leader is hastened, nourished by desperate popular loyalty and the nation's need to cope with the excolonialists. It makes no difference whether the government is despotic or not so long as its leader presents a lofty image of the nation to the world. Thus, Tunisians will be exultant if Habib Bourguiba, relying on their united support, can challenge the threats of Paris or Cairo.

Masochism is not what sends decolonized peoples rushing headlong into political bondage, but, as with those Japanese soldiers who plunged into a ravine and raised a bridge of corpses over which the next columns could pass, their self-effacement becomes a monument exalting their leader. In turn, the great man's triumph is supposed to rebound on them, much as the success of Brazil's football team eases the misery of fans in the Rio slums.

The universe of emergent nations is peopled with symbols, not to mention evil spirits. Neocolonialism is the most ominous and mysterious of these monsters. Its murky and debilitating influence must be counterattacked by a vigorous and radiant image: the face of a national hero. The leader's purifying portrait is displayed in every shop window in the capital in place of imported goods that deplete the state treasury (whiskey, luxury items, etc.) ; this, to stamp out such shameful commerce and reassure the "new class" of his adorers.

Yet the need for an apparatus of purification is not exclusively symbolic. This key actor, spotlighted, the voice of their common destiny, the object of every eye,[4] is indispensable to the masses if they are to resist the insidious pressures of foreign influence. Men must have someone to trust. The leader is such a precious symbol of the nation's spirit and is so eager to fulfill this trust that he cannot fail to be a savior.

Adolphe Thiers claimed to have helped establish "power in the shadows" at the time of the July Monarchy. That is just what colonized peoples fear. They want bold power blindingly displayed (although it be as burdensome as it is dazzling) : every sign of it points to the nation's autonomy and the morality of the regime.[5]

One need not observe the behavior of Egyptian fellahs or Cambodian peasants to understand the importance of emotions in the political sphere. The line that the French Communist Party followed for a long time showed that the personification

[4] Bourguiba frankly admitted that he lived in a "glass house."

[5] A. Sauvy, in J. J. Chevallier, et al., *Le Pouvoir* (Paris: PUF; 1956–7), p. 213: "Our real leaders are not our elected representatives. Political democracy is only a screen for economic oligarchy. . . . History teaches the governed not to be demanding. Yet it seems legitimate on their part to wonder, and to find out, at the very least, who their rulers are."

Jeremy Bentham considered "secrets" the most immoral of political practices.

of leadership can be based on a restless sentimentalism. Edgar Morin speaks of the militant campaigners who were urged to "do it for Maurice [Thorez]." A method that is effective among the French working class may prove even better among the emotionally volatile masses in Egypt or Brazil. And "for Maurice" is easily changed to "for Gamal" or "for Janio."

Especially in societies in which the family unit is dominant, an affectionate relationship with a "big brother" equipped with a first name, a special tone of voice, some idiosyncrasies, and only limited familiarity with the masses is guaranteed to make a hit. This is government based on a family-type relationship involving confidence, demonstrativeness, and passionate local loyalties. Jean Dupuy has pointed out[6] that demagogic dictators are interested less in paternal attitudes than in fraternal ones. Eva Perón played the role of sister to the *descamisados,* serving as intermediary between them and her husband, and argued thus: "This is the people's assurance that no divorce can separate it from its government, as the head of state would be forced to break with his wife in order to reject his people." Finally, "big brother" is behind the use of diminutives that speak affectionately of him: "Peroncito!" "Juancito!" Vargas and Castro lent their first names to their doctrines. Ben Bella was widely known as Aminedi (short for Ahmed), and Nasser is currently referred to as Gamal.

One example of the relationship between leader and people: a rich Egyptian merchant was called before the governor of Cairo. Worried sick, he appeared, wondering if he had failed somehow to observe price regulations. The first question upset him even more: "Don't you like the President?"

"Oh, of course I like him. Everyone knows I do. How can you ask such a thing?"

"Well, then, why don't you have his picture in your office?"

6 In *La Personalisation du Pouvoir* (Dijon: PUF; 1964), p. 140.

. . .

Should the gambling craze that dominates modern societies (parimutuel betting at French tracks, football pools in Italy, numbers-playing in New York) be linked to the rise of personal power? Would this make gambling a diversion for aimless people, a refuge in a fantasy world for those who feel powerless to change the real one? Among emergent peoples, such inclinations combine with a taste for perpetual dramatization of life in the form of ballet, psychodrama, or lyric commentary. Here, the aim is to lift the face of man's depressing or tragic lot, to woo the favor of mysterious powers, to conquer evil, or to turn the misfortunes of the masses into a joyous pageant.

The leader's presence on the platform, his speech, his ride through the capital standing in an open limousine, are the psychodramas of independence, of nationhood, of newly discovered power. The leader becomes an actor vested with a symbolic role, the nation's mouthpiece and the projection of its image. He is Robespierre at the Celebration of the Supreme Being on the Champ de Mars; he is Nkrumah, in his *kente,* addressing the crowd in the language of his coastal tribe, accompanied by the blare of hunting horns. Let us not forget that the word *personification* has actually a theatrical significance. It is the hero who gives form and meaning to liberty, who builds the sense of importance of the masses, who narrates the vision of national destiny.[7]

But such ceremonies also have their non-epic side; everything is not idealization. The *griot* (witch doctor) plays a major part in African societies and is the chief's admiring bard

---

[7] We quote once more from Jouvenel, for whom nineteenth-century ideologies of nationalism concealed an "all-pervading sentimentalism" and "made history into a romance of the person-nation, which, like the heroine of a melodrama, summoned a champion to appear at the appointed hour."

as well as his occasionally sarcastic jester. The chief can expect some sharp rebukes from him, or hymns of praise of which the fervor sometimes carries strangely ironic undertones.

What are the best examples from among so many rites of power and rituals of authority? They are woven into the political life of traditional societies, from New Caledonia,[8] where the *pilu-pilu* ceremony apotheosizes the chief in a pageant signifying the whole past and future structure of command, to the Congo, where the rite of investiture insures legitimacy but also promises the renewal of royal power.[9]

Rites build institutions. But it is a fair question whether their persistence in modern times (in altogether new forms) perhaps expresses a need for entertainment rather than a true belief. Or whether Hassan II's golden coach, paraded for Aïd-el-Kebir, is any more spiritually elevating than Queen Elizabeth II's. If the so-called underdeveloped masses cannot distinguish entertainment from ritual, and if they cling to a leader because ceremony has built him up or because he promised them bread and circuses . . .

While the leader awaits delivery of the bread, he promotes a loftier type of play with educational overtones, the theme of which is budding national consciousness. "Guided democracy" is a cultural festival, the real mystery play of nationhood.

The heroic and brotherly ties that coexist between chief and people—attributable as much to their efforts as to his will— are reinforced by modern audio-visual techniques. Of course, charismatic leaders initiated similar festivals in the past, and one can imagine what a celebration of the cult of Mars in

[8] J. Guiart, *Structures de la chefferie en Mélanésie du Sud* (Paris: Institut d'Ethnologie; 1963).

[9] G. Balandier, *Daily Life in the Kingdom of the Kongo* (New York: Pantheon; 1966).

Caesar's camp must have been like, or the Mahdi's entrance into Omdurman. Modern means of communication are not essential when Nasser visits Upper Egypt or Leopold Senghor makes a tour of Serer villages, but they lend incomparable breadth to the leader's every gesture, so much so that new nations nearly have gone overboard in using them.

Egyptian television carries five or six times more programs than French television, and it functions primarily to inform viewers of everything the president does or says (many sets are given out free because most people are unable to afford them). Every speech he makes, every new school he opens, is fully televised. So the cult of the leader is drummed in; he is constantly in the public eye on television as well as on the posters in all public places. "Big brother" is looking out for you. He never sleeps. He is always there. When he isn't making a speech or heading a parade, he is keeping an eye on you. Don't let him down!

This patient and omnipresent face is doubly admired because the common social purpose, which is the program, entails effort and devotion and must adopt a countenance both sensitive and familiar if it is to win approval. The leader is the smiling and respected face of the program, its bid for acceptance. In affluent societies the worker labors for an image that is dangled before his eyes: a vacation cottage or a car. In new nations a political program cannot be its own sole object of striving: it has to be masked by a disarming grin, a respected face, a mobilizing gesture.

Limits of
Personification

———◆◆———

*"Dictatorship: ultimate remedy in extreme cases.
In former times, a deity descended from the sky
to untangle affairs."*
—MONTESQUIEU, *Cahiers*

Strong as the incentives are to concentrate and personify power
in states seeking to free themselves from underdevelopment
and postcolonialist alienation, resistances to it appear in certain areas and in certain situations. They set immediate limits
to such power and are a measure of the risks it involves.

Decolonization is often, but not always, revolutionary.
When it has not coincided with the restoration of national
sovereignty, when independence has come about by agreement
between the colonizers and a ruling group that has managed
the transition from the old regime to genuine self-government,
it is to be expected that attempts to concentrate authority and
to personify leadership will arouse some opposition. "Heroic
leadership" requires a certain minimum of heroism: one recognizes it more easily in Ho Chi Minh than in Leon Mbâ.

In certain situations, a national figure who sought symbol-
status and the complete control of power it guarantees would
cause a public commotion on grounds of legitimacy. The
masses long to identify with a hero, but not just any hero, or
a mere agent of colonialism, such as Fulbert Youlou trying to
capture the image of Lumumba, or Kenyatta, who ran into a
storm of protest in the heavily populated areas of Brazzaville.

But even a "legitimate hero" can provoke public disapproval

by misuse of power. Of course, it is very difficult to draw the line between popular resistance and foreign intervention, both of which contributed to the fall of Abdulkerim Kassem and Kwame Nkrumah. Doctrinaire Arabic Moslems questioned Kassem's legitimacy because of his hostile relations with Nasser (who was the currently licensed spokesman of the Arab world) and the very conspicuous support he was getting from Marxist circles in Iraq. The widespread popular approval of Nkrumah, still evident on the eve of his downfall, reached a series of breaking-points over the flagrant abuse of power of which Pan-Africanism's standard-bearer was guilty: the death of imprisoned Joseph Danquah, his former mentor, tarnished his reputation badly.

Even in so-called underdeveloped societies, the masses eye their chosen leader very critically. They close their eyes to a great many things, including occasional corruption. But what they draw the line at in an independence movement is an individual threatening to take over the movement for his own benefit. The Algerians were devoted to Ahmed Ben Bella, who symbolized and was dedicated to the *thawra* (revolution). Yet they did not lift a finger to keep him in power: concentration in his hands had begun to resemble monopoly.

The concept of *thawra* conveys the sense of a collective whole, of equality. Personal power can be based on inequality if it expresses the will of a group through an individual. A leader who isolates himself in his own magnified image is no longer representative of the group. The masses look for identification. They will not ratify confiscation.

In the Arab-Muslim world the Koran is the law of the land only for the Moslem Brothers and a few fundamentalists such as Allal El-Fassi. But it pervades the general attitude to public affairs and adds weight to arguments condemning tyranny. Based on the premise that man surrenders himself to a superior being, it has tended to discourage any extreme form of personalized authority at least since the end of the Caliphate and the beginning of secular power, both in Arabia and in Morocco. Here, "democracy" is eyed with certain vague reservations that stem from the observance of a type of traditional social code, for example, the *Qaida* in Morocco.

In addition, exposure to a pluralistic tradition can be the source of organized resistance in countries where Western influence was formerly dominant. Of course, the prominence in Accra's top political circles of Geoffrey Bing, a former English Labor deputy, has not prevented Nkrumah's government from drifting toward dictatorship; nor have liberal French voices close to King Hassan's ear been able to alter the development of Moroccan monarchy into a theocratic state.

But in these countries, as in the Ivory Coast or Kenya, "democratic" alliances forged during the struggle for independence still carry a nostalgic fragrance of freedom. No organization worthy of the name is actually trying to loosen the grip of absolutism, yet the reflection of foreign institutions hovers over this new power, giving some of its policies a scandalous tinge. We have already seen that these European ties do not always play a constructive role. Still, it must be said that English or French political traditions, which have aided the rise of many Third World leaders, can sometimes check the overgrowth of personal power. In Egypt, Algeria, and Nigeria, foreign institutions have had such an effect.

As for the emergent nations of Asia, here too one can find a type of organized resistance in terms of the proverbial "mandate from heaven." The ruling power governs in the name of this principle. Sovereignty does not emanate from the leader; it is subject to repeal, dependent upon his actions. Thus, Diem was heaven's agent until the day his tyranny became so outrageous that he did not appear to warrant celestial approval. His place was no longer designated in that zodiac; he had to go, leaving no right of succession to his heirs, who, like himself, were under obligation to prove their divine mandate. Thus, the personification of power is subject to a not-very-effective criticism, but one at least likely to give a "form" to the popular feeling against abuses of centralization and personification.

Until a leader has eliminated all parties except his own and made his influence and style supreme within that party, so that his brand of leadership controls, there is always the possibility of a shift of power. So long as the reformist Egyptian Wafd survived (and even after its official demise), it challenged Nasser's power. The same was true in Tunisia, before and after Bizerte, when Bourguiba's impressive leadership harbored some "rotten eggs": there were even some dissidents within the Néo-Destour party itself.

Similar developments took place in Algeria when Ben Bella's former comrades took the reins of more or less synthetic parties and attempted to block his rise. So long as one sector of the political body (and this includes the trade unions, which in the Third World are primarily special branches of political organizations) retains its autonomy, it acts as an antidote to concentration.

On the other hand, personification could be the unconscious aim of some general conspiracy: it is conceivable that at a given moment everyone wants to see the hero incarnate the nation for a while. In Indonesia the various political groups chose to keep Sukarno in power to screen their infighting.

The intelligentsia seems bent on opposing any form of deification, but the situation can change. The court of Alexander the Great had its share of poets and magistrates. Giraudoux made great sport of poets who yearn for heroes: not every intellectual is a Galileo. There have been some great men who have loved to create gods before adoring their own handiwork. All the same, as a class intellectuals are likely to oppose this sort of thing.

The student groups are remarkably typical of the new nations. These nations, themselves adolescent societies, seek expression through what they call the "University"—which may include every age group from children to mature men. In Saigon, Damascus, and Mexico, they are destroying idols and forcing the most secure dictatorships to come to terms.

Students can be the leader's most enthusiastic promoters and then be the last to defend him (Ben Bella, for example). But they are usually the prime movers in the rush to glorify a hero. They were the principal agitators for Sukarno's ouster and for the long-overdue condemnation of Nkrumah's abusive power, and figured prominently in the struggle against a totalitarian framework for Moroccan monarchy. And sometimes their elders joined them.

Pressure groups can swallow heroic leadership if they are organized along modern lines and play their roles with the same patient hypocrisy that their European and American counterparts betray. While the political star performer holds the limelight, backstage dealings for export licenses or the price of coffee can be expedited. But experience has been known to teach some leaders the risks of closed-door operations: Nasser, Bourguiba, and even Lumumba were able to expose and prevent this type of arrangement.

As a general rule, national and foreign pressure groups are more at home under a parliamentary type of government. The word *lobby* itself refers to the rooms and corridors of parliament. Prominent personalities and their circles are excellent targets for such activities, as we shall see, and the multiparty system provides greater control over the representations of private-interest groups.

Feudalism, in its historic sense—which often obtains in the Third World—is inherently opposed to personalized power. A speculator can manage to live with heroic leadership, but a "lord" of Northern Nigeria or Southern Morocco cannot. Personal power depends to a great extent on an informal partnership of the people and their leader, who calls it "direct democracy."

Such a relationship can only undermine the very sources of marginal powers. The feudal lords of Andalusia get along with Franco because he protects them from a fate worse than himself, a glimpse of which they caught in 1936. But the magnates of Egyptian cotton and Algerian dates necessarily had to clash with the regimes of Nasser and Ben Bella, even if these two governments had been less outspoken about their socialist intentions. Beyond a certain point of identification, genuine state powers cannot be shared or superceded—and this is what feudalism requires.

We could regard the various churches confronting the power structure as mere pressure groups to which the preceding remarks apply. But this would undervalue the importance of religious forces in these nations, even in their organized forms. A leader like Nasser or Nkrumah (but not Batista or Fulbert Youlou) is unwilling to cooperate with the pressure groups, the sugar and aluminum lobbies. Usually he is a practicing member of the country's dominant religious group. Even when attempting to modernize or adapt religious practices to social life, he takes part in the activities of his own religious community. None of the present leaders of the Third World (except, of course, the committed Marxists), not even Habib Bourguiba, has adopted the position of Mustapha Kemal.

So the clergy is a partner to be treated with consideration, even with respect. In the interest of national power, it is often willing to concede some of its own influence. The Moslem clergy as well as the Buddhists and the officials of various blends of African religions render unto Caesar his due, and much more. But a silent struggle goes on. If Nasser's power has not been weakened by Azharist influence, that is because the Egyptian leader is fighting their mutual enemy, the Moslem Brotherhood.

Bourguiba's position is more uncomfortable. And while the Catholic hierarchy of Senegal is adapting itself quite well to the flamboyant leadership of Leopold Senghor, and even to his close ties with the peanut interests, Catholicism in the Ivory Coast is said to be resentful of Félix Houphouët-Boigny's growing power.

We have said that the former colonizer (or, for that matter, neocolonialist or former anticolonialist) can take to a strong man because he protects commercial interests and is likely to increase armament orders. But the hero may also turn out to be a nuisance: he may lose his temper (the Suez affair) or refuse to understand economic realities (Ben Bella and the commercialization of Algeria's agricultural produce). At that point the personalization of power becomes an obstacle and is labeled irrational. Murmurs of "chauvinism" can be heard, and the "strong man" becomes the "dictator." People claim that he was never elected, or was elected without a real majority. They try to oust him or to improve his government. But rarely does the defeat of personal power have its source outside the country; in almost every case, no matter what stories have been manufactured, the blow comes from inside (Ben Bella, and probably Nkrumah).

In the West it is dangerous to consider young people a class, although some thoughtful souls did so in France in the spring of 1968. This concept is better applied to the Third World, where youth constitutes a political force: rarely a critical factor in the life of personalized power, but a perpetual question mark.

Within its limits, does youth hold out the promise of a democratic tomorrow? Charles Debbasch does not think so:

. . . If they are given responsible positions, these freedom-fighters become the most dependable props of authoritarianism. The fact is that the split between the students and the ruling single party has much deeper roots. It originally grew out of the passionate political involvement of these elites. Medical students, literature and law students, all have a single ambition: to enter the civil or diplomatic services of their country. . . .

The important jobs are held by the generation that fought for independence, and that generation is not eager to be replaced by the new elites. Hence the persistent urge to unseat those who hold the reins of power. . . .[1]

But one need not be virtuous in order to fight vice . . .

[1] *Jeune Afrique* (May 3, 1963).

Representation and
Alienation

"The state, whose combined vigor and discretion ought to inspire confidence . . . obtrudes itself instead, flexing its muscles, shoving, bullying, and making clear to the citizen that he is in permanent danger. . . .

"The leader soothes the people. Years after independence has been won, we see him unable to invite the people's participation in an immediate task, incapable of really involving them in their future or launching them toward nation-building, and simply rehashing the saga of revolution, reviving the sacred ideals of the struggle for liberation. For fear of splintering the national middle class, the leader beckons the people to look backward, plying them with epic memories of the days of resistance."

—FRANTZ FANON
The Wretched of the Earth

No political myth is more gripping and intoxicating than the legend of the justice-loving ruler. The biggest fool can shout his name to the crowd, and suddenly all the wrongs of the world are righted: it may be Harun al-Rashid in one of his disguises, or France's Louis IX—Saint Louis—beneath his oak tree, or any of the kings who have had a cure for scrofula or injustice. Without this type of myth to lean on, tyranny would hardly be bearable—nor, at their inception, would even rationalized powers.

The curious thing about personal power is that, even in its declining stage, its holder seems to be "born lucky," always capable of new effort. When a parliamentary type of regime, whether bureaucratic or collegial, begins to falter (France's Fourth Republic, the Weimar Republic, or the last government of the Egyptian premier Nahas Pasha), faith in anyone and everyone collapses. But until disaster strikes "heroic leadership" fosters vague hopes and beliefs in individual virtue based on individual power; it continues to reflect some measure of what once was the common identity of a man and the crowd.

Whatever one may think of the methods or ideology that brought the leader to power, such marriages are usually impressive, and rarely prove fruitless. Admitting that the attainment of power presupposes the conquest of it and that its primary function is linked in some way to the severing of foreign domination, we can see that in the infancy of new nations the concepts of oneness, justice, and efficacy tend to merge.

The hero acts not only as mediator between the defenseless individual and the seething community, but as protector and refuge as well. Responsible for maintaining order, he often finds it simpler to impose his own will. Patriotism, a lust for power, and visions of dynastic immortality may inspire him. The problem lies in the transition from impulsive power to institutionalized authority—not through heredity (for what could be less heroic than to be "descended from") but through rational depersonalization and legalistic abstraction.

The power of the hero-founder is built around three themes: he incarnates and speaks for the nation in terms of ethnic origin, language, and aspirations; he guides the community, forging it into an active force; he dispenses justice (or at least attempts to) with due respect to custom as well as to social background. He is the exemplar, the leader, and the guardian spirit wrapped up in one. He unites representative, executive, and judicial powers, the separation of which has less significance for a twentieth-century Egyptian peasant than for an eighteenth-century magistrate of Bordeaux.

Whether personalized power can assure universal representation is a matter of controversy. In what or whose name does the hero speak? Who delegated or elected him? The argument goes on, erroneously, about this type of "democracy," which is both direct and directed. How many Third World leaders have been heard replying to a curious stranger's query as to whether elections would sooner or later put them in power: "Elections? They go on every day. The party and I, are we not daily plebiscites?" And, throwing open the windows of the presidential office that overlooks a balcony beneath which crowds gather from time to time: "Elections? We don't have time for them," as Fidel Castro told Chris Marker in *Cuba si*. "My legitimacy? You are it," was Perón's claim in Rosario in August 1950, before an audience of fifty thousand. And Nkrumah's answer to a Nigerian reporter in Accra in October 1965: "My power is the masses." (Three months later the same masses . . .)

Representation based on a plebiscite is in fact revocable, as in the case of duly elected British parties or of the most popular president of the Soviet presidium. Rejection, whether violent or not, justifies withdrawal of the leader's legitimate right to speak for the people. Of course, in weak nations that are prey to powerful and ambitious men, this falling out can be accelerated and even manipulated from the outside. But rarely is foreign intervention the decisive factor.

Its role was practically nonexistent in the case of Ben Bella, very slight for Kassem or Nkrumah, greater for Sukarno. But in none of these situations did foreign influence substitute wholly for action by the people. This could happen only if charisma had already disappeared, if "authority" as defined by Maritain had bowed to factual power, "raw power" in Russell's vocabulary.

Yet we should not underestimate the importance of this role (we are purposely using a theatrical term again). Because the people hunger for identity and unity, a time comes when the nation cannot dispense with a measuring-standard, an image, an echo of itself. This is the incubation period of statehood, when a gesture of Zaghloul establishes tradition, when Bourguiba's words set the style and Nyéréré's conduct creates the pattern for social behavior.

The leader is no less exclusive in matters of decision. Napolean once said that "one bad general is worth two good ones." And Bourguiba echoed: "Share responsibility? That's like splitting a boat that's adrift on a stormy sea "[1] The concept (or myth) of the pilot is shared by all who look out on "stormy seas." There are countless arguments to support it, and a narrow source of decision-making power is an initial aid to the growth of government. Personalized leadership works miracles when it comes to combating, rallying, repressing, or exhorting.

When Nasser reassembled the political fragments of the Egyptian nation, from the Wafd to the Communists and (for a time) from the Moslem Brotherhood to Ahmed Hussein's Socialists, he created a force out of anarchy. When Bourguiba broke with Salah Ben Youssef and took the helm by himself in order to solidify governmental control (a mere transition stage leading to independence, although it took intelligent political guesswork to discern that behind Bourguiba's elaborate rhetoric), he was doing a service to Tunisia.

When Ben Bella made his name the symbol of eight years

[1] Conversation with the author in February 1957.

of revolution in Algeria, he made a mockery of history but
rescued his country from chaos. And French repression gave a
decisive push to Moroccan nationalism by lifting Mohammed
V to leadership over that divided country, which had been
flirting with republicanism. The thinner the blade, the deeper
it cuts. In time of crisis, the greatest concentration of leadership produces the most effective action.

Dependence on the leader, whether he is Lenin or Kemal,
has its rewards during the heroic period when the pioneers
break ground, cross the desert, establish the law, and create
a new world. Just as the human body reacts to fear by sending
the blood rushing to the heart, so fear affects the social organism, strengthening its core and motor: the hero. Threats of
civil war, bankruptcy, foreign pressure, insufficient financial
resources, or an epidemic terrorize the community and serve
only to entrench the leader deeper in the national consciousness. Successful or not, he wins more credit than the Council
of the Hundred.

As for the justice-dispensing function, it is enough to cite
the legends telling of the hero's clemency to measure his popularity. The "just sultan" . . . How many leaders, conquerors,
has the Orient distinguished with that title? He is preoccupied
with the misery of his subjects, distinguishes false arrest from
equity, turns out the usurers and exploiters. Thus, after consideration of all the opportunities a leader has to redeem the
predatory political system he represents by making such a simple popular gesture as dismissing a minister or providing housing for poor widows, it is surprising that Third World
politicians are not so inclined to demagogy as one might sup-
pose.

The crowd likes to contrast its hero ("he") to a scorned or
reviled "they." "They" are exploiting us—if "he" only knew
. . . Because of the intense oppression most of these peoples
have suffered, cursing the multiheaded "they" has a tonic

effect; hopes are pinned to the solitary judge who does what "he" can once he has the facts, when "they" have stated their case. There will be a summons and attempted reconciliation beneath Saint Louis's oak tree, or in one of Prince Sihanouk's "popular audiences," or the *mechouar* of Rabat.

The Third World still has room for both its upright sultans and its benevolent despots. One has to have attended a session of Sihanouk's public court of justice, with the Prince presiding, to appreciate the ingenuity that underlies benevolence and the administration of justice. And just as personal power has no qualms about seeking support or participation of a purely sentimental variety ("Do it for Bourguiba"), pardon is granted or law interpreted on a strictly individual, if not arbitrary, basis. All one needs to do is catch hold of Ben Bella at a meeting, Nasser in his motorcade, Senghor in his native village: probably, everything will be straightened out, for the leader can do anything, and it is rare for him not to make the expected gesture.

If one of the Kairouan districts suffers a water shortage and fears an epidemic, if the schoolchildren of Treichville are so crammed into classrooms that they can barely hear the teacher's voice, if one of the Hoggar tribes has been without medical care for years, the problem falls into the leader's lap, for he is the Great Provider. Personal power is not always circumspect in its dealings, nor always conscientious about its methods, but as a popular system its virtue perhaps lies in the perpetual refuge it offers. Despite their positive influence, however, these are features derived from a romantic paternalism that does not cultivate morality or teach responsibility or prepare the structure of authority.

Equity rather than justice (or "Peronist justice" rather than social equality) characterizes this type of relation between leader and people. Of course, these "miracle healings" build credit from time to time, but even more important are the moral and political benefits that accrue to the miracle maker, whether or not he is aware of them. This type of mysterious and unilateral power tends to be short-lived, although it is useful on occasion for its shock value. Miracles can support the structure of the State as well as of the Church, but a miracle worker does well not to count on a prolonged stay in office.

After all, who can resist his own miracles forever? Few leaders of the Third World are likely to indulge the fancies that ruined Nkrumah—self-deification and professed immortality—but exercising unlimited power evidently unsettles the emotional balance of most of these heroes. Nasser's robust health and endless work-schedule alone keep him from being enbalmed like a pharaoh, when his incense-bearers push him in that direction by pressures inconceivable in our part of the world. When the *raïs* or *zaïm* or Supreme Commander or *lider máximo* opens the paper each morning to find himself the nation's inventor or savior, the redressor of wrongs or defender of rights, when his every movement is hailed as a national victory, how can he help growing a bit giddy? Leaders travel a great deal, and each contact with the outside can provide a touch of reality, an awareness of relative values. But most of the time, the hero, who is living a hallucination, meets other visionaries, and if there is any truth in the story that oracles could not look at each other without laughing, no one has ever reported that the demigods poke fun at one another. In Aimé Césaire's *Le Roi Christophe,* the newly elevated princes, dukes, and marquises are so impressed with themselves that they forget to mock each other. A Third World congress is like the court of King Christopher.

On home grounds the leader is constantly exposed to the cult of personality and its dizzying enticements. Let us take a look at his relations with the people.

. . .

At first, during and after the struggle for independence, he consciously expresses the ardent faith of the masses, each of his words an echo of their hopes. His mirror is the people, and the image he sees there gives him great confidence and inspiration. Soon the mirror encounter becomes a habit, and the merged images a device. Microphones enlarge his voice but not his audience. Yet the crowd is always there, applauding. It is not exactly the words that hold its attention now, but the memory of exciting moments of identification, of hearing him speak. Technique and suggestion replace fervor. Yet there is always a feeling of intimacy between them.

Picture the leader on the platform. He speaks in a rather monotonous voice, accenting his words sharply; he uses phrases that are meaningful to the audience in the darkened hall, whose warm acceptance acts like an undertow sweeping him on: this is the setting for Ben Bella's long affair with the masses. Now he speaks:

"Brothers, scouting is a noble activity which prepares citizens to serve the state."
"Yahya Ben Bella!"
"I am convinced that if scouting were compulsory, it would do a great service to Algeria."
"Yahya Ben Bella! Yahya Ben Bella!"
"Brothers, with your consent, I proclaim that scouting is henceforth compulsory in Algeria."

This is government from-the-platform and through-the-microphone; Egyptians and Tunisians live with it; Ghanaians, Indonesians, and many others came to know it; and this is the way Algerians experienced it. When a man has taken a major role in the independence movement, has recognized and reacted to the people's aspirations and then expressed them; when he passes for an ordinary citizen (but knows better) and possesses the art of rhetoric; when he is self-confident in his role of guide and is convinced that he is both chief and just an ordinary fellow—let this man speak, and his words will have the significance of acts, and the acts will have the force of law. Direct democracy? For a time, while the warm response of his audience signifies adherence and before it becomes mechanical.

Adherence depends on the representativeness of the leader, on the conformity of his ideas to those of the majority, and on the service he has rendered. When he speaks of socialism, as conveyed by the Arabic word *ichtiraka* (implying equality and the sharing of possessions), he expresses both a tradition and an aspiration; he is truly one with the Algerian people and their heavily burdened past, their uncertain and hopeful future. But this sanction has a deteriorating effect on its holder and may cause a divorce between prophet and leader if he cannot maintain his dual function of heart and heartbeat, voice and echo, if spontaneity gives way to routine and tricks of the trade, if what was once a dialogue with his listeners degenerates into a one-sided ritualistic digestion of slogans.

Thus the eloquence that was a source of power begins to wither, and the speaker hears only the sound of his own voice, his own protests of sincerity. He isolates himself, and the more highly he regards his sacred mission, the more likely it is that his audience will come to resemble the desert of the prophets and that his own soliloquy will intoxicate him.

Meanwhile, the slogans improve, the hymns of praise multiply. Going to hear the *zaïm* speak is like attending the performance of a great tenor in his most famous role. With every voice shouting the same slogans, doesn't it mean that they are all behind him still? And if they stopped supporting him, would they not be lost and betrayed? Where would the nation be? So the applause goes on through the night, the exalted leader staring fixedly past the microphone into the vast crowd echoing his chant. "Bung Karno, Bung Karno," "Ben Bella, yahya." The hero basks in the solid warmth of the faithful crowd. The warmth and faith are beyond question, for the sound he hears is that of his own voice.

If he can resist partial or total deification and keep his head on his shoulders, does this type of regime provide the leader with direct and natural authority during the initial stage of power, avoiding opposition, wasted time, and useless contradictions? The answer is uncertain. Anyone who has observed a national hero amid the active machinery of state knows that his representative and speech-making functions can overwhelm his executive duties, and that constant adulation encircles him like a net. Mustapha Kemal had not yet been trapped in it, but Nasser and Bourguiba have had to struggle against it.

One of the conditions related to charismatic power is the dilution of power within the leader's entourage. It is a perfect arena for hard-fisted, ambitious men, for in the vast shadow of the leader there is plenty of room for manipulation. The more respected, popular, and eloquent he is, the wider the field of play open to the camarilla. So let him talk and keep the crowd spellbound; his circle will mind the shop, applying pressure where needed and taking care of the interest groups.

Personalized power gives every appearance of efficiency. Once apprised of an event or a problem—a dam project, an innocent man condemned to death, famine in a far-off province, border rebels offering to negotiate—the leader gets hold of the facts, calls in experts, and telephones the minister of justice or the provincial governor or the general commanding the threatened area or the president of a national bank. The next day the leader is on the scene, giving orders to rescue parties, receiving the guerrilla chief, approving the plan for the dam (after making a very slight, but inspired, modification). The dazzled foreign banker, the submissive rebel, the pardoned convict, and the starving people acclaim him with one voice.

In the second phase the leader is conscious of having acted. He has paid a visit to the Zlass tribesmen; their wheat crop is as good as delivered. He has talked with a Kurdish insurgent; peace is "in the bag." He has seen the plans for the projected dam over the Sebou; it is half built already. Now he is free to turn to other matters. He has provided the impetus and left the follow-up to his experts; his cabinet will manage the rest. Anyway, he is due to address a meeting and afterwards receive a fellow leader.

But what is a cabinet but an amalgamation of forces, frailties, rivalries, factions, and loyalties just as complex as a parliament but more unpredictable and uncontrolled? The president's own brother is in charge of finance; his cousin, of public works; the best friend of his school days runs military affairs; the former vice-president of the party takes care of press relations. Each of them represents a voracious family and an impoverished region, a community and a generation, a party faction, a "nationalized" interest group, or a bureaucratic sector—all irresponsible.

"The raïs has decided." Now the decision must be implemented (that is, interpreted) and the method of approach outlined. If the leader's resolution is announced by Si Mahmoud, Colonel Mustapha is sure to be on his guard; he will find a chance to talk it over again with the president. "Technically impossible, Ya Rais. . . ." Personally, the Colonel would prefer to see the work done by another group and to start negotiations with another mountain tribe.

As it turns out, the leader's will prevails and is carried out in short order. Nasser, Bourguiba, and Houphouët-Boigny have cleared these hurdles and often have managed to sweep out executive scandals. But we should not underestimate the influence of a group whose figurehead often neglects to spell out details and whose laconic directives stimulate inner rivalries. When one of the clique has the leader's ear, that fact throws the other members into a panic. Nor are the group's activities controlled in any manner nearly so efficient as parliamentary supervision: each member of the clique has his supporters in the controlling party, where they are more easily concealed than in an Assembly.

The absence of supervision does not improve the team's behavior. The leader is of course beyond reproach—this is common knowledge, for who showed greater disdain for money than Ngo Dinh Diem (if not Kassem or Ben Bella)? One of the signs of the times is that power and wealth are coming gradually to be disassociated in societies that used to consider them inseparable. Power should corrupt at the very top, yet tropical Caesarism rarely assumes the splendid trappings that were to Sukarno's taste; it prefers the simple military tunic, the frugality of the barracks, receptions at which no liquor is served. Greed is not a common problem for these leaders. And if a few of them funnel part of their earnings as king or president into Swiss bank accounts as a cushion against uncertainty, more elect to end their days like Lumumba rather than like Farouk.

Yet these leaders are rarely bachelors or only sons or childless in marriage. "Families, I detest you," was the cry of André Gide. Here is a slogan that ought to be framed and hung in every presidential palace in the Third World. The absence of countless Madame Nhus or "Zouzou" Nahas would be a relief to the people, who ask only to believe and to admire: "familyarity" breeds contempt.[2]

Almost everyone has something to say about the entourages

[2] Cf. the idea of "amoral familyism" in Edward Banfield's *The Moral Basis of Backward Society* (New York: Glencoe Free Press; 1967).

of leaders. Thomas Kanza, who was foreign minister in the government that succeeded Lumumba's, had this comment:

> Many times, an excellent president or a capable and honest national political leader, who is decisive and respected, surrounds himself with a retinue of upstarts, corrupt and self-seeking men whose conduct, in the long run, discredits the opinion and the image of the nation, the government, and its chief both at home and abroad. Unfortunately, interfamily and intertribal loyalties guide most of the African leaders in choosing their immediate entourage.
>
> This intimate circle is not necessarily the government, meaning the ministers, secretaries of state, or high administrative officials. It is a kind of private court made up of special advisers, confident profiteers, and daily or nightly social companions.
>
> This new "breed" of men and women does more to influence the leader's decisions than his ministers or official technical consultants. Because they have unlimited access to the "boss," these members of the intimate clique form a kind of "invisible arm" of the state, providing their special services in addition to the official ones. . . .[3]

But we should also hear from a victim of the system, the former President of the Central African Republic, David Dacko, whose raw candor may well have been the cause of his downfall. He warned his colleagues:

> . . . the cabinet ministers have no sense of their responsibilities. They do not respect the dignity of their office. They abuse their power, which, in the long run, will discourage the people who supported them. Another danger that threatens the nation is the excessive use of alcohol,

[3] Unpublished memoir.

which most of you exemplify. And what is worse, you drink all day long and lose control of yourselves to the point at which you talk freely and publicly of everything that goes on in your own political group or ministry. It is a disgrace to the nation. . . .[4]

[4] *Afrique-Nouvelle,* October 20, 1961.

Few leaders are aware of the intrigues and practices they are harboring. For example, when one of Nasser's schoolmates who had become a successful industrialist without his friend's patronage called on the Egyptian leader, the visitor complained about widespread corruption in the government and the army. Nasser interrupted him: "Thanks for the tip. I'll look into it. By the way, how much did you have to pay to get this appointment from my secretary?"

II

The Rain Makers

Gamal Abdel Nasser:
Leader and Institution

"Blanqui is essentially a political revolutionist.
He is a socialist only out of sympathy. . . . He
was basically a 'man of action' who believed that
a small, well-organized minority, acting at the
proper moment, could lead the masses."

—FRIEDRICH ENGELS,
A Program for the
Blanquist Exiles

In Egypt, power is influenced more strongly than anywhere else by geographic, economic, and historical factors. Personification, in the forms of concentration and incarnation, found its promised land there at the beginning of history. Geography as well as the system of production had shared in creating a politico-religious ideology that of necessity took root in the fertile Nile Valley.

We need not accept Wittfogel's thesis that a direct and immutable relation links the water system to bureaucratic despotism, the program of land reclamation to the chief engineer's absolute rule over rural society.[1] Other influences have built and continue to build totalitarianism, from the Golden Age of Chinese culture to the era of the commissars, from the rise of Jesuit power in Paraguay to that of General Stroessner. The true picture is more complex, and Egypt, along with China, has had a glimpse of democracy from time to time.

---

[1] *Oriental Despotism: A Comparative Study of Total Power* (New Haven: Yale University Press; 1957), p. 12 and passim.

But if Wittfogel's argument, which stems from both Marx and Weber, has any value, it is certainly with regard to Egypt, especially since the harnessing of her waters, so necessary for her survival, developed into a program of dam construction, giving the ruling power supreme control over agriculture and industry—over life itself.

An equally important factor is the lay and distribution of the habitable land, which is densely populated and confined to flat strips that eliminate the possibility of guerrilla warfare and thus discourage revolt while helping to consolidate power. Also, Egyptian history has nurtured the tradition of pharaoh-worship, of a variety of Islam differing from that of Persia, Mesopotamia, or Syria in that it has produced more despotic caliphs than revolutionary prophets, fewer disciples of Ali, the popular branch of Islamic tradition, than of Muawiya, the sovereign arm. Everything tends to reinforce concentration and to sublimate the sun-god.

Important to this is the age-old heritage of centralized authority, which Ibn Khaldun characterized thus: "Some countries are destined for empire. The ruler need never worry about protest movements or revolt, which are rare: such is Egypt's case. . . . There we find only one sovereign and his obedient subjects."[2] And, on a minor note, around 1950 the actor-dramatist Naguib el-Rihani remarked to a friend: "Send me into the street in the general's uniform I wore in my last play; show me the Gardens of Ezbekieh and let me repeat the same speech there: I guarantee that Egypt is mine!"

Did the heritage of centralized authority influence Napoleon during his fifteen-month stay in Egypt? The rigid structure of French government has sources other than the Nile Valley, but the effects were at least reciprocal. It is more likely that Napoleon gave Mohammed Ali a few lessons in rulership and in-

[2] *Prolégomènes*, I, p. 338, translation quoted by Yves Lacoste in *Ibn Khaldoun* (Paris: Maspéro; 1966).

spired his Albanian-born pupil to impose a pharaonic regime on Egypt.

This was the government of modern Egypt's founder, who organized the country as if it were an immense state farm, altering its landscape and commercial orientation by introducing the cotton industry, taming the Nile by damming its delta and transforming peaceful farmers into Oriental conquerors. Moreover, this intense concentration became so firmly entrenched that even the decadent rule of Mohammed Ali's misguided and fanatical heirs could not uproot it. Thus, in 1944, when the Wafdist leader Abdessalam Fahmy Gomaa replied to the throne with a reference to "the will of the people," Farouk sneeringly answered, "My good Pasha, the will of the people emanates from my will!"[3]

Traditional centralized authority might have had less to do with shaping Nasser's power if the democratic experiments of 1850–1950 had not failed miserably. In fact, for many Egyptians democratic representation and parliamentary government were synonymous with foreign domination and palace intrigue. And the Wafdist party, symbol of independence and Western democracy, had made one concession after another to the British and to the monarchy and had become corrupt and demagogic.

We should take a close look at the "import label" on a certain brand of democracy in Egypt. The first "parliament" was organized in 1866 by the Khedive Ismaïl during the period when Egyptian sovereignty began to disintegrate and be replaced by Anglo-French domination. The first "modern" cabinet, formed in 1878, included two foreigners, one English, one French, who were the country's economic administrators. A year later, in 1879, a Legislative Assembly vaguely modeled after the House of Commons came into being. European dom-

[3] P. J. Vatikiotis, *The Egyptian Army in Politics* (Bloomington: Indiana University Press; 1969), p. 39.

ination (primarily British after 1882, when the officers' revolt failed) developed rapidly, along with Western-type institutions that placed the country squarely in European hands. The best example of this process of combined modernization and alienation was the constitution (the organic law) granted by the Khedive Tewfik in 1883.

In 1923, after nominal independence was proclaimed, King Fuad gave his people a new constitution, a body of law based on Belgian institutions as they existed in 1831—scarcely appropriate for the social and political realities of Egypt at the beginning of the twentieth century. In any event, that constitution was consistently violated by the throne until a new one, also "imported" but more authoritarian, replaced it in 1930. From 1935 to 1952, including World War II, the Palestine conflict and a period of relative calm, crisis, scandal, and social injustice were rampant.

As Abdel Amer put it: "Of her thirty years of constitutional government, Egypt spent ten under martial law or provisional regimes."[4] How could a democratic system, so obviously foreign-made and subject to the royal pleasure, be imposed on a people accustomed to disciplinary rule? Whatever the reasons, it is clear that what discredited the system was the way it operated (or was manipulated by the king and a class that catered to all his whims)—not the system itself, or the curious, imported constitution. As we shall see, the members of the officer group invoked it as their authority in the first days of the military government. In the years that followed, Nasser used it often as justification for his power.

While the people regarded parliamentary government as ruinous, indistinguishable from "the dominant interests of the great landowners,"[4] the nationalists were watching other political systems develop in countries hostile to Egypt's British

[4] *La Faillite du système constitutionnel égyptien (1923–52)*, (Paris: Doctoral dissertation; 1955).

enemy. To the young officers beginning to evaluate world affairs on the eve of the War, Italian Fascism, German National Socialism, and Francoism had great appeal, with their cults of youth, of efficiency, of patriotism and militarism, and their struggles against British "plutocracy" and French "bourgeois-type" institutions. The same fascination pervaded literary circles. In an essay on the Prophet Mohammed published in 1941, Abbas Mahmud El Akkad, one of the country's most celebrated writers, found it apt to compare Islam's founder to Hitler.[5]

Thus a number of Egyptians began to speak out in favor of governments that appeared capable of consolidating and organizing the foes of the British Empire: in the army, there was old Marshal Aziz el-Masri, a former Turkish officer long known for his anti-British and pro-German sympathies; in political circles, the lawyer Ahmed Hussein, leader of the "Green Shirts."

Just before the war broke out, a number of young army officers (including Gamal Abdel Nasser) were regularly attending Green Shirt meetings of the Misr el Fatat (Young Egypt) movement. The first Axis victories after 1940, followed by Rommel's astounding triumphs in the Libyan desert, aroused great enthusiasm among the Egyptians, as did the anti-British revolt unleashed in Iraq by Rachid Ali el-Keilani, notoriously an Axis sympathizer. Azis el-Masri tried to join forces with him, along with other officers who later appeared at Nasser's side.

Fascism's defeat in 1945 did not completely erase its charms. And Israel's victory in 1948 was attributed to the inept Egyptian parliamentary monarchy and served to revive the old prestige of totalitarian systems. Racism, which had not existed in Egypt, made its appearance. Denunciations of the "Zionist

[5] Nadav Safran: *Egypt in Search of Political Community* (Cambridge: Harvard University Press; 1961).

conspiracy" had the ring of a Goebbels diatribe, fostering thoughts and hopes of a similar caliber. Thus, in the early 1950's, in addition to the heritage of autocracy and the failure of parliamentary government, there was a vague attraction to dictatorship and personal power, the regime that was to follow on the heels of a coup d'état.

But outer forces were not the sole influences on Egyptian politics. Around 1950 the people had two images before them, two faces of power: Mustafa Nahas and King Farouk. They were typical and vigorous politicians. Nahas inherited legitimate charismatic authority from Saad Zaghlul, the "father of the people," who had set whatever standards and style there were. Nahas was a *zaïm* in miniature, almost in caricature. He was Everyman to the core: clownish and good-humored, open-minded and open-handed, all of which endeared him to the public. Thus, a certain political trend—democratic, demagogic, freewheeling—was colorfully personified in pre-Nasser Egypt.

Another policy, that of traditional and unrestricted authority, was also personified. Between 1935 and 1942 King Farouk had endowed it with a handsome, somewhat pudgy, but all-Egyptian, face. The face and the profile were gradually engulfed in a sea of flesh. His obesity became grotesque and provocative; his playboy fancies and utter unreliability were a public disgrace. When the summer of 1952 arrived, the Egyptian people were left with an extraordinary spectacle of public affairs to gaze upon, the joint collapse of an image and a form of government.

CONQUEST

An army officer named Gamal Abdel Nasser Hussein grew up in that climate. Son of a postal employee and grandson of a fellah with a few *feddans* (acres) in the village of Beni-Morr, near Asyut, in Upper Egypt, the stronghold of pious rural tradition, Nasser was born and spent some of his early years in Alexandria. It was a large and semi-Europeanized city, where the young Egyptian felt keenly the sense of alienation that pervaded his country. Lawrence Durrell's novels describe this well—Egyptians were like intruders there. In Cairo, where he finished high school, the estrangement was less obvious, but it was rampant in Faggala at the En-Hahda school, which had a reputation for "politicalizing" its students.

Young Nasser did not get along very well with his father, who had remarried after his mother's death, and he lived with his uncle Hussein Khalil, a veteran nationalist who all but enlisted him in various movements protesting the ubiquitous foreigners. He was wounded in 1936 while demonstrating with Ahmed Hussein's Green Shirts, a Fascist group. The demonstration was called to denounce the Anglo-Egyptian treaty granting Egypt political autonomy but committing her to an alliance with the West. He was also in contact with Hassan el-Banna's Moslem Brotherhood and with extreme left-wing organizations.

In his *Philosophy of Revolution* Nasser wrote that he was disgusted at being indirectly involved in an attempted assassination; yet everything seemed to groom this fervent young man for extremism, some form of Fascism, and terrorism, and we can imagine him sipping coffee with his comrades on the terrace of a Cairo café, seething as he watched the passing Rolls-Royces that belonged to Egypt's masters.

When he failed to enter the University of Cairo as a law student, he joined the army, which suited his activist leanings. He had never been a particularly good student, but he shone at the military academy. Stationed first in Mankabad, then in Alexandria, he went on to a garrison in the Sudan, always combining nationalist activities with his military apprenticeship. Between 1938 and 1941 he attracted a circle of protégés that remained intact until 1967: Abdel Hakim Amer, Zakaria Mohieddine, Anouar el-Sadat.

As we already know, the Second World War brought no more satisfaction to these young people than did their army careers. Egypt's support of the Allies aggravated Gamal and his friends all the more because London had no qualms about making and unmaking Cairo governments in accordance with its war aims. Thus, when victory came, it was not "their" victory.

In 1945, Captain Abdel Nasser began organizing his group of "Free Officers" and mounting his long-cherished campaign for a free Egypt. What really gave the project momentum was the Palestine war, which he and his friends labeled treason on the part of the Palace and its political allies: an officer group is most patriotic, and consequently most frustrated, immediately after a defeat. In the summer of 1948, the revolutionary officers' movement began to take shape, and by January 1950 it had a central committee with Nasser as president. Its program reflected whatever influences happened to weigh upon Gamal and his friends.

Three of those influences warrant particular attention. The first was the important Moslem Brotherhood, at its influential height around 1950 (despite the assassination of its leader the year before) as a result of its having sent commandos against the British in the Canal Zone. Through Anouar el-Sadat, Nasser came into contact with the *Morched* ("Supreme Guide") Hassan el-Banna, and some of his comrades joined the guerrillas against the English. But Nasser was already too preoccupied with current realities to give much attention to the Brotherhood's theocratic doctrine.

His second important contact was with the forward wing of the Wafd, notably with Ahmed Abul Fath, who published *Al-Misri,* and whom he met through the latter's brother-in-law, Saroit Okacha, also a friend of Nasser's. Major Nasser and his entourage circulated their ideas in this important democratic newspaper and formed alliances that would prove useful in the early days of power.

They also made enemies, however. Two of them, Lieutenant Colonel Youssef Saddiq and Major Khaled Mohieddine, were closely affiliated with one of the Marxist groups competing for influence in the intellectual community: HADETO (Democratic Movement for National Liberation). Nasser himself was frequently in touch with a young Marxist-oriented magistrate, Ahmed Fuad. The movement was developing a strong socialist undercurrent.

On January 26, 1952, Cairo burst into flames. The Wafdist government of Mustafa Nahas Pasha, in open conflict with London and facing a bloody engagement in the Suez Canal Zone, had invited anarchy—and incendiaries had seen their opportunity. Who were they? Who stood to benefit from the fiery spectacle? The English, the king? The Moslem Brothers? The Green Shirt movement, by then a "socialist" party? The Free Officers, forbidden by royal injunction to intervene or restore order "because there is a risk they might join the demonstrators,"[6] saw the handwriting on the wall. The government amounted to nothing but a heap of Cairo's ashes. The discredited monarchy would not even have to be abolished— but simply to be replaced by the state. Six months later, the Free Officers ruled Egypt.

Where did the July conspiracy promise to lead the country? Toward military dictatorship? A republic? Personal power? All we know about the July movement is that the officers acted independently, without political backing; that their objectives were both moral and patriotic, not bound by any ideology; and that the ringleader was a master strategist. How they intended to use their new power was another question.

6 Jean and Simonne Lacouture, *Egypt in Transition* (New York: Criterion; n.d.), p. 122.

At four o'clock in the morning of July 23, in their new headquarters the victors were gathered around the "boss" they had chosen and had sent for: Mohammed Naguib, already a personality and a symbol. Abdel Koddous, a journalist, asked Naguib what his plans were.

"To protect the constitution, to reform the army and the state."

"Will you actually take power?"

"No, the constitution does not allow it."

So they were looking for a civilian head of government. The conspirators settled on Aly Maher, a veteran politician, who had served as somewhat of a mentor to the king and his prime minister several times, and who was known for his anti-British sentiments. The newsman was asked to introduce one of the officers to the old Pasha, whom none of them knew. Abdel Koddous spotted a serious, thoughtful-looking officer who said nothing in the midst of the clamor—just the man for his mission. It was Nasser, whom he asked to accompany him. But Sadat interjected: "No, not him, leave him alone." Thus the reporter understood that Nasser was the key man and was being held in reserve for the task ahead.

A republican system of government was established at first, under the smiling aegis of good-natured Naguib. The officer group shredded the pros and cons of every issue: the fate of Farouk (death or exile?), how to punish the striking workers at the Kafr el-Dawar spinning mill, what regulations to impose on political parties . . . Nasser's views carried regarding the king and the parties. Today, his friends say he wanted to pardon the workers who were shot. That much credit we can grant him. His first steps certainly gave no hint that a Bonaparte had come onstage. Nasser was the brains of the movement, but there was no evidence that he planned to take it over.

. . .

How does one describe the ideas, the aims, the political thinking, or the motives of Gamal Abdel Nasser?

The man was thirty-four, a patriot and a Moslem. The latter allegiance provides a definite clue to his concept of power. He knew that although the authority of Islam is almost a situation, a condition that God has bestowed on a particular individual, endowing him with *hukm,* which the *beya* (oath of faith) sanctions, that authority is subject to *ijna* (consensus, either positive or negative). But he realizes that the principle of authority—a divine decree legalized by faith—almost always supersedes *ijma.* His attitude toward power is not cynical; at the same time, the religious side of it is not likely to foster any serious democratic ideals. Religion will simply point the way to self-deification in the pharaonic tradition.

Moreover, this ardent Moslem has certain historical and moral convictions, which Jean-Paul Charnay summarized in a study entitled *Temps social en Islam.*[7] For a Moslem leader, action moves in two directions: one reaching for inspiration into the past, to the time of the prophets, the golden age of faith, the other tending to focus on the present as a means of dominating the future by using tools of modernization

What dominates the religious thinking of Nasser? Does he lean toward prophethood and Mahdism, or does he stress willpower leading to rationalist theories (and practice) of the *nahda* (renaissance), of *thawra* (revolution) of *ichtirakya* (socialism)? In the context of his thought, appeals to "return to primitive purity" and to "recast oneself along modern lines" are not contradictory.

Hubert Michel made this observation about the serious

[7] Institut de Sociologie de Rabat (May 1967).

young leader, whose approach to power was slow and solemn, who wielded it with no restraints:

> If personalized power exists today in the Moslem states, it grew out of a loose concept of democracy which was translated into the notion of social and political liberation of the individual from "reactionary" forces, a compromise offered to twentieth-century industrial society whose welfare falls on the shoulders of the *zaïm,* the new leader of this reinterpreted jihad.[8]

All we know about this period of Nasser's career comes from his friends, Saroit Okacha, Anouar el-Sadat, and Ahmed Abul Fath. Fath, who began to oppose him more and more openly two years later, is the only one to suggest that Gamal was permeable to personal ambition.[9] Every other record seems to imply the opposite: *Bikbachi* (Lieutenant Colonel) Nasser, an excellent instructor in tactics at the military academy of Abassiah, organizer of the *Doubat el Ahrar* (Free Officers) conspiracy, was respected by his friends and considered a rank-and-file leader, not a "boss."

He was influential rather than imposing. He argued and tried to persuade, disregarding his rank and privilege. *Primus inter pares.* After his friend Khaled Modieddine had left for Alexandria on July 27, Nasser sent him a note that has a curious ring today: "Come back quickly; we must steer clear of dictatorship." But isn't this the language he used with his leftist comrades?

We do not know why or how he managed to stay out of the military and civil police records until July 23, 1952—either by his equalitarian sense or by his already disturbing talent for intrigue—or what kept the morose Colonel's real identity a

---

[8] "Le FLN et la personnalisation du pouvoir," in *Revue française d'études africaines* (April 1968).

[9] *L'Affaire Nasser* (Paris: n.p.; 1958).

virtual state secret during the following three months. His furtiveness, however, does not suggest that he was reluctant to take power. In any event, the success of a conspiracy depends on maximum secrecy; Nasser was never in contact with more than one or two of his colleagues at a given time. This lent the movement an air of mystery and intrigue, which had later consequences.

During the first weeks, Gamal's orientation seemed to be nonmilitaristic: he made every effort to seek closer cooperation with all the parties, especially the major one, the Wafd. He broke with it only after it became apparent that Fuad Seragguedine and his Wafdist allies planned to climb aboard the army train for a return to power without giving the least assurance that their political policies would change.

Throughout this period of power in the shadows, Nasser consistently gave the impression that he was attracted to, yet fearful of, responsibility, that power and its enticements frightened him. Prophethood was an anguishing burden. Did he ever doubt his calling? In his *Philosophy of Revolution*, dictated between 1952 and 1954 to a close friend, the journalist Mohammed Hassanein Heykal, he discusses the role that "awaits its hero." Is this hero the Egyptian people or Nasser himself? Looking back over the years, it now seems to have meant the man. But at that time he did not act like a leader who demands the limelight.

In his colorful biography of the *Bikbachi*, Robert St. John entitles a chapter covering this period "The Reluctant Dictator." The characterization was valid for a long time. Not until three months after the July coup did he authorize Abdel Koddous to mention him in his magazine *Rose el-Youssef* as the new regime's key man [1] And only in January 1953 did he take an official title: Secretary General of *Hay'Et el-Tahrir*

---

[1] Jean and Simonne Lacouture.

(Movement for Liberation), the first of many political organizations he founded for the purpose of implanting the regime among the masses.

Although the existent "provisory constitutional regulations" placed sovereign power in Naguib's hands "in order to protect the revolution," the face of the new power was Nasser's. Still, he remained in the shadows, usually in his private office, called the "Revolutionary Council," on the banks of the Nile. At that time he was just a straightforward and rather awkward fellow, somewhat round-shouldered, with a piercing and mournful gaze, sunburned, laconic, and unassuming.

His first real contact with the public came on June 18, 1953. Having deposed Farouk and exiled him eleven months earlier, the officers had set that date for proclaiming a republic: they had to declare themselves, for if the regime was to open negotiations with England over evacuation of the Canal Zone, it had to have some clearly defined status. A crowd gathered in front of the Abdine Palace, Farouk's former residence.

From the balcony of the building that became the headquarters of the Liberation Movement, a harsh yet warm voice, metallic and vibrant, rang out through the dusk, calling the people to support the Republic. He was finally at the helm. No mistaking it. The speaker's fervor left no doubt that this was not a mere propaganda exercise; he was a revolutionary. In any event, he was trying to find his historical bearings, to put his stamp on an upheaval that he carefully referred to as *thawra* (revolution, a lasting event) and not *inqilab* (overthrow, an accidental occurrence) as Naguib called it.

But his revolutionary zeal was already being punctured. Not until the beginning of 1954 did Nasser admit, again in his *Philosophie de la Révolution,*[2] that mass inertia had been a great disillusion. "We opened the way: but the reluctant

[2] (Cairo: n.p.; 1954), p. 21.

masses did not follow. . . ." His conversion to authoritarianism probably dates not from his seizure of power but from his awareness of that indifference on the part of those who had the most to gain from the Free Officers' coup. Would the people have fallen in behind the officers? And if so, would Nasser have seized control in the rough manner that typified the regime? In view of his great vitality, his constant reappraisal of situations, and his atttiude of aloofness toward democratic principles, the likelihood is doubtful.

In proclaiming the Republic, Nasser also made it clear that his term of invisible power was ended. On June 19, 1954, he became both Vice-Premier and Minister of the Interior, and his closest friend, Major Abdel Hakim Amer, was made a general (the only accelerated promotion that followed the 1952 coup—a fact to remember) and took command of the armed forces. At the same time, two other Free Officers were given key posts: Boghdadi, Minister of War, Salah Salem, Minister of Sudanese Affairs (of major importance at that time) and of National Orientation (propaganda).

As Secretary General of the Liberation Movement from January onward, Nasser controlled the basic political apparatus. The July victors emerged from the shadows and gave the regime its true color: neither white (despite their mild treatment of the king and their brutality toward the workers) nor red (agrarian reform and anti-imperialism), but simply khaki.

Yet militarism as such does not apply to Nasser or his cohorts, for it implies an unbroken military tradition, a link between Fontenoy, Tannenberg, and the direct experience of dramatic events. That was not possible in Egypt. Ibrahim Pasha's exploits and Orabi's revolt were too far in the past, and the Palestine drama was too tragic. For militarism to emerge, an army must be "caste-conscious," as it was in Germany, France, Japan, and Poland. Here, there was class-consciousness among the officers. These young men came almost exclusively from petty-bourgeois peasant stock, the small rural landholders who might own between five and twenty *feddans,* were able to send their sons to school and not miss them during the cotton harvest, but could not afford higher education for them in Cairo. When Mustafa Nahas's Wafdist government opened the military academy in 1936 to young men from poor or lower-middle-class families, he initiated a program of major importance, just as Saad Zaghlul had thirty years earlier by enabling the sons of peasants to enter universities, thus sowing the seeds of the modern intelligentsia, typified by Taha Hussein. In that same year, young men left the countryside in droves to enter the military academy, creating a "ladder of progress" within Egyptian society: Nasser and friends made a dash for it and thus managed to reach the top rung. But there was clearly no proud tradition to defend—it was simply a public vehicle for getting ahead. The army was a means, not an end in itself. And it was not by coincidence that all these men soon changed into civilian dress.[3]

Was this a military intelligentsia capable of reviving the Wafd and of substituting intelligence and direction for *esprit de corps?* Yes and no. It was, in that the intellectual level of the victors was relatively high. Nasser was partly self-taught and was blessed with energy and initiative; a clumsy writer but a born organizer and good speaker, he surrounded himself with men like Gamal Salem and Khaled Mohieddine, whose mental agility and curiosity perhaps made them the equals of their civilian predecessors. It was not, because for a long time the group was unable to create an original line of thought, cultural reorientation, a basic sense of intellectual freedom (hence creativity)—in a nutshell, what we would call an "ideology."

[3] Nasser himself retired from the army in 1955. Since that time he has not kept any military rank or title.

We have mentioned class-consciousness, an inexact term, but one that leads to some interesting comparisons. It recalls the career of Arabi Pasha, for example, leader of the officer revolt of 1880, which protested the favored treatment of Turkish army officers, foreign domination, and the corrupt rule of the khedives. An outburst of social and national frustration, completely alien to military posture, it awakened popular sympathy and was quickly snuffed out by the British. The movement taking shape in Egypt between 1952 and 1954 was of vaguely comparable inspiration. But Nasser was of a different cast than Arabi.

What they have in common is not simply their nationalism and social background; it is what one might call "Egyptianness." Whether or not Nasser's rise constituted a revolution has been and continues to be debated. However, the movement itself has a profoundly revolutionary aspect: the seizure of Egyptian sovereignty by Egyptians. June 18, 1953, marked the abolition of the monarchy, the Albanian dynasty that had reigned for a century and a half with the connivance of a court and its clique made up of Lebanese agents, Turkish cousins, Greek merchants, French experts, and English advisers. It also marked the nationalization of the Egyptian state, preceding that of the Canal and the economy.[4]

The officers looked beyond the nation's frontiers; most of them came from Upper Egypt, which faces unfamiliar Africa rather than Europe and the rest of the world. And though Nasser was born in Alexandria, everything about him—his complexion, carriage, blunt style, furtiveness, lasting grudges, sense of honor, and clannishness—all bespoke the *Said* (a descendant of Mohammed) and the Nile Valley, Egypt's cradle. He was bound by ancient traditions alien to the concept of a cosmopolitan nation.

[4] Egypt had scarcely become "Egyptianized" when she immersed herself in the United Arab Republic—a strange reluctance to take her own name.

So it is not surprising that young Colonel Nasser, with his lukewarm concern for democratic ideals, resorted to authoritarianism, ingrained in his own culture, in order to deal with initial political opposition and public apathy. Not militarism but Islam prodded him, after eleven trying months at the helm, to concentrate power and prepare, ever discreetly, the personification of authority.

To understand Nasser's approach to power, perhaps we should first separate ideology from organization and compare the July 23 regime to an enterprise headed by "managers" who balked at doctrine and at "politics" in general.

In an excellent essay, *The Organization of Egypt,* James Heaphey makes much of Nasser's disgusted attitude toward politics: "Political policies revolt the organization man." Nasser's own attempts to conceptualize his revolution are scarcely worth noting, but his planning and influence transcend the role of manager.

Do publications like *Al-Missa* and *Akhbar-el-Yom,* so patently bent on developing a political slant, deserve to be labeled "propaganda"? Was the 1962 Charter simply a wrapper for the projected power structure? Nasser is neither Lenin nor Mao, but his accomplishment (apart from implanting his own authority) in expanding the social-military regime of 1952 should not be undervalued.

Manfred Halpern said in referring to him: "By itself, military rule can be no substitute for the art of politics."[5] True, but Nasser's undertaking cannot be reduced to a military rule, or even to "a restrictive elitist cabal,"[6] as Amos Perlmutter puts it: first, because of the man's scope, imagination, and

[5] *The Politics of Social Change in the Middle East and North Africa* (Princeton: Princeton University Press; 1963).

[6] Institute of International Studies, University of California, Berkeley (report given in the "Seminar on Political Development," Harvard-M.I.T.: March 1966).

objectives; second, because of the close and active ties between
the July group and the Egyptian peasantry, the nation's sub-
structure; and finally, because the dramatic impact of Nasser's
statesmanship continually enlarged his undertaking, marking
it for disaster perhaps, but lending it all the same the aura
of myth.

CONCENTRATION

As of June 1953 it was public knowledge that Gamal Abdel
Nasser held power. Naguib was still Number One, but people
whispered that the "Good General" was only the Colonel's
colorbearer. As de facto president of the Revolutionary Council, Vice-Premier, and Minister of the Interior (Zakaria Mohieddine was in charge of the *mohabarat,* the political secret
police), and with the army under the thumb of his close friend
Abdel Hakim Amer, the Colonel had nearly total concentration of power. His taking the platform on June 19, 1953, may
have marked the beginning of personification.

The following year would tell the story, for it was the great
test of his power. Throughout the summer of 1953, the regime
rode down political opposition, suppressing parties, imprison-
ing their leaders, and even sentencing a number of them
(Abdelhadi and Farag) to death. The Wafd was broken, the
smaller parties were crushed. The Moslem Brotherhood grew
alarmed. They had survived the new rule but had not been
offered any deal that would allow them to gain the upper
hand. They were tolerated but considered suspect. Their mod-
erate-wing leaders, arm in arm with the most staid members
of the old regime, tried to come to terms with Mohammed
Naguib, who, it was said, frowned upon the new power's
bulging muscles.

But other factions within the Brotherhood were of a differ-

ent humor, and in January 1954 they loosed a wave of demonstrations at Cairo University. The Revolutionary Council met
and sealed the Brotherhood's fate. Naguib took issue and
roundly criticized the regime's policies, suggesting that the
army "return to the barracks" and demanding the right to
veto the decisions of his eleven young colleagues. There were
urgent calls for dictatorship, and the General offered to resign.
Nasser and his comrades accepted his resignation, and on February 25, 1954, Naguib stepped down.

Nasser was summoned before the officer group to explain
his position. "You choose power over the army. You try to
replace Farouk's rule with your own!" Nasser defended himself, claiming that revolutionary gains were won inch by inch,
through unrelenting struggle—and then suddenly dropped the
argument. "Remember Naguib. . . . I resign."

Cairo took to the streets: the beloved General Naguib,
whose appearance on the balcony of the Abdine Palace set off
waves of applause, had given them new hope of recovering
their lost liberties. And the crowd grew even wilder when he
announced: "We shall ask the people to elect a Parliament."
Nasser seemed headed for defeat.

He sought Khaled Mohieddine's support to counter the
pressure for dictatorship which was building in the junta (and
in his favor). Had he lost his democratic "illusions"? Was he
simply avid for power? Or did he believe that it was too soon
after the abolition of the monarchy for the country to handle
freedom?

At this point, I would like to mention two conversations I
had with Gamal Abdel Nasser, one on January 15, 1954, in
his office at the Revolutionary Council, the other, on the door-
step of his villa on March 5 of the same year, both of which
indicated the bare outline of a doctrine as well as Nasser's
characteristic pragmatism.

At the time of my first interview, the Colonel had just dissolved the Moslem Brotherhood and was carrying on secret talks with Britain aimed at clearing the Canal Zone—what one might call Nasser's second period. In the first period, covering the events of July 23 and the ensuing weeks, he seemed to have had no other objective than to free the people; the third period, after 1956, was to find him a popular leader defying the great powers and heading the march toward socialism. In 1954 he could hardly be called a popular leader: he was laconic, rather cynical, and convinced that firm discipline had to be enforced in order to maintain social stability.

Did he intend to restore constitutional government once Britain had withdrawn her troops? "No," he answered, "it wouldn't make any sense. In a year and a half we have been able to wipe out corruption. If the right to vote were now restored, the same landowners would be elected—the feudal interests. We don't want the capitalists and the wealthy back in power. If we open the government to them now, the revolution might just as well be forgotten."

The second interview was six weeks later. He had just agreed to hold the elections favored by Naguib, which he had recently considered so risky. Was the step premature? "No. We have talked for a month and a half, searching for a compromise solution. . . . We didn't expect to make such good progress. But now the British negotiators can no longer call us Nazis or Fascists."

Moreover, at that time he had already worked out a short cut to rapid restoration of limited democratic rights. He acted on three levels. First, bowing to pressure, he made concessions and let Naguib commit himself to the old-line politicians. Next, he stirred up the army against the "corrupt civilians." Finally, he appealed to the trade unions and the masses— having first prepared them through the army's propaganda services—to protest "the return of the pashas."

On March 28, it was *he* whom the crowd (perhaps not the

same crowd) cheered and acclaimed with the ringing cry
(which I heard): "Long live the Revolution! Down with
liberty!" A general strike broke out the next day "in support
of the revolution," and of reinstating Nasser. (He was already
reinvested with power but was not satisfied with a mere "technical" victory, for he wanted to obliterate the memory
of Naguib's victory the previous February. He won, but
with methods that were a far cry from his cautious steps
in 1952.)

This synthetic demonstration was to have far-reaching effects on his power and his emerging doctrine. It showed him
where his support lay, where it was uncertain, and who his
enemies were. The events of February, March, and April 1954
shaped his power. Because the middle class, the political parties, and the Moslem Brotherhood played Naguib against him,
because parliamentary government was the opposition's platform, and because the army and a segment of the working
class backed him solidly, "Nasserism" took on certain features: it was popular and military, authoritarian and plebian,
and secular.

Nasserism? The meaning of the word was still vague. His
power was developing a style, but it still had no doctrine.
Time after time Nasser had clutched at democratic ideals and
abandoned them as premature, only to reach for them again
later on and finally to oppose them in the form of parliamentary government. Nasserism was as yet only Nasser's power.
Its essence can be summarized briefly: the army, being the least
corrupt and most reform-minded organization, should furnish
the new regime's elite; democracy does not require representative government but involves a concerted governmental effort
to improve the people's existence; power was once the domain
of the rich, and therefore the transformation of Egyptian society must entail the divorce of authority from wealth. That is

perhaps the strongest argument in favor of Egypt's agrarian reform, which does not enrich the peasant so much as it destroys feudal landholding.

There was also a hint of the Boy Scout in Nasser during his second period, but he learned fast and shed most of his political naïveté. It was apparent in his conflict with the Moslem Brotherhood, which tried to have him assassinated in Alexandria the day after he signed the Anglo-Egyptian treaty.

It was an important incident. To a man as sensitive as Nasser, even if he had faced up to the wavering loyalty of the masses, the firing of those eight bullets on October 26, 1954, taught a profound lesson. "Ours is a white revolution," he would often say. But that evening, not long after the last gunshot rang out, he flung out his challenge in a piercing, emotion-choked voice: "Go ahead and kill Gamal! The Egyptian people have hundreds of Gamals who will rise up and show you that a red revolution is worth more than a dead one!" Two weeks later, six men were hanged in Cairo's prison; thousands were arrested, hundreds tortured. By the close of 1954, concentration of power was a fact.

Naguib, allegedly implicated in the Moslem Brotherhood conspiracy, fell from grace and was placed under arrest. The Colonel held all the cards. Although his election as President of the Republic did not come until June 1956, no leader had more rigid control of his country than Gamal Abdel Nasser.

The structure rose like a pyramid: the state, the government, the army, the party (the former Liberation Movement) were dominated, either directly or indirectly, by the *raïs*. Beneath him there were two organs: the Revolutionary Council, composed of officers whose political existence was dependent entirely on his favor (except perhaps for that odd personality Gamal Salem), and from which the "bad influences" (leftists such as Youssef Saddiq and Khaled Mohieddine) had been

removed; and finally the bureaucracy, in which the civilians—
good technicians or punctual bureaucrats—played second fid-
dle to the men in khaki.

On various levels were the army, riddled with factions but
loyal in the main, and mindful that its own prosperity was a
debt it owed the Free Officers; the trade unions, controlled
by hard-fisted managers who supported the government because it was industry-oriented and would protect their jobs;
and the peasant community, which was scarcely affected (only
8 percent of it at the time) by the redistribution of land, but
foresaw a slightly improved future in the reduction of its
taxes and in proposed wage increases.

Had the relation between citizen and government changed
since the coming of Nasser and his officers? "Lift up your
head, comrade. The days of oppression are over!" was one of
the slogans bearing Abdel Nasser's signature; it was printed
on mammoth banners that floated over Cairo the day after the
signing of the 1954 Anglo-Egyptian pact. Oppression? Yes,
in a sense. Life for the overwhelming majority of Egyptians
could be compressed into three words: "Haader ya bey"
("Yes, my lord"). Chattels of those who owned the land and
villages, the fellah had no alternative but to prostrate himself
in the feudal tradition, though he might sneer about it on the
sly. Then along came the young men in khaki. Many of them
were peasants themselves—their leader was still in close touch
with the fellahs of Beni-Morr, his uncles and cousins. They
were instituting agrarian reform and arresting a number of
"evil beys." In town, their manner—simple, straightforward,
unassuming—pleased the crowd.

This was the end of a particular form of oppression, one
manifestation of alienation and capitalistic exploitation (rather
than feudal exploitation, as the Egyptian ruling class inclined
toward absentee-management, relying on the law instead of
the stick). It was replaced by a domineering fraternalism that

was not unanimously appreciated, although its relative benefits colored the regime.

Nasser realized that the masses were not following. In March 1954 he saw that Naguib's proposed freedom had wider appeal that his own attempts to revive the revolution. His constant wrestling with these two elements and the choice he finally made—a revolution without freedom—followed. The fellah no longer prostrates himself before his bey (although the title has not disappeared completely despite the law). His attitude toward the man in uniform, or his representative, is not exactly one of respectful humility, but neither does it encourage dialogue. It is the product of discipline and caution.

Nasser's power had taken root by the end of 1954. By signing the pact that evacuated the British from the Canal Zone, he removed the principal deterrent to Egyptian independence, and by crushing the Moslem Brotherhood, he erased the gravest threat to his authority. But not until January 1956 did he attempt to provide a legal framework for his regime by proclaiming the authoritarian constitution, which Georges Burdeau has referred to as "technical Caesarism."

Perhaps the most important section of this document is Article 192, which provides for replacement of all political parties by a National Union, which is "a state party or merely a state agency for political control of the masses.[7] It is hardly surprising that this organization was inserted into the Constitution or that it has acted more as a disciplinary arm than as a revolutionary vanguard.

Of course, Nasser had been aware for some time that "a revolution requires a revolutionary elite or cadre (*jihaz thawri*) to undertake its organization, planning and leadership."[8] The National Union was never to play a progressive role in the

[7] Vatikiokis.
[8] Ibid.

area of leadership, any more than was the Arab Socialist Union, created in 1962. Was its apparatus too cumbersome? Or was the body itself too artificial, handed on a platter to the people, whereas a true party is born out of struggle? The same problem recurs throughout Nasser's regime.

He did not succeed in creating a healthy system with an opposition dedicated to the legal subversion and harassment of the inherently conservative state. The fruitful dialectic between party and state never had a start—not because the state naturally rules in a country marked by the three-fold domination of pharaohs, caliphs, and the tyrannical Nile, but because the dynamic, legendary personality of Nasser obscured everything else, and perhaps also because Communist groups and their allies exercised an option on militancy during the 1960's. Although Nasser was intelligent enough to appreciate their professional competence, and allowed some of them to serve him, he never considered them trustworthy "fellow travelers" or gave them the right to dissent.

In "revolutionary" Egypt, nothing very novel characterized the exercise of authority, at least until 1962. The village was ruled by its *omdeh,* the district by its *maamour,* the province by its *moudir*; the country as a whole had donned a khaki uniform and its customs had changed, but the style of power remained the same. Authority was tightly concentrated and rigidly subdivided. Whether the state was the Palace or Nasser, it was supreme. The only difference was that winds of change seemed to be blowing, even though at the village level they barely stirred the air. Nasser had vanished behind the cumbersome machinery of state.

Egyptian power had attained a level of concentration unknown since the days of Mohammed Ali, since the Court and the intelligentsia went their separate ways around 1870 and then clashed after 1919. The divorce between the khedive and Mustafa Kamal's nationalists, then between the king and the

Wafd, was abolished and resolved in the person of Nasser. By the close of 1954, the timid revolutionary of 1952 had become supreme ruler. He had only to make his image known to the people. Concentration, which was to take a variety of forms in the period 1954–6, had to be supplemented by personification. It took Nasser two years to consolidate power, four years to become the face of Egypt.

PERSONIFICATION

At first Nasser was not identified with Egypt. His family roots hugged the soil of Upper Egypt, and his youth and education plunged him into the seething urban nationalism of the 1940's. There was every reason for him to become the incarnation of restless Egypt, long suffering from lack of identity. But the first stages of his rise to power kept him on the sidelines as a national figure: the Egyptian people did not "recognize" Gamal because he did not recognize himself.

Did the trouble lie in his austere manner, his solemn speech, his crude way of appealing for order and hard work? The people, who expected a liberator, found themselves with a family tutor. Since the beginning of the century, the Egyptians had taken strongly to two leaders: Saad Zaghlul, who founded the Wafd and headed the first independent government, and whose exile and return to Cairo had profoundly stirred the nation; and Mustafa Nahas, Zaghlul's successor, not a great man but an appealing one, whose virtues and faults were equally attractive to the crowd—the quintessential Egyptian of the '30's.

They were eloquent and sophisticated men, patriotic but too concessive, loved like fathers and uncles. Then along came Gamal Abdel Nasser, a long-time protégé of Mohammed Naguib, whom the crowd took for a second Nahas—and who nearly was in February 1954. They took a dim view of the frowning Colonel alongside the Good General, weighing brotherly discipline against fatherly indulgence. They chose the second, but the Colonel won out. And they accepted Nasser even more reluctantly because the newly signed treaty with Britain naturally involved concessions and the Moslem Brotherhood was crying treason. As the students put it, wasn't the upright conqueror really "Colonel Jimmy," America's friend?

At the end of April 1955, Nasser suddenly emerged as the nation's acknowledged leader. He was governing Egypt and uniting her people. All it took was a trip to Bandung, and the Colonel, who had just been labeled a fascist by the opposition newspapers, found himself warmly applauded by imprisoned leftist leaders. He had challenged imperialism and spoken out for independence. Twenty months of tough negotiations with the British and a treaty that was grudgingly recognized as liberating had served only to make him distrusted. Yet his brief stay in Bandung, heartland of short-lived illusions (but symbolic of emancipation and dignity) won him popular acclaim.

Thus, Colonel Nasser's courtship of the Egyptian people may be said to date from his return from Indonesia: the marriage took place in 1956. Before 1955 his relation to the people was totally different from what it was the day he entered Cairo, April 22, 1955, his portrait flanked by those of Nehru and Chou En-lai, his jeep carried along by the mob to indicate the significance of the event: identification had taken place. Nasser was no longer the product of some secret Western intrigue; he spoke as an Egyptian nationalist about an Egyptian revolution that purported to be something more than a successful coup d'état. He spoke in the name of Egypt.

Six months later he had another rendezvous with the people. After the Israeli army had struck at Gaza in February 1955, killing fifty Egyptians, he had tried to obtain arms from Wash-

ington, London, and Paris. Endless bargaining ensued, as well
as attempts to commit Cairo to a Western alliance. Moscow
was more prudent and suggested that Egypt take her suit to
Prague. On September 26 the former Colonel, but by then
President, Nasser informed the country that Czechoslovakia
had contracted to sell arms to Egypt. Nasser was deeply impressed by the wild acclamation that greeted this speech: once
again, by defying the West and relying instead on the East, by
widening the lens of his diplomacy, he had triumphed. And
the Egyptian masses pictured him as the Nile Valley-dweller
rising against the invader, courageous enough to say "No"
and shrewd enough not to return empty-handed. Identification
evolved in the form of revolutionary nationalism.

The third stage of development arrived with the Suez crisis.
It had a strange beginning: to the supreme mortification of
Cairo's intelligentsia, Nasser chose to approach the West for
aid in constructing the Aswan High Dam. But there was strong
reaction against this in the United States, as well as in England
(irritated by Egyptian denouncements of her military positions
in Jordan and along the Persian Gulf) and in France (furious
at Egypt's aid to the Algerian rebels), the combined result of
which was a communiqué from John Foster Dulles advising
that "in view of Egypt's unstable economy," the loan promised
the preceding January would not be granted.

A week later Nasser gave his Alexandria speech, the Suez
Company was nationalized, and he was flouting the West. Each
Western attempt to humiliate Cario's government served to
lock Nasser and the Egyptian "underdogs" in tighter embrace.
And now there was indeed a marriage—dangerous, but exciting. For all those who had supported the Wafd and then
had sulked under the stern eye of their instructor during the
first three years of the revolution, Nasser became Gamal, he
who does not retreat.

Moreover, to mark this crucial encounter with his people,

the leader had created a style: his Alexandria speech caught the accents of everyday life, of country brawls and suburban banter (*nokta*). Nasser's famous laugh, exploding as he announced nationalization of the Canal, the laugh that sounded "hysterical" to Western ears, simply echoed the Egyptian people's sarcasm. "They"—the foreigners, the West, the rich —had been duped, made fools of, insulted by "him" (read "us"). Nasser had become part of the crowd: speaking its language, he was its spokesman.

The July 1952 tryst had restored Egypt to its most important social group, the rural petty bourgeoisie, although at first that class was represented only by a clan. The July 1956 assignation gave power a face and a revolutionary thrust. The Suez crisis, besides being a solemn ceremony, was a great leap forward: it was a charismatic situation involving dynamic incarnation, the creative force that implants standards and ideals. Its significance reached far beyond the event itself, causing a revolutionary transformation of the technocratic, reformist government Thenceforth, one crisis after another forced Nasser to assert and reappraise his leadership, he who was invested with *hukm*, the popular mandate bestowed in the Lord's name. He set about to restructure power that was already well centralized, and to step up ambitiously yet carefully the personification of authority, which was gradually becoming synonymous with the "conquests of the revolution."

The Suez crisis brought Nasser total domination. All the major decisions had been made by him alone: rejection of the Anglo-French ultimatum of October 30, the secret appeal to President Eisenhower on November 1, and the commitment of the same date to withdraw from Sinai, which was followed by acceptance of a cease-fire on November 6.

In January 1956, he had legalized his power by establishing a constitution with an all-powerful executive, and then getting himself elected (by more than 99 percent of the vote) to the presidency on June 6. He had put his power to the test and had emerged unscathed. But he was perceptive enough to realize that the relation between people and power had changed.

Before Suez, the relationship followed the formula laid down in his manifesto of 1954: he was the puppetmaster, they, a people-audience. During the action, the masses emerged as an active force: "From the very day the government called them to defend their country, organized and armed them . . . a radical transformation overtook these 'God-forsaken men' . . . and forced the dictator to risk a veritable revolution," observed Jean-Jacques Faust.[9]

So the "second revolution" unfolded. The first one, in July 1952, had been basically military. The second was economic. It took the form of a sweeping nationalization of Egyptian resources, previously controlled mainly by Europeans at Barclay's Bank and the Crédit Lyonnais, but now under the aegis of an economic agency.

Despite its ambiguous character and the bitter vengeance that motivated it, the program deserves to be called revolutionary for two reasons. It had broad popular support and pressure from the frustrated masses who had dedicated themselves as of October-November 1956 to "recuperation" of the national patrimony. In addition, Nasser, having suddenly lost the foreign technicians who had made the wheels of this semicolonial economy go round, was forced to call in two types of personnel, army officers and Marxists (whom he freed from prison and put in positions they were equipped to handle). So the new production system reflected the mixed economy rather than socialism. Yet it was an important step in the transition from capitalism to a planned society. Profit would still remain a basic objective of production and would

[9] *Etudes Méditerranéenes* (June 1957).

create a new class of officer-managers and state business-men.

The 1952 coup had brought a new set of men—small land-owners—to the summit of political power; the 1956 crisis handed the economy over to another group, still lower-middle-class, but for the most part urban and closer to the old-guard intelligentsia. Nasser saw to it that the second group (typified by such men as Colonel Mahmoud Younès, who had run the Suez Canal since 1956, Mohammed Ahmed Selim, an engineer and one of the "fathers" of the High Dam, and the former magistrate Ahmed Fuad, an old friend and strong advocate of planning) remained closely tied to the 1952 group. Moreover, the leader controlled national production as well as credit through his economic agency.

In 1958 economic sovereignty permitted him to start oper-ating the first five-year plan; in 1960, to sign an agreement with the Soviet Union providing aid for construction of the Aswan High Dam; in July 1961, to loose a fresh wave of nationalization decrees—what Cairo terms the "third revolu-tion"—covering notably a new system of distributing indus-trial profits based on a sharp rise in the income tax, apportionment of 25 percent of company shares among the workers, further nationalization of industry, and sweeping land reform.

But the opening of this "third revolution" was to put the government to its severest test: withdrawal from the United Arab Republic. Much as Nasser frowned upon the projected fusion of Egypt and Syria which was discussed at Damascus,[1] the proposal so brightened the future of a pan-Arab union that he could hardly refuse it. Then, too, his role was to bring unity, always a part of Egyptian tradition. But the heavy-handed "colonialism" that Cairo imposed on Damas-

[1] Claude Estier, *L'Égypte en révolution* (Paris: Julliard; 1965), p. 187.

cus, her obvious attempt to glut Syrian markets with Egyptian products, disagreement between the two armies, and most of all Egypt's far-reaching socialist program embarked on in June and July 1961, produced a coalition of Syrian nationalists and conservatives—and an explosion in September. It was the *raïs*'s first serious defeat.

Nasser, "less a man of action than of reaction,"[2] learned his lesson. Between 1961 and 1966 he made serious efforts to reorganize the government, arm it with a philosophy and a party structure, and widen its base of support. Although the post of prime minister was added to the hierarchy, it actually signaled not deconcentration, but a differentiation of functions—perhaps the start of modernization—and the creation of a political society.

DIFFERENTIATION

The Suez crisis marked the interval between the first and second revolutions, between the concentration of Nasser's power and its personification. The Damascus affair rallied Egypt, accenting the leftist trend of the third revolution (which began in June and was stepped up in October) and facilitating the transition from personified concentration to a slightly different type of personification bearing an ideological stamp. Having progressed from the revolutionary objectives of the years 1952–54 to an emphasis on organization, Nasser embarked in 1955 on the politics of diplomacy. Dialogue temporarily replaced monologue; the pyramid was not inverted but simply became more elastic.

On October 16, 1961, having announced two weeks earlier to an astonished (and undoubtedly relieved) people that

[2] John G. Campbell in *The Observer* (London, October 16, 1956).

"Arabs cannot fight Arabs," the *raïs* withdrew his troops from Syria and brought off a remarkable piece of self-criticism over television. This time the fault did not lie outside the country, in some imperialist intrigue, but inside, at the state's very pinnacle. He denounced "the political and organizational errors" responsible for the breach, and courageously admitted: "We overestimated our power. We were unable to guide the masses. We allowed reaction and opportunism to infiltrate our ranks. The state apparatus is outmoded." And he concluded: "What we must do now is build socialism." For Nasser, such a program no longer entailed merely the development of government control, the elimination of feudalism, and the establishment of a popular dictatorship. He realized that socialism also involves the economic and political interaction of people, a mass participation in the plan. Between 1962 and 1966 he would try to progress from mandatory overall planning of a mixed economy, with the private sector kept active and healthy, to a cooperative plan involving the various forces of production: technicians, workers, and elites. This policy may be described as the diversification of functions within the framework of centralized power, and had its origin in the 1962 Charter, which has the ring of a socialist manifesto.[3]

In this connection, we will not deal with the relation between Marxism and "Arab Socialism" (which Nasser was the first to call "scientific"). What concerns us is the interpretation of this major document, the product of long and lively debates among Nasser, his aides, and representatives of the new intelligentsia. It was no overture to democracy, yet for the first time since the leader had taken total control, he exposed himself to the criticism of a group that he did not dominate completely. The National Assembly meetings that generated the May 1962 Charter seemed, because of the existence of open debate, to contain the seeds of representative government. Anouar Abdel Malek covers this very interestingly in his book.[3]

Was this simply the whimsical diversion of a dictator, the work of a brain trust, or was it an opinion-poll and the germ of revolution? The answer probably lies somewhere between the last two. The debates that took place in the spring of 1962 did not "open Nasser's eyes"—which were already open. What they did was remind this faithful Moslem that *choura,* or consultation, is a rather effective method of learning the truth and avoiding the pitfalls of tightly concentrated authority.

The reform enacted several months later should probably be seen in the same light. A ministerial post with executive powers was created, nearly equivalent to that of the French prime minister, a modest office but nonetheless a decentralization of power. The fact that President Nasser awarded this post first to Aly Sabri, who was already acting as his vice-president or chief of staff, indicates that the step was a minor one. In practice, things had changed very little.

But two years later Aly Sabri was replaced by Zakaria Mohieddine: apparently the office carried more weight than people had thought. The former Secretary of the Interior's promotion came in conjunction with a "liberal" shift significant enough to discourage talk of a mere reshuffling of the innner circle.

The prime minister was responsible only for executing presidential policy (as in France), but just as the replacement of Debré by Pompidou (and later of Pompidou by Couve de Murville) was both the result and the cause of a particular reorientation, so was Mohieddine's advancement more than just a barometric indication. In fact, the President had offered another segment of the ruling class the chance to test its own views and methods. Under the circumstances,

[3] Anouar Abdel Malek. *Egypt, Military Society* (New York: Random ouse; 1968).

Nasser may be said to have shifted a fraction of power from the ideologists to the practical men.

In this respect, the leader made some headway in dealing with basic problems. The trend became even clearer in March 1964, during the National Assembly elections. There is no use pretending that this body was freely elected or had any real power. But every representative body—as Napoleon found out—introduces a certain amount of opposition. On November 12, 1964, and again on February 25, 1966,[4] Nasser leaned on this fact to squelch criticism of the role of communists in the Egyptian press and to refute arguments he himself had put forward ten years earlier.

And here is what the *raïs* had to say to the Arab Socialist Union's delegates, who met with him on May 16, 1955.[5] After pointing out various errors and failures of the old regime and some of its carryovers, items ranging from persistent unemployment in the countryside to the perpetuation of political policies alien to socialism, Nasser declared: "I believe that the era of revolutionary administrative measures is past. Now it is time for us to rely on the people's conscience instead of on government control." Then, turning to pure and simple political organization, the President went on, with the unique blend of candor, cynicism, and incisiveness which makes his comments so interesting: "Shall we create an opposition in the very center of the National Assembly which anyone who wishes can join? What I am trying to do is find a way to work collectively, not on an individual basis." Did the "individual" refer to his deputy or to himself? The fact is that a certain decentralization of power was developing in the United Arab Republic.

It is hard to say whether the first signs of political reawakening—timid parliamentary opposition, discussions be-

---

[4] Claude Estier, pp. 122–130.
[5] Ibid., pp. 230–38.

tween Nasser and Mohieddine of the private sector's role in the economy, press coverage of the pros and cons of birth control or planned production—had any effect on Nasser's power, which was consolidated by the Constitutions of 1960 and 1964 and rested upon four basic principles: Egypt's traditional centralized authority; the *raïs*'s dynamic leadership; structural inability to form a one-party system; mass apathy derived from long years of political nonexistence.

Nasser seemed to be making the third factor the target of his efforts to inject life into the mammoth structure of conservatism. Four months before his reelection to the presidency (in March 1965), he confided to a diplomat friend that he was considering not running in order to devote himself to "political organization without which we cannot complete the second phase of the Revolution." But although he was well aware of the errors he had made in 1953 with the Liberation Movement, in 1960 with the National Union, and in 1962 with the Arab Socialist Union, Nasser kept running up against the same problem: whether (as in the three preceding cases) to form a "people's party," which was likely to be bogged down by its size and factional strife, or to create an "elitist party," which would force the heretics or semiheretics (communists and reactionaries) into the opposition camp or into reorganization of their own ranks.

Until he could manage to bring together a consistent ideology and an informed elite, Egypt's leader could not possibly revive the political interaction he wanted, yet feared. Moreover, there was the problem of forming a party atop the power structure. Is it possible to create that which should have been the creator? It is the misfortune of coups d'état, born of a will to power, to retain their initial characteristics. The *Putsch* of 1952 developed into a species of revolution through its own achievements, not through the power it bred.

In many respects the Egyptian government has not progressed beyond the July regime: it still regards history as a conspiracy. There is a decided advantage in pulling off a bloodless coup, a palace revolution that costs the people nothing and requires only courage and ingenuity on the part of its leaders. But such an undertaking inevitably lacks a certain level of comradeship that can be forged only in the unique process of evolving and living by common principles entailing collective risks. In the eulogy he delivered in March 1965, when his old friend Nasser was re-elected President, Anouar el-Sadat spoke of the "rare phenomenon that constituted our people's encounter with Gamal Abdel Nasser." Rare phenomenon? Encounter? These are words that would never do for Fidel Castro or Ho Chi Minh.

The Wafd, despite its corruption and false pretenses, managed to survive for many years as an active national movement because it grew out of the 1919 upheaval. And Tunisia's Destour remains the only really solid party in the Arab world because Bourguiba and his followers forged it in the fires of struggle.

Is it too late now for Nasser and for Egypt? That would seem to be the case. A commando can change the course of history, but he cannot stand in for an entire people on the march. In March 1965 Nasser proclaimed that "the people's support of the revolution has been total." He forgot his 1954 pamphlet: "We opened the breach, we returned and nobody had followed. . . ." It is true that as of 1956 Nasser was no longer holding the breach singlehanded, and that in the fall of that year the erstwhile commando had become a national front. But the initiative, the impulse, and the surge are always in one direction only. Is there still time for Cairo to "rely on the people's conscience" and to loosen government control?[6]

6 Speech of May 16, 1965.

"We will lift them up in spite of themselves," Gamal
Salem said sarcastically to us when he was deputy prime
minister in 1954. In spite of themselves? Since 1956, power
and the people have come to terms and understand each
other a little better. But Nasser and his circle continue in
their role of harbor pilots and tugboat captains, bent on
getting ships across Egypt, from Port Said to Suez. The people
are being towed; except in emergencies, they do not "par-
ticipate" in the cult of the hero.

COMMUNICATION

On the other hand, Nasser never indulges in the extravagant rites of Nkrumah or Sukarno, not only because he
has a good memory for recent events, but also because as a
faithful Moslem he is forearmed against the temptation of
self-deification, a terrible sacrilege. Puritanism offers no
shield against this type of folly: witness Cromwell. But Islam,
in this case, is a good antidote. Though the pharaonic tradition pervades the entire network of power, it is seen by Egyptian Moslems as merely the product of extreme paganism.
Mussolini liked to be compared to Caesar, Stalin to Peter
the Great. But nothing irritates Nasser more than being
treated like a modern pharaoh.

Nonetheless, the cult of personality has assumed spectacular proportions in Egypt, and with legal blessing. To
appreciate the systematic adulation that is part of the ex-
Colonel's routine, one should attend electoral meetings, visit
cities, factories, inaugural ceremonies for the Aswan project,
or a reception for a foreign leader. George Bernard Shaw
maintained that men are not corrupted by power, but power
by men. In Egypt in 1952 neither Nasser nor anyone else
could tarnish what was "raw power," in Bertrand Russell's

language. Yet it took a great deal of will power on the leader's part to prevent the sunny psychological climate in which he basked from turning him into a Caligula.

He has won all kinds of praise, sometimes of an unexpected nature. During a visit to the Nile Delta in 1956, Gamal was swung aloft by the crowd and carried along to the rhythm of heroic-minded slogans. A wild-eyed old man stepped forward, crying out: *"El-Wahche!"* ("The brute!", or better still, "The ogre!") But make no mistake: this was an homage to the "strong man" who could stand his ground with the great nations, whose muscle was the very fiber of independence. Every Egyptian village, every section of Cairo has its cheeky *fettewa* (bully), and being equated with one of these local popular heroes was, for the *raïs,* the sign of his acceptance by the people.

But Nasser's glory usually comes in a more dignified wrapper. For example, the ritual of his entry into cities, or meetings and celebrations, or receptions for foreign dignitaries: greeted by waves of applause, the leader emerges from one of those gigantic and gaudily festooned tents that serve for marriages as well as funerals. Pumping his arm like a seasoned champion, he smiles and steps forward in his slightly bent, deliberate manner. He is the "great," the "generous," the "victor," and the "just." He is the "father of the revolution," the "nation's liberator"—a far cry from the mystical litanies once sung to Nkrumah, though the incense still is nearly overwhelming.

The person and the myth are treated perhaps in a more interesting and original way on television and radio and in the Egyptian press. Nasser follows the press avidly, more like a reporter than a head of state. Until 1961, he would hang around the pressrooms, supervising layout, correcting texts, choosing type and headings. Abdel Hakim Amer, amazed at his interest, said to Nasser one day, "My word!

You missed your calling, you should have been a news-paperman." Nasser replied gravely, "You're right."

His interest in the press became evident in a curious way at the very start of the regime. At eight o'clock on the morning of July 23, Anouar el-Sadat came rushing into the Ministry of the Interior along with several other officers, summoned Under Secretary of State Amar, and, before any officials arrived, absconded with the list of journalists who were being paid off with the ministry's secret funds. Part of the list was published in *Al-Ahram* in March 1954, during the Naguib-Nasser crisis, in an effort to discredit the General's old-guard retainers who made up the bulk of his support.

Thus the press was first among the old regime's hirelings to be "sewed up" by the Free Officers, and they kept their control. Pashas would be thrown out or arrested, foreigners expelled, high officials "purged," and seventeen years after the revolution the only faces still around that could be connected with the monarchy and its political allies belong to its partisans in the press. Naguib interpreted this, in December 1952, as Nasser's intention "to rule by results, not causes, and to win men's minds by any means."

A few months later, Aly Sabri turned in a report to Nasser recommending "concentration" of the press. This program was gradually achieved, and from 1956 on was financed by unpublicized funds drawn from the nationalized economy or from semipublic or private sources. The press response was so great, especially during the early years (when industry still flourished and there was semifree trade), that the *raïs* decided to launch a number of new newspapers, *Al-Chaab, Al-Gumhuriah, Al-Missa,* plus nearly a hundred magazines.

In 1954 it was television's turn to be reorganized. Under the banner of "national consciousness," a campaign of folklore entertainment was opened. Radio followed this up with new programs: for example, the *Arab Voice,* broadcast in Hebrew.

Nasser himself, aided by his "scribe," supervised these information- and propaganda-feeding activities. Each spectacular success of the regime warranted careful layout and headlining; antigovernment plots, the lighter side of the news, were held in reserve for scoops. Nasser had good reason to tell Abdel Hakim Amer that he was a frustrated newsman.

Propaganda themes began to take shape in the *raïs's* mind.[7] Before the new regime could "take," there had to be a clean sweep of the old one. And the cooperation was nearly overwhelming. Nasser was obliged to take a hand personally in toning down the encomia. Except in *Al Ahram,* there was talk of nothing but "national heroes" or the origins of Islam. And anyone with a sensitive ear could catch some familiar echoes: the monarchy had tried desperately to sustain itself on the same arguments. Nasser knew the power of words: in February 1953 he ordered that new slogans should run counter to the old ones. The profaned cult of Farouk was to be replaced (temporarily) by a cult of impersonality.

During a speech in February 1953, in an out-of-the-way village, Chebine el-Kom, the leader began unobtrusively to build his image: "Our problems have been the same for centuries; it is not the problems that are important, but men. . . . Men must be of good will and at the same time humble in the service of their country." He added that reason must dominate the revolution. The nation is like faith, he went on, and we know Allah through reason (*Allah, 'erefnah bel akl*). Nasser did not embrace traditional "obscurantism," by using the sacred language of the Koran, which had "made language into

---

[7] Ibrahim Farhi is my source for many of the observations here and all the Arabic quotations.

a class". The revolution "must cast down idols" (*"ibadate el asnam"*).

It is interesting to note that on that day of his first public address, every phrase focused on personal power, tyranny, legitimacy, the relation between leaders and militants, and the loyalty of the masses, which is "more important than their abilities." It was as if he felt, either instinctively or unconsciously, that he owed the people a profession of faith.

Didn't Islam have its leaders? Mohammed was one of them. Nasser spoke of the Prophet as a realist, a political leader. The words he used, words that recur in his speeches whenever there are great crises or events, had double meanings, both secular and sacred.

Was his choice of religious terms purely instinctive? Whatever the answer, Nasser's metaphors, always folksy and colloquial, had a way of stressing his (and by extension, the government's) fairmindedness; he was the upright judge whose code of honor was the people's welfare (Port Said speech, Autumn 1955). From 1952 through 1955, his metaphors remained neutral, ambivalent; he made frequent use of tautology (a technique that is somewhat reminiscent of de Gaulle). His syllogisms were dead ends; he was not there by accident but because of what he called "logic and reason" (speech at the University of Cairo, 1954). "We are not going to create personalities; the only acceptable authority is moral law, events, and necessity. As long as your leaders agree on these necessities, they deserve your attention and your confidence."

Nasser had time on his side (speech to the Liberation Movement, July 1955). His existence depended on results: but results may be slow in coming, "may take five, six, ten, or twenty years." Meanwhile, don't pass judgment or prejudge. The leader and his power are only what the people make them, one day good, the next, bad; time will tell.

And until the verdict is in, power stands guard. The ruler is transcendent, but not a "dangling puppet." "The leader is not a star performer": he represents only the people and the reality *(wak'ei)* of Egypt. Like the people, he is everywhere, omnipresent *(saher fi kol hetah)*. Nothing escapes his eye, neither good nor evil.

The same themes were repeated on radio and television and in the press, as well as in pamphlets, on the screen, in religious services, in advertising and various types of popular imagery ranging from sugar dolls to color prints, from biscuits to actual questions asked, and even to the artless, gaudy paintings that decorated the pargetted walls of alleys and villages. *Nasser is the institution.* And the champion of what has created it: "dignity" *(karama)*. A beautiful vision, which political vicissitudes, the erosion of power, and the stifling atmosphere of flattery gradually would alter.

And already, on July 26, 1955, propaganda chief Salah Salem stated over the radio: "He is moving away from us, in our very midst, through his own humility, as the Saviour did from his disciples. But among us there is no Judas!"

"He is becoming part of our history," Mohammed Hassanein Kseykal wrote beneath a photo taken in March 1956, showing Nasser with his friends, who even then kept a few steps behind him (except Amer, on the edge of the foreground). "Liberty, justice, Israel, Bandung, land reform, these are steps on the path to greatness. He is the shepherd. What if he fails? Then it was bound to happen."

In Nasser's rhetoric, the "I" is not supreme. The "we" reigns instead—not a "we" of superiority or collectivity, but of coresponsibility, shared by the leader and the masses. It is a mixture of joint deception and sincerity. This is how he expressed it: "The more we fool ourselves," he said a few weeks before Suez, "the more you will have to help us. We are not like some outgoing minister but are here to accomplish our task together. We are united by evidence [*badi-hiates*]. And you have a share in our failures." And in 1955 he made this statement to the public: "We fought a revolution against injustice. What have *you* done? The enemy is not simply imperialism, it is within you."

Later on, in June 1967, on the heels of disaster, he spoke at first as if he were mediating a dispute. Although forced at the very end to say "I," he put everything else in the third person. Only at the last, pathetic moment came "I am resigning." Two days later, after his "return," he asserted that Allah had not made the world in one day. You—the people —must get to work, you are the ones who should tell us, guide us.

Thus, Nasser's recurring theme is the impersonality of the leader, who is detached and objective—the weight-holding bar of a scale—and for whom history, the revolution, and his own person are faceless entities, necessities, a neutralizing "fatality" (*kada wa kadar*).

But with the growth of personification, the leader sought to distribute responsibility, at least in the people's consciousness: "What can I do if you are not prepared? I can't do everything. Even if I know all there is to know, how can I take a stand for or against something. . . . This is *your* job" (speech on February 28, 1967).

We have emphasized the strong bond linking the charismatic leader to his followers: Weber's theory described the relationship between this visionary figure and the masses as well as between the leader and those who have heard and answered his call—two magnetic fields. Apostles are the most reliable indicators of charisma; the palm-bearing host follows later. Nasser's undertaking has similar divisions.

The 1952 movement began as a brotherhood under the

direction of an intuitive and cautious grass-roots leader who knew how to implant his ideas, how to spread and enforce them. Once his influence was firmly established, the sharing process began. Diffusion "on the second level," or mass participation, could·occur only afterward and, as we have seen, with varying success. But the leader's charisma acted upon the officer group that made the long journey at his side. And their comradeship survived the ups and downs of power, despite the chinks that developed.

Nasser's seizure and consolidation of power was not a lone man's adventure. The careers of Bourguiba, Sihanouk, and Nkrumah uncover the tensions experienced along the path to prophetic leadership. Until 1967 Nasser seemed an exception to this rule. He was a rank-and-file leader who did occasional solos, and his partners were near at hand and usually dependable.

All along, his entourage had three notable features. Its members were young men who stepped into public life simultaneously, with no record of distinction and no political reputation or ideological proclivities (except for Marxists such as Khaled Mohieddine and Youssef Saddig, or a Moslem Brother such as Abdel Raouf). They were soldiers, bred on discipline, accustomed to a degree of anonymity, for whom orders were orders. And finally, these men were products of a tightly organized and centralized society, most of them from poor or extremely modest backgrounds, where these factors are even more predominant. In short, they were good raw material for a leader.

At the same time, there were leveling influences: their ages ranged from only twenty-nine to thirty-four at the time of the *Putsch;* they were close in rank (five lieutenant colonels, seven majors) and had similar backgrounds. Apart from Sabri or Okacha, sons of the middle class, they were the type of fellow who makes a sandwich of *foul* (a bean mixture) his evening meal because it costs too much to eat out, who buys a small second-hand car on the installment plan and piles the kids in for weekend outings.

They were a gang, a *Brüderschaft* with a great deal in common, who stuck together for better or worse. They were unanimous in accepting Gamal as their chief. Khaled Mohieddine was the first to oppose him, taking Naguib's side in 1954. But he lost out and went into exile for a period. That odd personality Gamal Salem faded from the picture in 1955; he disagreed with Nasser but would not come out and fight. Then came the rupture with Boghdadi, who condemned the regime's leftist leanings and favored better relations with the West; and in turn with Kamaleddine Hussein, whose ties with Islam took too reactionary a turn in 1962–63.

But until 1967 these dissensions did not amount to much alongside the Bourguiba-Salah Ben Youssef clash that lasted from 1955 to 1961, or the FLN crisis in 1962, or the relations between Nkrumah and Danquah. The Egyptian military revolution remained relatively easygoing, like the people it purported to be liberating, and coherent, like the society it sought to modernize, despite the fact that team spirit did not generate communal spirit, or consultation (*ijma*).

What distinguishes Nasser's power from that of certain Eastern dictatorships is the discussion that went on within the leadership. A number of men developed close ties with Nasser on the level of his friendship with Abdel Hakim Amer or his camaraderie with Khaled Mohieddine (in spite of the latter's political conduct), and perhaps even Saroit Okacha (who escaped disaster though his brother-in-law was the rebel Ahmed Abul Fath).

But this in no way made for a community of power. Despite long-existing bonds of friendship, men like Zakaria Mohieddine, Anouar el-Sadat, and Aly Sabri were close colleagues but not influential advisers. Mohieddine was oc-

casionally able to win a point—if it happened to agree with
something the *raïs* had already considered. By and large,
however, the leader's intimates had no real impact on his
actions. He was the guide, and intended to remain so. His
companions could not expect to limit or channel the personification of Nasser's power. They were good at carrying out
orders and giving advice, like generally obedient consultants,
but were they ever equal to a debate that the leader might
have welcomed? Or perhaps his remarkable ability to listen,
which impressed Nehru and Adlai Stevenson, was reserved
for foreigners.

Nasser sometimes gives the impression of forgetting he is
the leader, but then suddenly comes alive during a discussion,
or when he is listening intently to someone's opinion: Abdel
Hakim Amer's, for example. At the time of the Syrian affair
in September 1961, the Marshal convinced his chief that any
attempted repression would lead to disaster. That precedent
would have a tragic echo.

SECOND THOUGHTS

We have already seen that the personification of power governing a community is in direct relation to the impact of
internal and external events upon that community.

At the start of 1967, the situation in Egypt was not conducive to the normalization of authority. The United Arab
Republic, beset by problems of overpopulation, diplomatically
isolated, financially impoverished, enmeshed in the Yemenite
dilemma, and still lacking a political structure capable of
promoting modernization, was more firmly than ever in the
grip of revolutionary leadership and further away than ever
from systematic diversification of government or a dialogue
between power and the public.

On April 6, 1967, Israeli planes raided Damascus in reprisal for commando strikes originating from Syria and opened a new and critical phase of the Palestine conflict. Nasser still dominated Egyptian politics, but was nearly as isolated on his heights as he was in the entire Arab—and non-Arab—world.

Apart from Marshal Amer, his entourage consisted only of orderlies, clerks, and staff officers. The Marshal, who was known to give him his cue on occasion, was himself under fire for activities in private life, and was no longer so sure of political favor. In the public sector, people were not very excited over the Palestine issue. But hostility to Israel had become ingrained. They had heard once too often that her army was weaker than it had been in 1948.

On May 10 Nasser was almost certain that the Israelis were on the verge of striking at Syria. He opened his own game of dissuasion, moving troops into Sinai, recalling the Blue Helmet forces first from the Gaza Strip and then from all along the Israeli border, occupying Charm el-Cheikh, and entering into secret negotiations with U Thant and the White House. A month of bluffs and gambles brought him to the morning of June 5, when he waited for over six hours to learn that his air force had been wiped out on the ground in less than fifty minutes.

The *raïs* was too experienced a strategist to nurse any further hopes. For four days running he tried to maneuver, to get help from the USSR and the United Nations, even the USA. Toward midday on the 9th, he saw defeat staring at him. And his instinctive reaction was to personalize it as one of his responsibilities. Convening the staff of the Arab Socialist Union, he announced his decision to resign in favor of Zakaria Mohieddine. He incarnated defeat as completely as he had incarnated the nation. He was disaster personified.

At about seven o'clock on the evening of June 9, this is

what he told the country very matter-of-factly on television, his voice, like Egypt, anguished, his expression, like his army, bewildered. Beginning with an account of the disaster, he went on painting details with dismal realism, then suddenly announced just before concluding: "I am retiring from public life. . . . My comrade Zakaria will take over my duties. Follow him."

The reaction was fascinating, perhaps unprecedented, and casts a strange light on this extreme case of the mythical incarnation of a nation.

In *Israël et les Arabes, le troisème combat*,[8] Eric Rouleau gives a marvelous description of the wave of sympathy that engulfed the vanishing leader. The author notes that the public did an about-face: in the morning, having learned of their defeat, they blamed Nasser alone and were ready to send him packing; that evening, the news of his retirement made them cling to him as their sole refuge, their teacher, symbol, and breath of life: "Gamal, Gamal, don't desert us, we need you . . ."

The wails of protest over a vanquished chief's well-timed departure (and he was to blame as no chief ever was, for he had overplayed his hand, had exposed the country and the army to disaster, had hurled defiance without considering that it might be returned in kind, had threatened a nation that was stronger, healthier, and better equipped than his own) in a sense were a cartoonist's tribute to a particular relationship between the leader and the people, the act of incorporation, of swallowing.

A leader is not expected to make the sun rise, but instead to impose his physical presence in an immediate way; this is all the more important when he is at fault and feeling guilty.[9]

---

[8] (Paris: Éd. du Seuil; 1967), p. 135.

[9] A brief precedent: On Napoleon's return from Waterloo, the people of Paris entreated him to stay in command. But only of Paris.

Napoleon III, William II, and Hitler did not experience this intimate and pressing complicity, the avid demand for partnership. I and the people? The people and I? *We* as one are humiliated and suffering, like Beckett's hobos and the children of *Mother Courage*. We share the same circle of Hell.

But these magical moments, rich in psycho-political drama, reveal another facet, also noted by Eric Rouleau,[1] of the shifting relationship between power and authority. Shortly after Nasser's "farewell," which Parliament was preparing to debate, the vice-president of the Assembly entered a post office, identified himself, and handed one of the clerks a congratulatory telegram addressed to the new president, Zakaria Mohieddine. And would you believe that this bureaucratic "doormat" threw back his shoulders and refused to send the wire, calling it treason! The official called in a policeman to arrest the presumptuous clerk, and lo and behold, the *chaouich* in turn balked at the order!

Authority remained on the side of the defeated and resigning man, though he himself had transferred power to a trusted follower. And this happened in the world's most discipline-bound nation, most submissive to the blows of history; a drowning man was rescued despite incontrovertible evidence that he was doomed. Therein lie the power and significance of Nasser's leadership.

It is not really important to know whether he was sincere that day or was feigning an exit in order to win public support. In any event, he was taking a chance with a people that had been dealt a crushing blow. What nation would not have sanctioned the fallen leader's decision?[2]

So here was Gamal Abdel Nasser kept in power by an instant plebiscite. But power in the aftermath of a defeat also repre-

[1] P. 137.
[2] Prussia, following Iena. Renan pointed this out with some surprise. Prussia was the domain of hierarchy.

sents justice. And how can you render justice when you bear the principal burden of guilt? Naturally, you will want to put the army's top brass on trial; but what do you do when the chief of staff, a close friend and the only man in the entire country who still holds up his head, Marshal Abdel Hakim Amer, can counter you with the fact that the army's defeat was the fault of the *raïs* who ruled out offensive warfare, the key to victory? A military argument, yes, but the people expect to hear it.

Whether there was any plot among the Marshal and his aides to keep the army from being involved in Nasser's exploits is not the question. What is important is the first serious tremor that shook Nasser's power: the actual or alleged suicide of Abdel Hakim Amer. This was the final appearance of a pluralistic principle in Nasser's Republic, the ultimate phase of concentration—and a muted echo of collective responsibility.

Nasser incarnated the state. By erasing his military image, his other self, the leader purified himself, smashed the sword of defeat and waited to receive a new one. The Marshal's death, whether provoked or directed, takes on the ritual significance of partial suicide—a substitute for the aborted suicide of June 9. Personified power can divide itself in two and start a new round of Abraham's sacrifice.

But the public rescue in June altered the foundations and the nature of Nasser's power; it was no longer autonomous and now owed its existence more to the people than to the presence of foreign hordes on Egyptian soil. Who made you, *raïs?*

In February and November 1968, the Egyptian masses indicated to their leader that they were prepared to take on responsibility, which was personalized thereafter to the same degree as was his power.

On February 21, 1968, twenty years to the day after the mass demonstration of workers and students against Sidki Pasha marked the birth of the Egyptian Left, the work force of the Helwan arms-manufacturing plant, twenty miles from Cairo, rose in violent protest against the lenient sentences handed down to certain army chiefs. The police fired on the workers, who were soon joined by students echoing their demands for the death sentence. The *raïs* became directly involved. "You're sleeping, Nasser! Wake up, Gamal! We want a free press!" Elections were held in May. Once again the leader was upheld; Israeli forces were camped along the Canal.

November brought another warning shot. Just as they did in Paris that May, students demonstrated first against restrictive regulations governing entry into universities. But in El Mansura and Alexandria, groups of Moslem Brothers joined the protest, giving the movement a radical edge. The universities were shut down and ringed by army troops. Demonstrators clashed with police, who opened fire; army helicopters hovered over the cities; twenty died and hundreds were wounded. Yet the movement spread. On November 25 workers joined the students in Alexandria. Did this mark a resurgence of the 1946 worker-student front that Nasser and his predecessors feared so much?

Protest slogans were becoming more and more significant: "Gamal, use your army against Dayan, not us!" "Heykal, you promised us liberty, you give us police bullets!"[3]

A drastic reappraisal was taking place. Was the fresh "mandate" of 1967, the public renewal of *hukm,* being re-

---

[3] *Jeune Afrique* (December 1968). Heykal, Nasser's spokesman, had just published an article inviting the students to join in an "open discussion."

voked at its source by the masses? Here is what an objective journalist, observing the Cairo scene at the end of 1968, had to report:

> Two posters are plastered by the thousands all over the walls of Egyptian cities. One shows a scowling Nasser, jaw set, standing guard over two "fidai," their machine guns in hand. The other pictures the grinning, languid-eyed, well-shaven playboy President soaking up public approval. This is the silent strong man the country leans on. . . . Why should they go to the trouble of replacing Nasser with a mere reflection incapable of transmitting his magnetic "aura," his semihypnotic effect upon a people galvanized by his very presence?[4]

Two images are a lot—when the holder of personified power is struggling for survival, one face, even if it is morose, is better than two pleasant ones. Do the anxious, dispirited Egyptians imagine themselves in the smiling leader's image? Do they see him as the man they resurrected on June 9, 1967? Personification? Yes, but how credible is a double mask if one of them blurs the other?

The result of Nasser's essential failure as Egypt's responsible leader in June 1967, immediately followed by his triumph as both incarnation and personalized myth—in other words, the unwarranted value accorded to an authority whose claims to power had been destroyed and even abandoned—has been to make his charisma ambiguous. Not to mention the whole network of altered relations among the man, the masses, and the functions of building and protecting the nation; among the leader's mission and the people's freedom, the collective identity, the modernization of the state and the development of the national product; among being, having, and doing. The real problem is the interaction between the leader and the state.

---

[4] Yves Courrières in *France-Soir* (December 14, 1968).

How is a leader's potential to be measured? By his ability to create. Create what? Institutions, the very antithesis of his image as refuge and incarnated miracle. This is the point at which Nasser's journey should end—and precisely when the "miracle" ceases to emanate from him toward the people, but instead from the people toward him. Once the masses have rescued, reinvested, restored, and appropriated him for their own account, it is easier for them to evaluate what they had a right to expect.

We have indicated why the Egyptians had reason to distrust democratic institutions in the form of the sample imports offered them, which they associated with the colonial era.

Despite their justifiable resistance, the people still are eager for institutions that promise a modern way of life, stable social relations, and permanent political structures—in short, their existence as citizens freed from the spellbinding apparatus of prophet rulers.

The charismatic leader, personified by his own extraordinary abilities and technique, has the task of founding an institution for which he can only prepare the ground. If he perpetuates himself by clever manipulations or is perpetuated by public emotion, he fails the test. His glory must of necessity be fleeting. As to what is the right season for genuine personification, it moves like a pendulum between charisma and the creating of institutions.

Ibrahim Farhi has said of Nasser: "Because he did not recognize or could not resolve Egypt's problems, he incarnated them."[5] Thus he creates, in the plebeian style of national populism, and for a too-numerous people, the modern version of what in antiquity were the atmospheric myths, the makers of harvests and of catastrophes.[6]

[5] *L'Express* (Paris, 1968).

[6] Such was his burial, on October 1 1970: a hurricane. Eighteen years of boldness, adventure, courage and manoeuvre ended in a storm of despair, fear and love, of rites of possession and attempts to change death in a frantic nightmare. "Gamal, you are alive!"

Habib Bourguiba: Prophet of a National Bourgeoisie

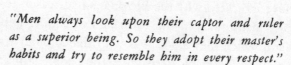

"Men always look upon their captor and ruler as a superior being. So they adopt their master's habits and try to resemble him in every respect."
—IBN KHALDUN, *Prolegomena*

Moving from Egypt to Tunisia, and from the realm of Gamal Abdel Nasser's power to that of Habib Bourguiba's, we find one common factor and two important differences.

Tunisia, like Egypt, was a markedly unified country before the era of its independence. It had a uniform language and culture. Centrifugal forces or tribal movements played a minor role; Ibn Khaldun's theory of cyclical tribal thrusts is less applicable to his own Tunisia than to Morocco. Tunisia's government was another bearing the stamp of the Turkish bureaucracy and subsequent remodeling under European colonial administrations. This was no ragged society overtaken by independence, but rather a nation in search of itself which had already attained some of the goals of development. The country's lack of natural resources created an urgent need for the exercise of power, but the elements of both a nation and a state were already present.

Was there any reason why Tunisian independence, having that much to build upon, could not evolve democratically— the normal path of development, according to Western standards? Did conditions demand a hero? In any event, Bourguiba was on hand. He fought for normalcy using abnormal tactics —if revolutionary leadership be considered abnormal. Unlike Nasser, he was never troubled by the moral problem of dictatorship. While Egypt's leader approached absolutism with a Moslem's puritanical misgivings, the double standards of one who reads the English-language press, and a beggar's guile, Tunisia's chief headed in the same direction with complete assurance, never seeming to question his own abilities, his preeminence, or his mission. Power fascinated Nasser, but made him uneasy; for Bourguiba, it was simply a fact.

But the difference in their attitudes is not solely psychological and cultural in origin; it is also a basic political datum. Bourguiba seized power and held it with mass support, whereas Nasser attained it only by dint of a conspiracy that left him isolated amid his a band of lieutenants and a public plagued by uncertainty. Bourguiba did not have to deal with the foundations and the balance of power: they already existed, owing to his own labors and organizational efforts in the period prior to independence.

Nasser's lack of a broad, flexible base of organized support, coupled with his principles and his political inexperience, account for his dizziness on the heights. Bourguiba's power was grafted onto the Neo-Destour and, in a sense, has been strengthened and shielded by it; Nasser's, on the other hand, sprang only from his own temerity and the undefined longings of the Egyptian masses and is forever imperiled by the intelligentsia, the elite, and the professional politicians. Bourguiba, buttressed by the Neo-Destour, is secure.

Tunisia is a long-established community. Her history does not go back sixty centuries like Egypt's, but at least three thousand years ago Homer's and Virgil's heroes are said to have ruled over her. The seat of Carthaginian grandeur was there. Jugurtha battled the Romans on her soil. And though the province that the victorious Romans added to their Empire, along with Moslem Ifriqya, had different boundaries (they encompassed nearly all of the present-day Constantine), Tunis soon emerged as its cultural and commercial capital.

The Hafsid dynasty consolidated the Tunisian community between the thirteenth and seventeenth centuries. Andalusians driven out of Spain by persecution set up manufacturing centers there. The Mosque of the Zeitounia became one of Islam's major cultural centers, and Ibn Khaldun added his own fame to his country's prestige. In the eighteenth century a new ruling power joined the sequence of Carthaginian, Roman, Vandal, and Arab conquerors. But Turkish domination did not alienate the populace, and the Hussein dynasty functioned as a national monarchy (as had that of the Fatimites, who emigrated to Egypt, or of the Hafsids, who came from the Western Maghreb).

One can certainly question the existence of any modern nationalist spirit in the Tunisia of the Husseins, as French conquest did not run up against determined resistance. But throughout Tunisia's eventful history, in which foreign powers played an extensive role, the relative stability of the Tunisian community encouraged the development of her political roots, her social codes, her systems of trade and communication in advance of most of her neighbors. It also accounts for the uninterrupted religious and cultural unity of this ancient Arab-Moslem country, where large numbers of *zaouias* did not overly fragment the spiritual community.

Nineteenth-century Tunisia under its beys, just like Egypt under the khedives, had the urge for progress in addition to recognized boundaries and an established cultural existence. Along the same lines as the efforts to institute constitutional law under the beys Amhed and Sadok, General Kheireddine, Ahmed Bey's minister and the author of an essay on nationhood (a type of introduction to Western institutions for

Moslem consumption), attempted to apply some aspects of European fiscal and administrative procedures to Tunisia. Colonialism did not discover a somnolent Tunisia, but instead a land of active and promising development.

If French rule did anything constructive for Tunisia, it was to promote, between 1881 and 1914, what was to be the nation's cornerstone: a three-rooted middle class derived from a small bureaucracy (*mamlouks*), a merchant class solidly organized in trade guilds (*baldi*), notably in Tunis, and a rural group with moderate-size landholdings, predominating in the Sahel. One of the most original contributions of the dying Hussein dynasty was the development of the Sadiki school in Tunis (founded in 1875 by Kheireddine), where rural middle-class boys (parvenus in the eyes of the city folk) could get an education.[1] One of them was Habib Bourguiba.

Everything encouraged the colonial administrations to develop responsibility among this youthful elite. But from 1911 onward they did just the opposite. This by-passing of potential subadministrative personnel created intense frustration among the educated middle class and forced over into the radical anti-French opposition even those who had long considered French rule an instrument of social change and intellectual development.

Tunisia's independence movement is divided into three distinct phases, which correspond to the three branches of the Tunisian middle class: *mamlouk, baldi,* and rural.

A movement called the Young Tunisians, modeled after the Young Turks, developed before the First World War under the leadership of Ali Bach Hamba, who was of Turkish origin. The watchword of this basically urban middle-class group was "modernization." Although they did not reject French control *a priori*, they were more sympathetic to Turkish reform

1 Clement H. Moore, *Tunisia Since Independence* (Berkeley: University of California Press; 1965), pp. 24–5.

policies. Development rather than nationhood was the keynote. The movement had little support outside Tunis and was favored more by the bureaucracy (*mamlouk*) than by the tradesmen (*baldi*).

The second phase stressed nationalism and religion more than modernization: Abdelaziz Taalbi, who preached in the Zeitounia Mosque and who wrote a pamphlet called *Martyred Tunisia*, called on the Tunisian intelligentsia to throw off French rule. Its inspiration was neither xenophobic nor fundamentalist, and the movement campaigned for a constitution (*Destour*), from which it took its name. Like its predecessor, it had an urban middle-class base, but appealed strongly to the commercial community; schooled in the rhetoric of Islam, it tempered its oratory with the commonplace language of business and trade and rapidly (between 1920 and 1922) gained the vast popularity that within the space of ten years dissipated its erratic extremism.

Then along came Bourguiba, a typical product of the Sahel's rural bourgeoisie, its peasant hardiness quickened by daring exploits on the sea.

THIS LIVING AND HISTORIC SYMBOL . . .

His background is especially significant. "I was born," he tells us, "into an honorable family that had known hard times, several of my relatives having suffered from the beys' repression following the revolts that took place in the middle of the last century. My father was hard pressed and had to join the army. . . ."[2] All the important facts are here: the rise of the middle class, the climate of nationalism, despotic government, and recourse to public service. The Sahel is a region of arbori-

[2] *Cinq hommes et la France* (Éd. du Seuil, 1961), p. 109.

culture, with fishing another source of revenue, but the Sahelians cannot feed themselves from the land any more than the Tonkinese can from their rice paddies. And like the Tonkinese, the Sahelians respond to deprivation by pouring their talent and energy into urban administrative jobs, thus acquiring an understanding of government which is the very foundation of Tunisian development, and especially of Bourguiba's power.

The surprisingly typical career of this leader was marked by each stage of his education, from his earliest training at the Sadiki school, then at the Lycée Carnot and the École des Sciences Politiques in Paris. There is no better illustration of the cultural and social advancement of a lower middle-class country boy during the period of the French protectorate. A Tunisian Balzac would have turned this into a realistic novel; Bourguiba made it his autobiography. On his return from Paris in 1927, fresh from the experience of a school where liberalism was all but a religion at the time, married to a Frenchwoman who bore him a son, and having developed contacts in Parisian leftist circles, Habib Bourguiba gained admission to the Tunis bar and proceeded to discover his own country: a society bound hand and foot by tradition and abandoned to colonial power.

His years in Paris were not instrumental in settling his attitude toward conditions at home. As early as 1922, at the age of nineteen, he was a nationalist, active in Taalbi's Destour party. Not until 1928, however, did his outlook mature and broaden onto the plane of political analysis from which he viewed social injustice in the same light as colonialist alienation. Bourguiba then devoted himself to the legal defense of peasants disposessed by industry—and to reorienting the nationalist movement along modern lines, widening its support. This regenerative process was accomplished in three stages.

First, he chose "his" team: Dr. Materi, Bahri Guiga, and Tahar Sfar, the heirs of Tahar Hadda, the modernizers of

nationalism. To say the group was his is exaggerating, for
Habib Bourguiba was its youngest member. But the fact is
that a man who is destined to hold power singles himself out
very quickly. Why was Bourguiba's leadership so immediately
evident? And why did Bonaparte take command at Toulon?

He broadened his influence through the press, writing for
La Voix du Tunisien, and then founded his own organ, *L'Action Tunisienne,* in 1932. His articles in both papers were
unusually vigorous and broad-minded. On the subject of
colonialism, for example, he wrote: "Are we talking about a
degenerate, dying people? This means progressive absorption,
assimilation. Or, on the other hand, are we talking about a
healthy and vigorous people, forced by international competition or temporary misfortune to bear the yoke of a foreign
power? In itself the contact with a more developed civilization
has a healthy effect. It causes a virtual renaissance."[3]

Finally, he shaped and disciplined the Destour so that it
flourished. The fact that he was able to rule one party for
twenty-five years was owing to his extraordinary ability to
influence and dominate a movement whose double target was
the French protectorate and the national leadership. His apprenticeship to power first involved assembling a team. These
young men, who were at the crossroads of the two earlier
trends in Tunisian demands—the constructive modernism of
the Young Tunisians of 1907 and the Destour party's militant
nationalism of the twenties—sat in judgment on their elders,
the disciples of Taalbi (Salah Farhat, Ahmed es-Safi) and intransigent conservatives.

In the early thirties the nationalist party was like a dignified
academy in which politics took the form of melodious rhetoric
on stubbornly stationary themes. Lawyers, tradespeople or
civil servants—hardly one of them looked beyond Tunis or

[3] *La Voix du Tunisien* (N.p.: February 1931).

his own nose. Nobody had really made an effort to join forces with groups who were accomplishing things over the border. They were middle class to the core, bound by convention, background, and local interests. They were nationalists somewhat by conviction, mostly by emotion. What would happen if they were taken at their word?

Bourguiba himself was a politician who intended to be taken at his word and to act upon it. His objectives were independence and modernization for Tunisia. Conflict was bound to erupt shortly between those whom Peyrouton, the military governor and a clever manipulator of ambitions and interests, called "the concaves and the convexes," which gives a fairly accurate picture of the basic reserve of one group and the restless energy of the other. Although at times Bourguiba seemed caught up in the petty schemes of the party's old-guard leadership, his stubborn optimism prevailed.

In March 1934 he held a meeting of the young dissidents in Ksar-Hellal, a village in his native Sahel. There, among the olive trees trembling in the breeze from the nearby sea, he launched the Neo-Destour party as if it were a ship. For thenceforth all the others would be nothing but the "archeo."

But this was beyond the realm of confrontations between generations. Here was the line of demarcation between quaintness and reality, rationalization and action, a club of shawl-draped elders and a party of conquest. Bourguiba turned his roving eye on the rest of the world and saw vast movements on the march in the Soviet Union and in Fascist Italy. He studied the organization of rising parties in France: La Rocque's PSF, Doriot's PPF, Bergery's Frontism. He was already familiar with the machinery of the SFIO and the French Communist Party, to which his first lawyer, Berthon, had exposed him (without seeking to justify it, it seems).

All these examples provided him with very few ideological principles, but he looked to them for inspiration in building his own structure. The doctrine of this "party" can be found only in the person of its leader. Was it, strictly speaking, a party? Or simply a gathering of Bourguiba's supporters? Or, still more simply, one of the many "independence fronts" that flourished from the Atlantic to the China Sea during the era of colonialism?

One need not be cynical for fear of seeming naïve. It is true that the philosophy of the Neo-Destour, haunted by fascist goblins but saved from that pitfall by Tunisian finesse and the leader's democratic ties, is practically indefinable except in terms of Bourguiba's aims: Tunisian independence and modernization, glory for the chief. But occasionally these objectives were given an ideological expression: "Tunisia is on the path to rationalism; the Neo-Destour is the apostle of Reason"—an echo of Robespierre and Royer-Collard.

It is also true that the movement's social and economic bases, the peasantry, the middle class, and the proletariat, gave it the appearance of revolutionary middle-class movements, which elsewhere produced radical or fascist parties.

The Neo-Destour was neither of those. What we can say is that it was and remains the major modern type of party in the Arab-Moslem world (neither the Syrian Baath nor the Algerian FLN nor Morocco's UNPF, its nearest rivals, possess the same efficiency-fostering cohesion). Of course, the Egyptian Wafd preceded it chronologically in attempting to win mass Arab support based on "democratic" themes and European-type institutions. But the vast movement led by Saad Zaghlul and later by Mustafa el-Nahas depended on patrons and could never free itself entirely from the domination of adroit feudal barons who encouraged the party to adopt a popular image behind which they could preserve their essential privileges.

Habib Bourguiba's party borrowed from major Western parties not only ideas and techniques, but also a plan, an organization and objectives that were concrete instead of mythical or mystical. With the advent of the Neo-Destour, the Arab community progressed from religion to politics, from suggestion to strategy, from the imaginary to the real world. Needless to say, both the party and its leader have made numerous errors. But through the Neo-Destour a unit of the Arab world ceased to see collective action as a prophet-led caravan on some desert journey, and saw it instead as a low-cost and highly profitable effort to solve one or more historical problems. As Jacques Berque put it: "It offers an escape route from the pernicious syndrome of intransigence/opportunism and substitutes another combination: radicalism/historical authenticity."[4] With Bourguiba, this region of the Maghreb replaced prophecy with analysis and mob impulse with mass action.

From 1934 onward, the main features of the party, with Materi as president and Bourguiba as secretary general, were its organization in local units modeled more or less after European communist cells; the provincial, rural, and generally modest origins of its leaders and cadres, in contrast to the staff of the first Destour; the new leaders' concern for creating ties with the masses, using simple language and concentrating their activity in the areas of greatest deprivation; also the desire to bolster the political organ by a trade union arm, which later became the well-known UGTT and played as important a role in the independence movement as the Neo-Destour itself;[5] a clearly modernist ideology, outspokenly democratic even though such principles may not exactly have guided its

[4] Le Maghreb entre deux guerres (Paris: Éd. du Seuil; 1962), p. 263.

[5] Which does not mean that Tunisian trade unionism, even in its native form, dates from the Neo-Destour movement.

As far back as the close of the First World War, M'Hammed Ali, that colorful personality who was Mustafa Kemal's driver and somewhat reminiscent of American working-class leaders, had led a union struggle that took hold among the masses. But his political vision and his principles were not equal to his courage. He fell by the wayside.

leaders' actions; a realistic and flexible strategy, so consistent that it came to define the leader's policy.

For what was Bourguibism, then, if not a modern brand of Machiavellianism, a blend of shrewdness, patience, and reliance on force which outshone the performance of any other contemporary Arab political chiefs (except, as always, the Egyptian Wafdists, who were bound at the time by treaty commitments with England).

Supported by this rigid organization and broad doctrine, the dashing and colorful Bourguiba, who soon dominated an entourage comprised of Mongi Slim, Hedi Nouira, Ali Belhaouane, and Hedi Chaker, set out to negotiate with France. We will not deal with that side of the picture, as our subject is not Bourguiba the diplomat but rather Bourguiba as a leader in relation to his followers.

We should also remember that the show of force he made in April while ill, like some hell-bent chivalrous charge, brought him under arrest once more. But four years of harsh prisons allowed him to impose his leadership more firmly than ever. Against a strong current favoring collaboration with the Axis, the colonialists' foe, he managed to make his own policy of cooperation with the Allies prevail, principally because he believed they would win.

A letter he wrote in 1942 to Dr. Thameur, who directed the party in his absence, carries some extremely significant and forceful remarks: "And if, in spite of everything I say, all of you are not convinced, obey me anyway! I'm giving you an order. Don't argue with me! I take full responsibility before God and History!" A Neo-Destour pamphlet reprinted this text with a comment from its action committee: "As Si El Habib says so . . ." Thus the Neo-Destour joined the victors' camp.

Habib Bourguiba returned to Tunisia in the spring of 1943 to find only the remnants of a party. That setback led to his

"hegira" to the Orient, where he remained for four years that
seemed like centuries to him. His absence, and the absence of
his near-suffocating influence, resulted in a number of promo-
tions, freer movement inside the party, and above all the sudden emergence of a man who was to gain wide notoriety:
Salah Ben Youssef, a young lawyer from Djerba who took
Bourguiba's place as secretary general.

On his return from the East in 1949, greatly disillusioned
by what he had seen and experienced there, Bourguiba found
his party reorganized and led by much younger men, some of
whose attitudes he could not understand. But the strength of
his reputation and personality was such that he soon recovered
his influence, particularly as he got along well at that time with
Salah Ben Youssef. And with the latter's support, he embarked
on a second round of conferences and attempted cooperation
with the French. In December 1951, after eighteen months of
illusions and palavers, the break came. On January 18, 1952,
Bourguiba gave a speech that was tantamount to a declaration
of war against the intransigent colonizers.

There was another show of force, but this time Bourguiba
faced it in a more favorable climate and on more solid ground.
What was the sociopolitical climate? Abdel Wahed Boudhiba,
using information provided by Georges Gurvitch, described
it as follows:

> In the precolonial period, Tunisian nationalists inte-
> grated themselves into the multiarmed bureaucracy and,
> by the same token, into Islam's "omma" . . . In the
> 1950's, they were becoming part of the fabric of the
> Tunisian nation. . . . Habib Bourguiba was the living and
> historic symbol that made the "national horizon" finite
> and gave it a quadruple significance: social, political,
> psycho-dynamic, and symbolic.[6]

[6] La Formation de la nation tunisienne, address delivered at the Conference
on Sociology (Royaumont: 1965).

As to the Neo-Destour, the machinery that had been forged at Ksar-Hellal withstood pressure and repression. It had gained broader support, and its trade-union arm—for how else can you describe the UGTT?—had considerable national influence, which the French authorities deferred to more than did the party. Thus, at the height of the 1951–53 conflicts, when the top Neo-Destour leadership was in prison, nationalist activity was directed quite openly by the UGTT's general secretary, Ferhat Hached—whom European terrorists, forerunners of the OAS, cut down with their machine guns on December 6, 1952.

But Bourguiba's hour was approaching. French opinion had shifted, world pressure was increasing, and the Indo-China war was headed downhill. In July 1954, after concluding the Geneva Pact, Mendès-France went to Tunis and in his Carthage statement committed himself to make good the promises of many French spokesmen. Several months later, Habib Bourguiba and Edgar Faure signed agreements assuring internal autonomy. By the beginning of June 1955, the leader was back in Tunisia.

He was given a triumphant welcome. But the party he founded, the cadres he trained, the activists he inspired, all seemed even less recognizable than they had in 1949. Was he reluctant to take up the reins of political leadership, as he admitted to the author in 1961? His aides (and there were more new names: Bahi Ladgham, Taieb Mehiri, Ahmed Mestiri, and Mohammed Masmoudi) easily persuaded him to take the party's helm again.

Bourguiba had to meet two concurrent threats, after those of 1934, 1938, and 1952, and they were equally trying: the test of unity in the face of "Youssefist" dissidence,[7] and the transition from the opposition camp to the seat of power after independence was won, soon after autonomy—even sooner than the leader had hoped.

[7] Activated by Salah Ben Youssef.

Bourguiba surmounted the first challenge by arranging to have his rebellious rival and the latter's closest satellites eliminated, and also by holding the first well-organized public congress of the party, at Sfax in November 1955. As for the second challenge, the test of his power, the Neo-Destour handled it better than most similar organizations. For what is more difficult than totally converting revolutionary principles and tactics into those of a government party? The Neo-Destour, built like a war machine against the protectorate, had to cast aside its armor and become a system for insuring stability and order, for erecting the state—an explosive substance was destined to serve as a tool of progress.

With its unwieldy structure and rigid operation, Bourguiba's party had the good sense to limit its objectives to the practical sort. It chose its battlefields wisely, skirting those which served essentially nationalist aims, except for two absurd and ruinous ventures: Bizerte, a veritable "retreat forward," and land nationalization in 1964. Secularization, the support of women's rights, and planning were decisive factors in developing Tunisian society, although Bourguiba's opposition to strict observance of Ramadan fasting, considered harmful to the national economy, ran into stubborn resistance and still continues to do so; the party's leadership has not recognized the strong attachment to Moslem tradition which pervades a large section of the country.

Bourguiba's most commendable reform has been in the area of reappraising economic priorities. He developed the concept gradually, but the change itself came about in a solemn manner, on February 8, 1960, the second anniversary of the Sakiet-Sidi-Youssef raid.[8] Summoned by the party to hear the "supreme commander" speak, the people expected to hear

[8] On the eve of the Maghreb conference in Tunis called to discuss the Algerian question, a squadron of French planes bombed and strafed this village, destroying it almost entirely and killing over 100 civilians. (Trans.)

some nationalist battle recalled or a public policy outlined. "The most urgent battle is not Bizerte," Habib Bourguiba declared, "it is the one we must wage against underdevelopment"—a decisive statement from a man whose entire career had been focused on political and legal struggles, on questions of sovereignty, prestige, and status, relying all the while on demagogic arguments and impassioned appeals to nationalism and the most elemental longings of the masses. He was no longer telling them that the enemy was the foreigner, the handiest target, but that it was poverty, which is not so easy to erase. And who is to say that the Tunisians did not know this all along?

STRUCTURE AND STYLE OF A POWER

"Revolts are not led essentially in the name of nationalism, but in the name of an overpowering desire for dignity. When the rebels can assuage this desire through institutions whose every detail has been organized by their leaders, success is bound to follow. When there are no institutions, there is chaos."

—In an interview with
JEAN DANIEL *in* L'Express, *September 1, 1960*

The prerogatives allegedly enjoyed by Bourguiba are nothing compared with the power he exercises by virtue of his personality, his influence, his style of rule, and his relations with the elite and the masses. Yet it is important to know something about the institutional framework surrounding this "sacred monster," one of whose legal maxims is that "in order to remain strong, power must not exhaust itself in ramifications," and who replied to a question about Tunisia's political "system" by saying: "The system? I am the system."[9]

9 Clement H. Moore, p. 104.

The Constitution of June 1, 1959, legalized a de facto situation: the absolute power of the Neo-Destour (renamed the Destour Socialist Party in 1964) and its chief, Habib Bourguiba. When the leader had abolished the monarchy in 1957, he had added the comment that he could reinstitute it for his own benefit but "preferred a republic." Moreover, he had publicly favored an "American-type" presidency.[1] What he did not mention was that he would alter the system somewhat by putting Congress to sleep.

Elected for five years and eligible to hold office for three terms,[2] the chief of state "called a halt to government policy-making and assumed the function himself," merely "informing" the Assembly and designating ministers who were responsible to him alone. He proposed laws "in conjunction with the Assembly," but his proposals had priority. He was empowered to legislate by decree upon the Assembly's recommendation or when it was not in session, which simplified matters. Summarizing his powers, a Tunisian magistrate described Bourguiba as "the regime's organic motor"—a motor with no apparent brake, for the elections following the adoption of this constitution gave Bourguiba 99.1 percent of the vote for President of the Republic. He was the only candidate.

In fact, the only group the leader had to worry about and rarely, at that, was the old Neo-Destour party, now the Destour Socialist Party. The Assembly functioned only as a registry, and the government functioned as a society of chief clerks who usually were consulted privately. The remaining organ was the party's Political Bureau (also known as the Central Committee or the Council of the Republic). Most of Bourguiba's major decisions were made after he had met with the Political Bureau, which had a counseling role but ultimately could be overruled by the leader.

[1] In an interview on Swiss television, September 6, 1957.
[2] Bringing the end of his final term to 1974.

The top echelons of the party, all members of the Political Bureau, had more to say than the ministers (they were often the same people, but the party, a satellite of Bourguiba's, superseded every other hierarchy), yet they would never bring themselves to oppose him. The Tunisian jurist Ridah Abdallah puts it thus:

> Total submission to the party leader builds a homogeneous movement and welds men together with a common sense of discipline and duty: to attack the chief is tantamount to sacrilege. There is an emotional and mystical bond between the people and him. . . . Stronger than any institution, this emotional bond linking the people to Bourguiba is the very foundation of the regime. . . . He is their all, they only hope . . .[3]

These remarks are significant enough not to require further elaboration of the structure of Bourguiba's power, the modifications brought to it by the Congress of Sousse in 1959, at which the decentralizing powers of the federations were practically eliminated (the leader maintained that the dual powers of governors on the one hand and commissioners on the other made no sense because "both are emanations of my person"[4]), and then the Bizerte Conference in 1964, at which, in the guise of promoting socialism, state control finally was consolidated.

We get an idea of Bourguiba's image of himself from some of the letters he wrote in 1952 while a prisoner of the French on the Island of La Galite. "If my life were taken, the people would suffer an irreparable loss in losing not so much their leader and moral counselor as the fruit of all their past sacrifices." (Besides being the motor of Tunisian history, he was already embodied in it; not animating force, but substance.)

---

[3] "Le Néo-Destour depuis l'Indépendance," in *Revue juridique et politique d'outre-mer* (October–December 1963).

[4] Clement H. Moore, p. 128.

Several months later he amplified this: "As the creator of
Tunisia, I have renewed her human substance."

And one should also read the speech he gave on March 20,
1966, the tenth anniversary of independence:

> Having been the major artisan of Tunisian history for
> thirty-five years, I believe I should shed some light on the
> critical moments in our struggle. . . . Those events ought
> to be recalled so that the new generations may reflect
> upon this long journey of ours, this exalting epic which
> brought Tunisia to independence, whose origin was my
> work for *La Voix du Tunisien* and, especially, my article
> entitled "The Evolution of a Protectorate" on February
> 13, 1931.

All the elements are here: the essentially creative role,
attempted mythification, strict personification, and a didactic
tendency, one of Bourguiba's traits that we will mention
again. As an example of his pedagogical bent, a story is told
that in Le Kef, in December 1962, a visitor asked him if he felt
any political bond with the most illustrious of "pre-Tunisians,"
Hannibal. He made no pretense of modesty, as anyone else
would have. Instead, he thought a moment and, pointing to
the neighboring mountain, replied: "No, my ancestor was
Jugurtha, who fought the foreign invaders on those peaks. A
patriot, like myself, not a conqueror. Alive or dead, I am
responsible for this nation's destiny."

These are the words of Bourguiba, who rules as you or I
breathe, without giving it a thought. You would think that
his most remote forebears had received Tunisia as a fief and
that egalitarian Tunisia had no other wish than to submit to
one man's will. With his magnetic eyes, decisive gestures, and
ringing speech, he rules.

Habib Bourguiba must have felt some resentment at being
the child of a small, impoverished, colonized people. His broad

understanding and imagination and his vitality would have qualified him to lead successfully a populace far greater than Tunisia's four millions. But the scope of his power makes up for his modest work space.

Is it charismatic power? In his excellent book on contemporary Tunisia,[5] Clement Moore says it is not, in view of the highly secular nature of Bourguiba's acts and doctrine. This seems to be an extremely narrow interpretation of charisma, which is, as we see it, the irrational yet apparently irrefutable dimension of an individual's dynamic authority over a group. In terms of this definition, Bourguiba is a charismatic leader like those other, much more secular prophets Simón Bolívar and Mustafa Kemal.

Furthermore, the lay aspect of Bourguiba's power should not be overemphasized. He has fought the tenacious hold of Islam, but when necessary he can act as a miracle-worker (*mordjeza*). He knows the roles of prophet, oracle, and seer. He is perfectly at ease extolling religion as both spiritual imperative and social structure. Thus, in December 1958, while visiting a village that had no mosque, he was heard to exclaim: "What a disgrace for a Moslem community to be deprived of a temple where the name of God is glorified and whence the muezzin sends out his call to prayer!"[6]

Although Bourguiba does not take a stand on the social role of religion, he tends to emphasize Islam's dynamic role:

We Tunisians believe it a useful daily incentive in the struggle for progress. . . . Instead of snuffing out this attachment, calling it fanaticism and a holdover from ancient times, we regard it as a motivating force. Do we

[5] Already cited.
[6] Charles Debbasch, *La République tunisienne* (Paris: Librairie de droit et de jurisprudence; 1962), p. 146.

not have it to thank for every great undertaking of the
Moslems, every conquest that has led them from the
China frontier to Poitiers in France . . . ?[7]

He does not look for arguments, yet nothing annoys him
more than being coerced or even contradicted. Three years
ago a friendly visitor inquired whether he would not benefit
from the criticism of his close advisers: "I am perfectly agree-
able to it," replied Bourguiba, "but for some reason, they
don't care." After thinking better of it, he added: "Anyway,
when you have a Bourguiba, what's the point in arguing with
him?"

His relations with his aides and entourage are thus rigidly
formal; the give-and-take is only superficial. He is paternalistic
toward his people, reflecting a culture in which the father has
unlimited authority and punishment is meted out as generously
as affection. Habib Bourguiba speaks of the Tunisians as an innocent and lively household whose prime needs are to be fed,
educated, and kept in tow. But what might have remained only
paternalism gradually became didacticism.

In addition to being a leader and paterfamilias, Bourguiba
also sees himself as a schoolmaster. His speeches, aside from
being exhortations to loyalty, are also courses in history,
political science, economics, hygiene, and domestic manners.
Of the numerous cornerstones he has laid, the greatest number
has been for schools, and he gives prime consideration to his
relations with the young. His government is first and foremost
a school system.

Leader, cadres, masses. This triangle is the fabric of political
life in Tunisia, as it is for her neighbors, except that only in

[7] Press conference on March 29, 1965, cited by Michael Camau, *La Notion
de démocratie dans la pensée des dirigeants maghrébiens* (1969).

Tunisia are the cadres so solidly organized in a party worthy of the name.

There are factions at both extremities of this essentially single-minded community, and a certain degree of friction between the leader and the cadres. This is unusual for such a country, or for any developing nation, and these tensions serve as reminders that history, social stratification and geographic factors fashion political life.

The historical explanation of this tension between the leader and the Tunisian intelligentsia is familiar enough. We know that the particular stage of the Tunisian nationalist movement which led to independence was reached in 1934 with the founding of the Neo-Destour party at the Congress of Ksar-Hellal. That congress became a forum for debate, a confrontation, and already marked a rupture between the young elite, headed by Bourguiba, and the old Destour party. So there was open dissent from the start, and it continued to characterize the development of the nationalist movement.

An event, classic in the history of colonialism, followed this congress: the arrest of the Neo-Destour leaders. This was an extremely significant period because while Bourguiba and his comrades were held in a concentration camp at Bordj-Leboeuf, on the edge of the Sahara, there was incessant personal and factional strife in the core of Tunisia's political leadership.[8] Bourguiba was freed by the Popular Front in 1936, only to be reimprisoned after the events of 1938. And another test of political unity began. A comparison to Sartre's *No Exit* comes to mind. Can prisoners establish a bond of trust among themselves? The experience of Tunisia's leaders had a lasting effect on their future relations.[9]

[8] This episode gave rise to the publication in Tunis in 1969 of certain documents under the title *The First Test*.

[9] Similar circumstances affected Ben Bella and his lieutenants and, as we shall see, Nkrumah and Danquah.

Speaking of a plot against his life which he had just exposed at the end of 1962, Bourguiba said to me, "You know, it was nothing alongside what I had to go through in my relations with the other Tunisian leaders. Prison hardships are much worse than attempts on your life."

After he was freed and had negotiated the 1955 agreements with France providing for internal autonomy, Bourguiba returned to Tunis. There was a fresh wave of conflict, groping, and uncertainty. In June 1955, the new faces and attitudes he discovered in high political circles left him confused and surprised. Although he himself had done much to transform the national consciousness, he found that in his absence it had progressed a good deal on its own. Some of the people had changed so much that he began to wonder whether he could continue to lead a group of strangers. He toyed with the idea of retiring from political life and becoming a sort of Gandhi —if indeed he had any talent at all for that role. This rediscovery of Tunisia was to lead to another test: the conflict with Salah Ben Youssef, the party's general secretary, which brought to a head the divergences between the exiled leader and the party that had developed in his absence.

This historical picture helps to explain the relations between the leader and Tunisia's political chiefs. But there were other elements that weighed: geographic factors, for example. Except for Egypt, Tunisia is said to be the most strongly unified of the Arab countries, with no ethnic problem to face and minimal provincial factionalism. Yet political life is regional, each group having its own local character. Tunisians have strong local attachments, and even in the Tunis suburbs there are district clubs functioning each under its own name.

But the most important and active communities are those of the Sahel and the Djerba regions, while Tunis, Sfax and the Cape Bon area have emerged as secondary centers. The rivalry between Sahelians and Djerbians deserves particular attention because, to a degree, it touches upon the major issues separating the two most widely known leaders, Bourguiba and Salah Ben Youssef, and also because it has deeper implications in the areas of culture and human relations and in the economy.

The Sahelians played an outstanding role in the emergence of modern Tunisia. The Neo-Destour leadership had always been largely Sahelian; Ksar-Hellal, the party's cradle and the site of its first congress, is in the very heart of the Sahel. Nor was that an accident of history, for in this region, intellectual achievement had far outstripped economic development, making it a community ripe for creative activity and public service, opportunities that this poor and overcrowded province could not provide. What happened to the people of the Peloponnesus or of Kabylia is what happened to the Sahelians.

We can understand why, in very recent times, this group, which had entrenched itself in the bureaucracy, came to represent economic statism while its Djerbian rivals retained control of private trade. Apart from their clashes over specific political issues, there was constant interaction between the adaptable Sahelian group, which became integrated with the party first, and then with the state—which is practically the reflection of the party—and the Djerbians, principally a merchant group that dominated the private sector of commerce and whose interests naturally conflicted with the aims of an increasingly planned and state-oriented economy.

One might well compare the role of the Djerbians in Tunisian political and social life to that of another meridional group, the Soussis of present-day Morocco, who are also small tradesmen and opposed to state control, though for basically political reasons.

Perhaps this antithesis between Sahelians and Djerbians appears a bit simplistic. Let me add a comment on the Tunisian economy that Bourguiba made in my presence: "The awful thing in this country is the teeming presence of the third sector." One may substitute "Djerbians" for "third sector."

The Sahelians themselves belong to the first sector: they are an agricultural petty bourgeoisie. Moreover, the Sahel is a region of small towns where a certain communal, even democratic, tradition has grown up which had its influence upon the party's founding doctrine and, later on, the state's, even though that doctrine subsequently took a more authoritarian turn.

The third point is the different relationship between the leader and the masses on one hand and the elite and the masses on the other. Bourguiba and the Tunisians evidently relate to each other in a special way. He is called the *zaïm*, although he is not very fond of the word, probably because of its strong Oriental overtones. In any event, it describes the close bond between a leader and his people which is characteristic of this type of power. The irrational, magnetic, and unimpeachable evidence is there, linking an individual and a crowd and establishing the framework of this kind of power.

We have used the word "irrational": it comes to mind. Is it exaggerated? Jacques Berque, defining the relationship between leaders such as Bourguiba, Ben Badïs, and Allal el-Fassi and the masses, writes that these chiefs "provide this nebula with a polarizing signal. They instruct the masses from the lexicon of a new life."[1] In this concept of a lexicon, of teaching and of a new life, there is less irrationality than learning and enlightenment. We do not use these words haphazardly, and in describing the Tunisian regime we would be tempted to speak of that enlightened despotism which was the glory of another world.

So there is an immediate relationship between the leader and the people.

[1] *Le Maghreb entre deux guerres.*

The ties are different when it comes to the nation's elite. It is evident that the Tunisians do not accept the word, the authority, or the decrees of their political chiefs in the same spirit or in the same light that they accept Bourguiba's. Two types of relations exist. The state party does not act as an intermediary to convey Bourguiba's power; there is a dual set of relations: between the leader and the masses on one hand, between the party and the masses on the other. And because the machinery of state tends to limp and lag, this involves certain risks.

To improve the poor relations between the cadres (which he had been influential in forming) and the masses, Bourguiba founded what he called the Destourian School of National Cadres (not the school of Neo-Destour cadres), to show how far he went in placing the good of the state before that of the party. The danger is that the party may cease to generate ideas or to enrich the political scene, that it may no longer act as a counterforce to the state and as a source of change, but simply as an association bent on acquiring and maintaining power. Bourguiba stated to the directors of this school:

> My objective is to rebuild the nation's prestige by raising the level of its entire elite. Only in this way can the state meet its responsibilities or social imbalance be eliminated. Our struggle against underdevelopment and for education of the masses is in itself a promise that we will succeed, that we will give all citizens a share of responsibility in order to narrow as much as possible the differences that separate them from the elite; this is the authentic democracy for which we are striving and working.

As to the present situation of the Tunisian community, only one aspect of which is represented by the leader-cadres relationship, we may perhaps conclude that it jumped too abruptly from anticolonial struggle into self-government, by-passing the

stage of political ripening—in other words, from total commitment to an individual, to total and unquestioning self-
acceptance.

Bourguiba, a realist who knows that Rome was not built in
a day, is also a tribune who sets the Forum buzzing, a gifted
orator whose eloquence occasionally sideswipes reason and
who often lets himself be carried away by his own soliloquy.
This stateman, whose chief contribution to contemporary Arab
history is probably his replacement of prophecy by politics, has
been known to play the prophet or the muezzin and to chant
his message so movingly that his own voice takes the place
of political objectives.

He blazes up, sometimes forgetting himself, and is left at
the mercy of words that were better left unspoken. And, unlike
other Arab leaders, in trying to match his words to his actions,
he tangles himself in some risky venture: the Bizerte affair, for
one. In that Palestinian enterprise he stood up boldly to the
demagogues but perhaps had not foreseen the pace, the scope,
or the consequences of the affair at the time of his famous
press conference in Beirut. And the realist was left to repair
the prophet's misjudgment.

No one is surer than he of what Pierre Rossi has said of
him:

> No state has ever come into being without the presence
> and the thrust of an individual's authority. To build last-
> ing order from such confused elements as nations, fami-
> lies, and mass movements, there must be injected at a
> given moment, under the control of one man, a grand
> and powerful vision and a precise knowledge of reality.[2]

2 *La Tunisie de Bourguiba* (Éd. Kahia: Tunis; 1967).

Bourguiba is so sure of it that the book from which this passage comes, and in whose format he has obviously had a personal hand, is illustrated exclusively with photographs of him.

Here, then, is the regime founded, molded, animated, incarnated, symbolized, epitomized, and perhaps a bit bewildered by the man Clement Moore calls a "presidential monarch,"[3] in whom can well be seen the prophet of a middle class condemned by poverty, bureaucratic expedients, and the miracles wrought by "heroic leadership."

PROMOTION THROUGH CRISIS

To have a compelling purpose, to believe in one's calling, to translate it into significant political action, forging it into an effective, adaptable instrument that serves the aspirations, the interests, and the creativity of a social class—in this case, the petty bourgeoisie—is not enough. All these assets must be made something permanent.

Patrice Lumumba, Ahmed Ben Bella, and Janio Quadros had consolidated those elements, but their power could not withstand certain pressures—in the first instance, of the banking interests, in the second, of democratic demands, and in the last, of extortionate conservatism. Habib Bourguiba himself survived a number of stormy episodes, and each time managed to solidify his power as well as his authority. Every crisis furnished him with additional reasons to impose his leadership more firmly and mythify it more boldly; in short, to embark on a new stage of personification.

We will not return to the conflicts that beset the Neo-Destour from 1934 onward, when its leaders were first imprisoned, but will deal with those which confronted Bourguiba's power:

[3] *Tunisia Since Independence.*

in 1955–6, while it was rooting itself; in 1959, over the issue
of a free press and while there was still a choice between a
"ruling democracy" (see Georges Burdeau) and enlightened
despotism; in 1962, when a military conspiracy threatened his
life; in 1965, with the emergence of "worker opposition," as
Moscow termed it in the 1920's; in January 1968, when, from
the very core of the party's leadership, complaints arose that
the last vestige of democratic procedure had vanished in
that the leader did not consult his trusted advisers before
making decisions; and finally, the student demonstrations of
March 1968, two months before the Paris outbreaks.

The crisis at the end of 1965 was the gravest threat to
Bourguiba's rule. Because it burst triumphantly and confidently
onto the scene, pitting the leader against his most promising
lieutenant and nearly causing his overthrow, it had far-reaching effects on the future course of the regime and shifted it
permanently onto authoritarian ground, fixing the style of
Bourguiba's power.

One should bear in mind the preceding events of that year,
the "supreme commander's" triumphant return to Tunis on
June 1, his acclamation by the mob and the chorus of officials,
and the historic and apparently irreversible nature of this
popular "rite." Bourguiba believed himself the elect of the
Tunisians. He reciprocated their love. He gave himself to their
fervent adoration. The future was his. He would be careful
not to abuse all this honor, as he confided to a French diplomat
whom he continued to call a friend.

Three months later, the situation was completely reversed.
Salah Ben Youssef, the only political chief with a following
at all comparable to his own (and very remotely comparable,
at that), had represented Tunisia at the Bandung Conference
that April and had denounced the agreements between Bourguiba and Edgar Faure. Not satisfied to carry on his campaign
from afar, he returned home, rejoined his strong band of

political allies, and embarked on a prolonged and systematic program of defaming the leader. And the same populace that had wildly acclaimed Bourguiba in June now turned a receptive ear to Ben Youssef's message. Was this what the Tunisians took for fervent loyalty? Was yesterday's savior today's traitor? "The ancient instinct for anarchy regained the upper hand. . . . This was the greatest disappointment of my life," he admitted ten years later in a tear-choked voice.

The tense and uncertain period from September through October 1955 marked the onset of Bourguiba's disillusionment, his distrust of the people, which, added to his Caesarist temperament and the trying experience of founding a pauper state, is at the source of his absolutism.[4] The people did not deserve to be consulted. General de Gaulle is said to have taken the French for sheep. What Bourguiba thought of the Tunisians in the fall of 1955 was told us one December day in 1962 in Le Kef: "There is no Saint-Germain-des-Près here. Everything has to be spelled out, explained and directed. These people need a guide. Democracy? It would frighten them."

As we know, the 1955 showdown gave Bourguiba the upper hand: Salah Ben Youssef did not dare take issue with the Sfax Congress, and that settled his defeat. Bourguiba remained master. He had no intention of sharing his crown and was prepared to antagonize or even alienate those whose support had swung the balance in his favor: the majority of the Destour ranks, of the peasants of Cape Bon, the Medjerda Valley, and the Sahel who had been able to voice their opinion, and above all of the trade unions, then under the leadership of Ahmed Ben Salah.

Thereafter, Bourguiba's power never ceased to expand,

---

[4] "I insisted that the mission entrusted to me by the party's National Council should not be precisely defined: that I should control events." (Speech on March 20, 1966.)

from the inner party to the Assembly, from the government right up to the pinnacle of the state. The bey was deposed, the fellaghas (guerrillas) suppressed, the Youssefist opposition virtually crushed, and Islam's leaders were politely advised to back the regime. Two years after his return in June 1955, Bourguiba had achieved mastery of Tunisia without compromise or hypocrisy. If he did not replace the Hussein dynasty by his own, he was motivated less by consideration for his people than by the knowledge that modern history has little use for crowned sovereigns.

Then the second crisis began to gather, much less dramatic than the first, but affecting Bourguiba deeply because it was touched off by two of his closest comrades: Mohammed Masmoudi and Bechir Ben Yahmed.

Those two men, close associates of Bourguiba in all his negotiations with the French, founded the newspaper *Action*, which aimed at encouraging moderate and constructive criticism of national politics. Throughout 1958 they supported the leader's programs, occasionally expressing some mild criticism—notably over the condemnation of Tahar Ben Ammar, former prime minister and wealthy landowner, who was accused of malfeasance though the misconduct of many other prominent people in Tunisian upper-middle-class circles had been overlooked; and over the trial of the Youssefists, which was handled in much the same manner as the "people's courts" in the East.

The criticisms expressed by the two men and by *Action* amounted to high treason. The Neo-Destour Political Bureau accused the authors of "systematically slandering President Bourguiba's policy by threatening the very foundations of republican government . . . through a treacherous campaign to sow disorder." The Fronde was broken from the outset: Masmoudi was barred from the Political Bureau and Ben Yahmed's newspaper was virtually outlawed—the party "withdrew every iota of confidence and support" from it, making continued publication extremely hazardous.

In short, Bourguiba had gone on a rampage, taking a direction that went beyond authoritarianism into fascist territory. But no discordant murmur rose from around his altar. And three years later, when the directors of *Action*, revived under the name *Afrique-Action,* tried to warn the leader against the dangers of despotism, they were stopped short again.

In December 1962 Bourguiba faced an entirely different kind of challenge: a military conspiracy was uncovered involving Captain Maherzi, his closest aide and confidential assistant. Was it actually a Youssefist plot to assassinate him? Having been in the courtroom during this trial, we are inclined to say that the evidence against the defendants was far short of incontrovertible. Still, a number of officers and two Youssefist activists were shot. A "national council" of the Neo-Destour took advantage of the situation to enlarge the President's powers by giving him the right to choose the members of the party presidium.

In 1965 conflict broke out over the issue of trade-union autonomy and the right to promote the specific interests of the workers. The protagonist was Ahmed Tlili, leader of the UGTT (Tunisian National Trade Unions) after Ferhat Hached and Ahmed Ben Salah; he also remained a member of the party's Political Bureau and Assembly vice-president.

On July 31 a special session of the union's central committee did a thorough housecleaning and swept out every last "Tlilist." Ahmed Tlili left Tunisia; in Paris, where he stayed for a while, he told us that the session of July 31 "is part of a vast plan to monopolize power. . . . The two stages that were the most difficult to surmount were the 'integration' of the UGET[5] and the 'conversion' of the UGET. . . . I did every-

5 Union Générale des Étudiants Tunisians (National Student Union).

thing I could to avert an open conflict: it was useless. . . . Now, the maturity of the Tunisian people, the swelling ranks of its elite, and the dynamism of its young people enable it to manage its own affairs and achieve a democratic economy and social progress."

The head of state retorted: "Contrary to the lies Mr. Tlili tells, democracy is not in danger in Tunisia. Bourguiba is neither a dictator nor a despot. . . . The restriction of civil liberties is a purely temporary measure."[6]

The dressing-down had its effect: two years later, in March 1967, when a heart attack almost took the President's life, Tlili asked to return to Tunisia; scarcely had he touched home soil when he announced that "President Bourguiba has brought democracy to Tunisia . . . shouldering a task that he alone could accomplish." Tlili died the following year, but not before he had voiced[7] new doubts about the government's methods of operation, and especially the relations between political authority and the remnants of the trade-union organizations. Criticism, honorable amends, and restrained comment (*Ketman* in the Persian tradition): this was the dialectical process of Tunisian politics.

A similar type of affair unfolded early in 1968. In fact, for the first time, a member of the tight inner circle of leadership made his exit by resigning before the usual charges of "indiscipline" or "treason" against the nation could be brought. Ahmed Mestiri, secretary of defense, considered Number Four man in the party (after the President, Ladgham, and Ben Salah) and "held up as an example of raw, tough militancy," announced that he was retiring from the public scene, commenting that "the most important thing for a citizen of a civilized state is to know in advance the

[6] Speech to the National Assembly on October 30, 1965.

[7] In several private interviews, one of which was in Tunis in April 1967 with the author.

state's intentions; otherwise, we have arbitrary government."[8]

Mestiri saw evidence of such arbitrary government in the fact that responsible officials were never consulted. One of his colleagues assured us at the time that for over five years the Council of Ministers had never been convened in full session; the head of state usually did his consulting on a person-to-person basis or with small groups, enabling him to assert his own influence. Furthermore, the same Tunisian minister told us that there was no longer room for even the most cautiously worded disagreement with the leader, as it might enrage him to the point of endangering his health.

Had Mestiri hoped to induce a popular backlash by resigning and publicly airing the grounds for his decision? If there was one, it was well concealed, and the Destourian Socialist Party set up meetings throughout the country to denounce the former minister's position, which was "incompatible with the principles of honest militancy," to approve his disbarment, and to salute "the chief of state's democratic and farsighted leadership." Bitter repression followed; in two weeks, four hundred people, mostly students and workers, were arrested and convicted.

But the judicial aspect of the crisis wounded the regime's moral authority very deeply: from the methods of interrogation to the harassment of foreign attorneys (one of whom was Mme Renée Stibbe, widow of Pierre Stibbe, who had been the most courageous lawyer to defend anticolonialist militants), from the conduct of court proceedings to the arrest of numerous Tunisian defense attorneys—the government was responsible for withholding justice on a number of accounts. Without attempting to pass judgment on Tunisian justice or to interfere in the country's sovereign affairs, *Newsweek* magazine, on record as favoring Bourguiba and

---

[8] *Le Monde* (Paris, January 30, 1968).

his regime, entitled its coverage "Tunisia Self-condemned."

Among the prisoners in the dock, trying to turn the trial into an inquest into personal power, were about twenty members of a group called Perspectives, whose Paris-based publication riddled the Bourguiba government with Marxist-inspired criticism. When a foreign reporter asked a high Tunisian official what the group represented, he retorted in a muffled voice: "Come now! They're Bourguiba's successors!"[9]

What of prison as a test of politics? As a school for the nation's cadres? As the means of conveying and transferring charisma, as the diploma attesting to the transformation of personified power into institutionalized authority? The "Supreme Commander" has traveled that route. But perhaps he is looking for new ways to perpetuate his achievements.

Once again everything was back to normal. But not for long. A few weeks later it was the students' turn to dissent —as if there were a concerted effort to put the regime to every possible test, the young intelligentsia taking up where the party cadres, the military, the unions, and the press had left off.

In the statement he made in 1965, Tlili had referred to the integration of the Student Union. That process, carried out in 1964, had left some open wounds, for in addition to the students' unfulfilled demands for free and independent discussion, the problem of finding work for an expanding educated class threatened them with the prospect of unemployment. When the Israeli conflict shook the entire Arab world in June 1967, violent demonstrations erupted in Tunis. Many students were arrested and sentenced. One of them, Ben Jennet, known for his left-wing sympathies, was accused of trying to burn down the United States Embassy and was given twenty years at hard labor, a sentence that brought strong reaction from intellectual circles.

[9] *Le Nouvel Observateur* (Paris, September 16, 1968).

Six months later a wave of discontent began to roll through the universities, where there was little sympathy for the Bourguiba government's support of American policy. In November, students called a strike protesting the Vietnam war. They booed Hubert Humphrey when he visited Tunis in January 1968.

On March 15 a meeting was organized at the University of Tunis to demand Ben Jennet's freedom. The police tried to intervene, but students and professors barred their way. A scuffle led to the arrest of nearly twenty youths. A round of strikes and demonstrations ensued, and by April the situation was inflammable.

PERSONAL POWER ON TRIAL

Each of these challenges, insofar as Bourguiba rose to them, added to his instruments of power and accelerated the personification process, which he never ceased to advance, spontaneously yet with a Machiavellian eye for detail.

One such confrontation deserves particular attention because it gave the liberal faction and "hard-line" Bourguibists a chance to air their grievances during the course of an unusually interesting debate. Each side was completely candid, and the discussion of personal power, while transcending the Tunisian scene, focused most penetratingly on the nature and scope of Bourguiba's power.

The affair occurred in the fall of 1961. Two months earlier Bourguiba had launched the battle of Bizerte, largely as the result of French blunders and the ruthlessness of General de Gaulle, but it turned out so badly for Tunisia that there was reason to question Bourguiba's application of absolute power.

In addition, the Tunisian President, who was as quick to

appease as to inflame, had suddenly declared his readiness
to talk over the situation with France in early September.
Moreover, the attack and cease-fire decisions came as a total
surprise, catching most of the leadership off balance. Hence
the deep frustration summed up in an editorial in *Afrique-
Action,* the successor to *Action* after the latter came under fire
in the 1959 crisis, and still under the editorship of Ben
Yahmed and Masmoudi.

Published in 1961 under the title "Personal Power," this
article commands respect for its courageous honesty even
upon rereading more than seven years later. Judge for yourself:

> Individuals and the masses have a kind of irrational
> and constant need to rely on, to cling to, somebody. And,
> for a nation, this "somebody" is always on hand to re-
> spond to the desire. In the twentieth century, we see not
> the abolition of monarchy but its transformation into
> power that differs from it only in two respects: it is
> not inherited, it is seized (and consequently must be
> guarded); it cannot be bequeathed, and thus creates the
> permanent problem of its inheritor. This is personal
> power, wielded by men who are presidents of republics
> and, in reality, untitled monarchs. . . .
>
> *   *   *
>
> In Tunisia, on the day the monarchy was abolished,
> Bourguiba told the National Assembly: "I could, if I
> wished, install myself as monarch and found a dynasty.
> I prefer the Republic."
>   This is quite true. Today, legally and factually, he
> holds greater power than the Bey and the Resident Gen-
> eral combined. . . .
>
> *   *   *
>
> Because it is efficient when its holder can, by vigilance,
> compromise, and constant alertness to the popular will,
> maintain a balance; because democracy has too often re-

duced nations to impotence, instability, and chaos; because it is more tolerable than dictatorship, against which
it sometimes provides a bulwark, personal power is today
the most common type of power and offers, in the short
run, apparent results. . . .

* * *

In the short run—but what after that? History is so full
of examples of personal power that, at the first sign of
laxity, the first tremor, turns into dictatorship—catas-
trophic for those who live under it and for him who
practices it—that we Africans must give serious thought
to the destiny of the power we have sanctioned. Because
personal power is in an individual's hands, it is a most
fragile and precarious thing. Because it nurtures pride
and scorn in its holder, submissiveness and servility in
others, it is inherently dangerous to the moral well-
being of a nation. Because it does not stimulate the search
for factual truth or thoughtful appraisal and discussion,
it can easily be disoriented in the real sense of the word.
Finally, and most important, because it leaves no heir
either by law or through its own foresight, it dooms the
nation, its faithful companion, to chaos. . . .

Afrique-Action put itself out on a limb with this article, all
the more so when its criticisms were echoed by the *Tribune
du Progrès,* the extreme left-wing weekly of Dr. Slimane Ben
Slimane, who wrote: "The Tunisian people, so well 'organized,' so well 'represented,' has virtually no voice in any
matter. It has nothing to do but listen and applaud."

The "supreme commander" struck back on two fronts.
First, he ordered one of his mouthpieces, the editor of the
Destourian daily *Al Amal,* to put the insolent critics in their
place. Then, in a speech to the party cadres on October 18, he
lashed out at "backstairs maneuvers": "Anyone is free to
criticize party actions, but let him do it within the party

framework or else get out of the Neo-Destour party" (note the artful dodge involved in labeling as critics of "the party" those who specifically referred to "personal power"). No sacrilege was committed, for he did not choose to recognize it as such, and the leader could show great magnanimity: he did not bear down. In a series of talks with Masmoudi and Ben Yahmed, he appeared moved, but his own master. He took the position of an offended man, not an avenger. (However, *Afrique-Action* soon left the scene. As for the *Tribune du Progrès*, it was banned two years later.)

But even more startling than the President's reaction was the rebuttal of *Al Amal*, for it summarized to perfection the behavior and arguments of Bourguibist stalwarts, those for whom "the entire population must feel, think and act as one man under the President's leadership."[1]

The term "personal power" recurs with tiresome insistence in general conversation. People gargle with it. They find that it vibrates in measure with anyone seeking a target for criticism. . . . What is at stake is the policy of power, not the exercise of personal power itself. . . . Why resort to these cautious procedures? They only mark the extent of the mystification. . . . The responsibility of power was entrusted to the President under the control of the Assembly and the people—which elects him directly. [Here again we find the theme of direct popular control, one of the most familiar illusions of personified power.]

The current power happens to be Bourguibist power, deriving its name from the man who inspires and animates it. . . . But every Destourian is responsible for this power. . . . That is why we consider an attack on Bourguiba as an attack on all the party militants, who

[1] Ridah Abdallah.

form a phalanx behind the leader. [Thus the personification of power tends to conceal itself behind the depersonalization of responsibility.]

Moreover, to link the Chief of State to errors committed by those in the ranks below would constitute further mystification. . . . An attack against him is equivalent to ingratitude toward a benefactor. . . . [Another classic argument of those who defend this type of regime: any errors are the fault of the "entourage" or the "lieutenants".]

Democracy is not a fortress that can be taken by assault; it is a discipline that must be acquired. In Tunisia's case, two indisputable facts must be kept in mind: the overwhelming personality of a man and the powerful organization of a party, the Neo-Destour. The man has given Tunisia her present-day appearance. He has distinguished himself by his intense determination, his clairvoyance, which borders on occultism, a brilliant mind that functions with breathtaking speed. He has so often caught off-guard those who thought to influence him that his close advisers have become somewhat wary. [Here again the distinction is made between the hero and his supporting cast in order to blame the latter's relative mediocrity for the extremely narrowed nucleus of decision-making, and to build the leader as the source of every splendid initiative.]

He is no Machiavelli because he has too much feeling to be one. He is strict, but not dictatorial, for it would hurt him to feel unloved. [This feature is revealing because of its emotional dimension: let's not make our chief suffer by not loving him.]

This is the man who has changed Tunisia's destiny so completely that he considers her his own creation. It would not be fair to deny him this, for it stems from affection more than from possessiveness."[2]

[2] Al Amal (October 20–23, 1961).

The above argumentation acquires even greater interest, or perhaps savor, because the text of it was both inspired and edited by Bourguiba himself. Appeals to geopolitical realism are answered by nakedly sentimental echoes, the most twisted logic by outbursts of fervor and loyalty.

But *Afrique-Action* was not about to be silenced in spite of that. A second article, subtler but quite as pointed as the first, questioned the exercise as well as the foundations of power *"à la Bourguiba."*

There is personal power and personal power. The kind Bourguiba holds in Tunisia was secreted by History. It discharged itself "on its own," imposed itself naturally, and the Tunisians welcomed it. And—as we ourselves did—supported it.

Today, we believe that Bourguiba's personal power is one of the best examples in the world; that it is suited to Tunisia's present condition, but that it owes it to itself to develop: it is our duty as responsible Tunisians to suggest for our countrymen's consideration the direction we believe this development should take.

We have said that personal power—wherever it exists, and in Tunisia as elsewhere—can save itself and save the country to which it applies if it is careful to:

avoid slipping into totalitarian dictatorship, with its contempt for law, men, and institutions, which would send it to disaster (even at this moment Ghana offers an example of this);

prepare the way for its heir and lead the country step by step toward a structured democracy. . . .[3]

But it was too late, if indeed it ever had been possible, to counteract the spontaneous yet deliberate proliferation of authority. Bechir Ben Yahmed soon transferred his paper to

---

[3] *Afrique-Action* (November 1, 1961).

Rome and later to Paris,[4] from where he remained on cordial
terms with the leader; Mohammed Masmoudi was to accept
once more the post of Tunisian Ambassador to Paris. Some
friendships fare better at a distance.

"THE CHILDREN OF BOURGUIBA"

The chief of state or "supreme commander" occupies a place
in Tunisian life which is beyond imagination: in the daily
press, radio news reports, televised or cinema newscasts,
he is not the first, he is virtually the unique subject. His
portrait is everywhere: in government offices, public administration buildings, railroad stations, and airports, in shops
and often in private homes.

In presidential elections (he is the only candidate), he
draws a near-unanimous vote. He crisscrosses the country,
touring cities and villages where the entire population is
marshaled to greet him, with banner portraits floating from
public buildings. When he goes abroad, the entire officialdom
and representatives of various national organizations accompany him to the airport. They are there again when he returns to Tunis; his return may, on occasion, become a solemn
event: in 1966, for example, after he had toured the Arab
countries and had aroused strong opposition at the mention
of Israel in Amman and Beirut.

The President has a number of residences (some of which
are palatial) in several Tunisian cities. In the domain of
innovation, in one respect he has outstripped his Third
World rivals: his wife, Wassila, is also the object of a public
cult. His speeches dispense advice and directions to every
sector of the population: the National Assembly, the unions,
national organizations, youth, women, teachers, the medical

[4] Under the name *Jeune-Afrique*.

profession, the sporting world, the army, artists, religious circles. Moreover, the institution founded to re-educate homeless children is called The Children of Bourguiba.

The chief of state is everywhere. Everything flows from him. Everything speaks of him. He speaks of everything. Religion? Morals? There seems to be nothing he considers outside his "private domain."

We hear him plead for temperance to an audience of workers he is trying to discourage from drinking up their wages: "Bourguiba himself has only been able to achieve his great task at the price of enormous sacrifices. He could have spent his youth drinking and merry-making, but he rejected that easy path. . . . Man must dominate his pleasure instincts and resist the temptations of vice!"[5]

Television, in Bourguiba's hands, can turn into the likes of a courtroom over which he presides as the nation's conscience, its arbiter, and the emanator of *umma*. In September 1966 he appeared on the screen standing between two people—a learned Moslem (reputedly unfriendly to the regime) and his French wife, against whom the former had initiated divorce proceedings. Here was the supreme commander as judge, condemning this "Moslem reactionary who is under the false impression that a wife can still be repudiated," an act that "will harm the good reputation of Tunisians all over the world." Never! And before a magistrate has had a chance to rule, the good scholar's suit is rejected. Justice incarnate, reason in action, the nation in one man, all have spoken. What more is there to say?

The same scene is repeated three months later on the home screen. This time it is the story of a young doctor sent out to the country for two years of practice in accord with the government's formula. His assistant, a local young village

[5] Speech on October 30, 1964.

woman, is pregnant. The *zaïm* has heard about this, and
here he stands, paternally, between the sheepish young man
and the terrified girl, performing the marriage ceremony.
"Let this be a lesson to you!" he warns the public.

Intervention in religious matters is also part of his routine. His guiding principle is that "Islam has liberated our
minds and enjoined us to reflect on its laws so that we may
adapt them to human progress."[6] "Religion must bend with
and meet the needs of the times . . ."[7] In short, for him,
Islam merges with *ijma,* the majority opinion, and with *jdid*
or modernity. It is a flexible religion that invites constant
reappraisal and has the lofty features of reformism and the
adaptable framework of progress on the march.

And when Bourguiba takes charge of modernization, he
also involves himself in the perpetual reconciliation of religious principles and political demands. The broad powers
of interpretation he assigns himself as leader of "this Moslem
state [which I have] rescued from colonialist degradation"
also cover his decrees. "To accomplish a productive task,
you may break the fast with a clear conscience: this is my
'fetwa.' "[8]

So the prescriptions pile up until the *zaïm* comes to resemble a caliph, a combined Caesar and pope: "As spiritual
leader of this country's Moslems, I declare that each of you
will perform just as worthy a duty [as making a pilgrimage
to the Holy Places] by giving what you would spend for the
trip to institutions for social progress or by investing it in
industry."

A number of examples will illustrate how Bourguiba's
relations with the public typify this ambiguous authority

[6] Speech on August 2, 1956.
[7] Speech on February 5, 1960.
[8] *Fetwa* is the opinion delivered by Moslem legal authorities.

based on sound argument and the magic of mass persuasion. This two-pronged thrust, this resort to traditional witchery in the name of progress, constitutes the novelty, the color, the efficacy, and the fragility of Bourguiba's power.

Here we are on the first day of the month of Ramadan 1964. Habib Bourguiba mounts the plaform shortly before noon to address an audience 90 percent of which has been fasting since dawn. As he is about to begin his harangue, he raises a glass of lemonade to his lips, like Moses striking the rock, and sips it in a leisurely way while his famous eyes, the color of the dawn-lit sea, dart over the hypnotized crowd. He starts to speak, explaining his sacrilegious and creative act: "You 'are permitted' to drink during Ramadan, for the 'holy war,' that is, the effort to unite Islam, is first and foremost the battle of production. Conserve your strength so that you may work hard; learn to interpret the Prophet's teachings."

A few months later, the leader visits the marketplace in Le Kef. He asks the price of oranges. They tell him. He stops short, thunderstruck, and falls into one of his angry fits—almost Churchillian, but tempered by Mediterranean lucidity. Seizing the fruit and passing it out to the neighborhood children, he summons the petrified merchant to appear before him, and that very evening the fruit-seller becomes economic assistant to the governor of a small southern town. "Now you will know better than anyone how to deal with fraud! And every time you tell this story, I want you to describe Bourguiba's wrath!"

But it is Monastir that rounds out the scenario of the "supreme commander's" power. His native city had already become a sort of pyramidal Versailles, the pre-mausoleum of Bourguibism. The streets there are named Habib and the enues Bourguiba. The sea reflects the color of his eyes, the storm winds the timbre of his voice. You will find him strolling there in his official autobiography; he speaks of "the builder."

To those who may remark timidly that these buildings must have cost a fortune, he retorts, with jaw outthrust, eyebrows in battle formation, eyes afire: "This is the way I chose to provide work for Tunisians, to keep them from starving, to revive artisanry! An old stucco worker was dying of hunger. Two years ago I commissioned him to decorate a banquet hall. Working for Bourguiba renewed his will to live. Pride and gratitude have brought him back to life: an eighty-five-year-old man!"

He has still other arguments. "Do we dare leave our descendants ignorant of what we were? Building a palace for which someone has dared criticize me is presenting the image of our renaissance to the Tunisia of the future. It is a legacy!"

Bourguiba's popularity just after he had won autonomy for the nation was extraordinarily enthusiastic, spontaneous, and nearly unanimous. In the twelve years that followed, this enthusiasm cooled considerably. Many people thought that independence meant the solution to all problems. Disappointment was inevitable even if no errors had been made. And, of course, many were.

The President has kept the support of his stalwarts: principally the men and women in his entourage, his "court." Opportunists? Many of them are undeniably sincere, believing that Tunisia is independent today because of him and that of all the underdeveloped nations, she is among those for whom the future looks brightest.

Others criticize certain of the President's decisions (Bizerte, or the appropriation of *colon* landholdings). Although embarrassed by the outlandish cult of personality, they still feel it to be to Bourguiba's credit that the nation has recognized certain priorities that will encourage her growth

panding the educational system, legal reform, improving the
status of women, family planning, developing Islam along
clearly modern lines, etc.) For them, the personification of
power was and remains a necessary evil for Tunisia.

The necessarily silent opposition falls into three categories:

those who cannot tolerate either the cult of personality
or the fact that after thirteen years of independence they are
no better off than before, whereas certain privileged persons
are benefiting considerably from the regime;

a good many intellectuals who feel that the regime pre-
tends to be socialist but really is not, who deplore the absence
of any serious opposition, who condemn the "new class of
privileged people" and denounce the opportunism of the
regime's stalwarts;

the most rigid adherents to orthodox Islam and Arabism,
who claim that Bourguiba has abused his power by setting
foot in the religious domain; his rulings on Ramadan offended a sizeable group of Moslems. But these stirrings of
the fundamentalist (*taqlid*) faction against the modernist
(*jadid*) faction and those called "Sarabina" (people from the
Sorbonne) have never become an active force.

Yet somehow the extravagances of personification and
leader-veneration do not seem to weaken their credibility.
Who can claim he has known a Tunisian audience to snicker
or shrug its shoulders during one of Bourguiba's "performances"?

One or another of his philippics against orthodoxy may
raise fears, this or that threat may encourage disbelief, one
of his many diatribes against Cairo and the leaders of the
Arab East may sow anxiety in certain sectors of the population
in which there are deeper attachments to Arab-Moslem fra-
ternity, to *umma*. But what he has to say is always listened
to and applauded—except by the small Youssefist remnant,
the communist fringe, and a large proportion of the intelli-

gentsia—even though his credit has fallen somewhat as a result of the spring and fall repressions of 1968. Grumbling is heard here and there, especially in the leaflets that the leftist opposition prints and distributes in Paris.

In January 1969, *La Tribune progressiste*[9] reported the leader's remarks in Sfax the previous December: "The helicopter I have acquired has changed my understanding of Tunisian reality and the national problems I have struggled with for forty years. . . . I was already aware that all across the country communities are scattered and nomadism is still an open wound. But what struck me as new and deeply impressed me is the large proportion of our people living in poverty or seminomadism. It is worse than anything I imagined."

And *La Tribune progressiste* unleashed its mockery at this learning-by-helicopter and the belated discoveries . . .

But these "bad apples" are a recent crop. You should accompany Bourguiba on one of the junkets he still makes to the Sahel, Cape Bon, or the Medjerda Valley to appreciate the significance of his "natural" authority, his techniques of mass communication, and the overwhelming support he enjoys. The *zaïm* is both the thunder and the rainmaker, the speaker and the echo, he who assumes the right to expand, with only slight alterations, a latent universal truth into The Truth, and The Law.

The press, radio, and television, meetings, tours of the provinces, solemn visits to cities, groundbreaking ceremonies for public works projects, receptions for foreign heads of state —all these are the instruments of this dramatization of authority. The myth is no limp and shapeless entity; it is planned, measured, and delivered accurately and forcefully every day.

[9] Published by Tunisian Marxist students in Paris.

To give an idea of this psychological barrage—the very persistence of which tends to imbed this person in the collective consciousness—we have made an unsystematic analysis of the front page of *L'Action,* the voice of the Destourian Socialist Party, during the first three months of 1967, a significant year because Bourguiba was seriously ill (hence, this period was an index of the warmth of his relations with the masses).

The procedure may seem monotonous, but it measures the intensity and the nature of Bourguibist personification of power. (A Moroccan friend who helped me with this project was amazed at the extent of Tunisian propaganda.) Before we smile at the scenario, let us remember that, in another climate, it might be more sophisticated and certainly would be more deceptive.

January 1, 1967: An enormous picture of Bourguiba smiling at a little girl who symbolizes 1967 covers the front page. The editorial exalts "Bourguibism," which has "elected to create an adult people."

January 3: An editorial entitled "Reliance on the People" recalls Bourguiba's arrival in Ksar-Hellal thirty-three years before and the difficulties encountered by this "young lawyer and determined nationalist" vis-à-vis the Destour leaders "who [had] never really accepted him"; it extols the virtues of this tireless and seasoned fighter.

January 4: A three-column photograph shows the smiling Bourguiba leaving for Ksar-Hellal. The headline quotes the President: "My confidence in the people has made our strategy pay off." An editorial by Aboulkeir is also devoted to the events of 1934: "Bourguibism was born, and with it a people determined to defend its right to live in dignity."

January 5: A photograph of the President, smiling as always,

is captioned by the report of his return to Tunis after the
Ksar-Hellal trip.

January 6: Covering four bordered columns is a photograph
of Bourguiba during a work session devoted to the redevelop-
ment of metropolitan Tunis.

January 7: Two-column headline: "This evening the chief
of state will tour the *souks* [marketplaces] in Medina in
honor of the 27th of Ramadan," will hear a talk and will
receive a woman prizewinner in a radio contest. Eight photographs show the President giving his New Year address in
Carthage.

January 8: Photograph showing the President celebrating
the night of the 27th of Ramadan, accompanied by a three-
column text.

January 10: Two-column photograph of the President visiting a group of schoolchildren.

January 11: Bourguiba chairs the meeting of the Committee
on Socialist Studies.

January 12: Broadest grin thus far, in a photograph captioned:
"The chief of state receiving European businessmen." Surrounding him are Moslem leaders extending their greetings
for Aïd Seghir. Texts of several greetings to the President
and his wife from individuals or, more precisely, from com-
panies, banks, and cooperatives.

January 14: Three-column photograph of Bourguiba receiving the "glossary of Takrouna" from Mr. Klibi.

January 17: Headline: "Tomorrow, anniversary of the beginning of the revolution."

January 18: Five bordered columns, commemorating the fif-
teenth anniversary of the revolution, with a photograph of
the President and members of the Committee on Socialist
Studies of the Destourian Socialist Party. On page 5 there

are various documents and a photograph taken in Bizerte on January 13, 1952, in which the "Supreme Commander exhorts the Tunisian people to armed struggle." On page 4 a banner headline and a photograph show the President receiving the vice-president of the Ford Foundation.

January 19: Headline announces the "Supreme Commander's address to the Committee on Socialist Studies," the text of which appears on page 5.

January 20: Bordered text: Bourguiba receives representatives of the Common Market. A photograph is captioned "In their battle against underdevelopment, as during the struggle for independence, President Bourguiba and his Party appeal first and foremost to men."

January 21: Report of a session of the Council of the Republic accompanies a photograph with Bourguiba in the center.

January 22: "Appeal to Bourguiba" (in bold-face type) issued by the Committee for the Preservation of Freedom in Lebanon (in small light-face type).

January 25: Three-column photograph of the President hanging a portrait of Ferhat Hached in his office.

January 26: Photograph of the President receiving Mr. Slim.

January 27: The editorial recalls the fruitful discussions between the high judicial echelons and "the state's chief officer . . . who has inspired this nation with the cult of modernism and progress . . ."

January 28: Photograph showing Bourguiba at the construction site of the new presidential office building.

January 29: "President Bourguiba's work schedule": a photograph shows him examining plans for a low-income housing facility.

January 31: Bordered photograph shows the President receiving Ahmed Alaoui.

February 1: "Tunisians ought to have a serious interest in moral and civic values," President Bourguiba declares.

February 2: Six-column text of Bourguiba's speech on educational reform.

February 3–8: The Roumanian president visits Tunisia: photos and speeches of Bourguiba and Stoïca fill each issue.

February 10: Photograph shows the chief of state receiving Prince Bernhard.

February 11: Photograph shows Bourgubia receiving André Schenk, special adviser to the French Ministry of Agriculture.

February 12: Photograph captioned "The chief of state vacationing in Ousseltia."

February 14: Photograph captioned "President Bourguiba talking to a group of French experts."

February 15: Two-column report: "suffering from a slight illness, President Bourguiba returns to Tunis today."

February 16: Headline: "The head of state returned to the capital yesterday." Photograph accompanies.

February 17: Bordered headline: "Members of the Maghreb Committee for Education wish the Chief of State a speedy recovery."

February 18: Headline: "The Chief of State receives Mr. Bahi Ladgham."

February 19: Headline: "Wishes for the chief of state's prompt recovery."

February 21: Headline: "The head of state has recovered."

February 24: Photograph shows the President, "still convalescing," conferring with Bahi Ladgham.

February 25: Photograph captioned "Lebanese ambassador bids farewell to Mr. Bourguiba."

February 26: Headline: "President Bourguiba delegates Mr. Masmoudi to represent him at the bedside of Mr. Allal El Fassi."

February 28: Bordered headline: "A meeting between Bourguiba and Hassan II inaugurates the laying of the new North African cable."

March 2: Headline: "Neo-Destour born thirty-three years ago." Pages 6–7 given over to this event, including two pictures of Bourguiba, taken in 1927 and 1930. Eulogy of Bourguiba's efforts, his "impassioned· speeches," "his sincere patriotism," his "alertness."

March 3: Photograph of the leader and an unnamed colleague examining plans for "greater Tunis."

March 4: Bordered headline: "Meeting of the local unit of Halfaouine-Bab-Souika presided over yesterday by Bourguiba." Photograph indicates how Bourguiba listens to militant interventions "for three hours." Article entitled "Bourguibism, or the sense of proportion."

The leader's statement is given under a six-column heading. "I was lucky enough to survive every ordeal," Habib Bourguiba declared, evoking Kant and the existence of God, the divine spark, and moral arguments (as logic cannot establish God's existence).

March 5: "Thirty-three years ago to the day, the young leader Habib Bourguiba took arms against parlor nationalism": thus began Aboulkheir's editorial on the birth of the Neo-Destour party and the "symbolic value" of Bourguiba's presence at a meeting of a local party unit.

March 7: Photograph shows a delegation of pilgrims visiting Bourguiba.

March 8: Photograph shows Habib Bourguiba receiving Pakistani envoys. The editorialist, speaking of the pilgrims' visit the day before, emphasizes that the Supreme Commander put special stress on the "necessity for Moslems to combat illusions as well as injustice."

March 9: Bourguiba interviewed by Radio Montreal.

March 10: Photograph shows Mongi Slim with Bourguiba.

March 11: Picture of Bourguiba presiding over a session of the Council of the Republic.

March 12: Photograph shows Bourguiba receiving two women who have won a radio contest.

From March 13–15, no mention is made of Bourguiba, who on March 14 suffered a serious heart attack. The silence is significant.

March 16: Headline: "President Ould Daddah of Mauritania has visited Bourguiba."

First presidential health bulletins appear, issued the night before. He is better.

March 17: News of the President's health relegated to page 5, along with good wishes from Tunisian and foreign sources.

Ill fortune does not sit well with the leadership. Only when he is reported "doing better" does personification renew its full swing.

March 18: Four-column headline: "Tunisian people relieved by steady improvement of President Bourguiba's health." Editorial: "Relief takes the place of unbearable anxiety, and today the Tunisian people breathes easily again." Then text goes on to extol "the man's bursting vitality [and] endless activity [which] concealed the fact that his constitution might one day weaken," and the "feeling of love and gratitude" which this illness "reveals" between him and the Tunisians.

March 19: Headline and photograph: "Tunisia reassured" (five columns); "Innumerable messages" of good will. The editorial ("Tunisia's Conscience") is devoted to "the profound shock we have experienced"; it speaks of a "great test," of "anguish," of "the nation convulsed" by Bourguiba's illness, which is an index of the "affection" shared by everyone. "This universal attitude" results from "a feeling of gratitude and thankfulness" on the part of the nation, "conscious of the asset she possesses in Bourguiba," this "legendary figure" and "national hero" whose courageous acts are "beyond the ordinary." He is "the people's conscience," "he symbolizes action and dignity, faith and generosity, integrity and probity."

March 21: Headline over six columns with accompanying photograph: "Yesterday the public saw Bourguiba on T.V."; health bulletin; messages of comfort. The editorial entitled "An Immense Comfort" is once again given over to the "great ordeal" Tunisia has just undergone, the strain of which is now eased. On page 4 there are two photos of the illustrious convalescent.

March 23–30: Text and photographs relating to Bourguiba's health.

March 31: Large photograph of President Bourguiba, "still confined to bed," holding the hand of one of his physicians. More messages of good cheer.

THE LEGACY OF THE SYMBOL

Habib Bourguiba has an audaciously noble concept of his mission. Sometimes he speaks of it as the Prophet's mission (which could be taken for sacrilege were the comparison not handled adeptly): "In assuming it, he [the Prophet] was conscious of being guided and upheld by God, whose Angel Gabriel transmitted the command to him—which he executed. He had no reason to ponder the consequences of his acts. Unfortunately, this is not my situation, for there is nothing to assure me that my first step is the right one."[1] But then, he still has a second chance . . .

Should Bourguiba ever begin to doubt his prophetic calling or the all-embracing nature of his image (incarnation, model, symbol, sign), he would only have to glance at the daily press, which takes its inspiration from him. On March 19, 1967, Moncef Jaafar wrote: "Habib Bourguiba is not merely the epitome of a successful chief of state, of a master politician, of an inspiring leader—he is greater than that: he is the one who lives in each of us, witnessing our every act, guiding our conduct, shaping our noble and generous acts."[2]

Out of his understanding of the vast scope of his role, from its very beginnings at Ksar-Hellal, Bourguiba has fashioned what we might call his doctrine. It is founded on the two principles of legitimacy and unanimity.

At the conference on the Maghreb held at Aix-en-Provence in November 1967, Bruno Etienne spoke on the theme of "the new normative role of law in North Africa," distinguishing between a legal system unsound in many respects and characterized by the conflict between its principles and social practice, and legitimacy, the product of history, a kind of consecration of the leader by the militant, emancipated masses.

Nothing could be closer to Bourguiba's philosophy. For him, his seizure of command and the crises he met between 1934 and 1955 imbued his power with the "validity of history." It is rare, he says, "for the pattern of a man's life to parallel a people's existence . . . to such an extent that their destinies be-

---

[1] Address to the National Assembly, October 2, 1964.
[2] L'Action (March 19, 1967).

come one."[3] It is solid, unquestionable legitimacy, he maintains, because it is founded upon "unanimity."

This demand for a unanimous expression of popular will
("unanimous" signifies "one"—and a people thus united finds
natural expression in a single leader) stems from his respect
both for *umma* and for the voice of the majority. Bourguibist
doctrine is profoundly opposed to pluralism and diversity.
Critics are faithless dissenters; opponents are traitors or blind
men, people who are crippled from having divorced themselves
from the crowd, which is the inspired and informed majority
vouched for by the leader.

In his thesis on "the idea of democracy held by leaders of
the Maghreb,"[4] Michel Camau explains this demand for
unanimity by the fundamental "unity" of the Tunisian people.
But we cannot be so sure that Bourguiba is entirely convinced
of that unity. During a discussion of the personification of his
power with Bechir Ben Yahmed, his Secretary of Information
at that time, the Supreme Commander pointed out that his
seemingly excessive authority had no other purpose than to
keep the Tunisians together. Otherwise there would be chaos.
Is this a reflection of unity, or the need to harmonize discord?
The result is the endless ceremony of collective identification

Is the leader in a position to hand on the symbolic apparatus
he has erected with such tedious persistence? Is it possible to
bequeath this type of power, whose partisans have described
it as prophethood and even "occultism"? Bourguiba even more
than Nehru—whose authority, it was thought, could survive
through heredity—faces this problem: the post-mortem projection of power that is allegedly essential to the welfare of
the community, the survival of charisma, the permanence of
the symbol.

At one time Bourguiba did not consider this a vital question.

[3] Speech on June 1, 1959.
[4] Law Faculty of the University of Aix-en-Provence, 1969.

He seemed to believe that the party he forged would generate its heir or heirs, the "caliphs" to come. Only after the military conspiracy of December 1962 did the Supreme Commander become preoccupied with the problem of succession. He discussed it quite freely with party activists during the Destour Congress in Bizerte on October 22, 1964. He hinted at his concern in a statement to Philippe Herreman of *Le Monde,* who noted what a stir his proposals for succession had provoked among the delegates. "What would you expect, since they love me," the leader said. "I mentioned it to point out that the Central Committee must find me a successor. But this isn't something imminent. . . . In the meantime, I have to consider the future of the state. The great problem in a democracy is the transfer of responsibility."

Responsibility, yes. But what of the symbol? What becomes of the type of leader who expresses far more than he represents and signifies far more than he decrees? The question was still pending three years later when Bourguiba came close to death on March 14, 1967. His physical existence had never been so imperiled, his mythical presence never greater, to the point where he himself was obsessed and distraught by it, totally involved, like Alfred de Vigny's Moses, in the naming of his heir. This is how he described it two years later to Thierry Maulnier:

> Two years ago, I had that cardiac trouble. They thought I was going to die. People were weeping in the streets. They felt abandoned. I had only one thought: What will become of them? For the job is not done, far from it. . . . I must stay fit. If . . . something happened to me, all the old problems would be back, the country swept by factionalism and dissension, everything we have tried to do threatened with destruction. I need ten more years . . .[5]

[5] *Le Figaro* (Paris, January 10, 1969).

Anyone visiting Tunisia in the late spring of 1967 found it a lost and bewildered country, anxious and frightened by the leader's close call with death. It wasn't exactly the climate of the Millennium, but when a man comes to be identified with a community, it experiences a fearful trauma when that man's life is in danger. Can Tunisia survive the loss of the one who "created" and then "incarnated" her?

Mr. Sayah, party leader, replied to this substantially as follows: Of course, each of us has given serious thought to the catastrophe we have just been spared. But since the Bizerte Conference, everything has been arranged so that the country will be able to survive that ordeal without a setback: the Council of the Republic, comprised of government officials and members of the party's political bureau, was created for this purpose. This Council, when convoked by its Secretary General, Bahi Ladgham, will nominate the new chief of state and will elect him.

But this type of power is always more strongly personified than they who have had some part in it would believe. Less than nine months after Mr. Sayah had made his remarks to us on January 28, 1968, Bourguiba, apparently recovered, informed the party's Central Committee that he wished personally to designate his successor "in order to insure better the continuity of government." Moreover, the leader candidly made it perfectly clear that this arrangement would not be legalized until 1969, "the year marking the third renewal of the presidential mandate"—certain evidence of a healthy optimism.

Much has been said to the effect that the suddenness of the decision, coupled with its personal nature—more personal than the Tunisians were familiar with—had something to do with Mr. Mestiri's resignation. For in fact, the perpetuation of the Bourguiba-made "environment" was discouraging if not aggravating to some of the more doctrinaire party leaders who were concerned about bridging the future. But wasn't that bound to happen? Could Habib Bourguiba afford to risk a single vote by failing to secure his reincarnation, his privilege of transferring the symbolic apparatus?

Personified power in its current Tunisian form has some highly dangerous aspects. By grounding all opposition and preventing the free discussion of opinions, by protecting the façade of national unity, a façade that in fact does not exist, the regime runs the risk of incurring future difficulties if it does not choose to "inject" a few doses of democracy into its own bloodstream, as Maurice Duverger put it in a lecture that to his credit he delivered on the scene. Yet it amazes anyone familiar with Tunisia and her lively intelligentsia to see how easily many cultured and "liberal-minded" Tunisians appear to accept certain facets of personal power.[6]

Is Tunisia obligated to this type of organized incarnation for her present statehood? Although disfigured by many repressive features, the task accomplished twelve years ago has positive aspects that may have a decisive bearing on the country's future. Could such a task have been achieved without the mythification of Bourguiba, a dynamic process in areas as important as cultural orientation, emancipation of women, and religious development?

The Neo-Destour's leader will at least have founded what is known as Bourguibism, which, in the Arab lexicon of political science, may well one day replace the term Machiavellianism. For the Tunisian leader will have taught his Eastern contemporaries, just as the Florentine minister taught the Renaissance Christian West, that politics is the art of adjusting one's immediate ends to the means currently at hand.

[6] The situation was the same as late as spring of 1969. But how long can it last?

Where the rule of all or nothing and the incantations of whirling dervishes had held sway, Bourguiba enforced his policy of "stages" and of the respect for reality. From Tunisia even to Algeria, and from the Congo to Palestine, he pleaded for truth to become the bulwark of politics. It is a rich legacy. And so is what Abdel Wahed Boudhila has described:

> The haunting vibrancy of *Tonnes el-Fatat* (the image of Tunisia as a girl) of the heroic years, the prestigious image of the leader *(zaïm)* who became the Supreme Commander in the struggle and President *(raïs)* in independence, the epic sea-flight to the Orient, and the crossing of the desert: these are the strands of the Jungian myth of the hero. These myths, or rather these shared memories, are the symbolic stanchions of modern Tunisia's values . . .

It is one thing to propel, to symbolize, to incarnate—and another to build foundations. Bourguibist charisma will have played a positive historic role. Has it already become part of Tunisian history, dissolved in the past that the leader so ardently recalls?

There is a place for incarnated leadership in the founding of a new society, i.e., in revolution. Thirteen years after the establishment of the Tunisian Republic, can we call the vast and daring enterprise known as decolonization a revolution? Tunisia's collective identity has been aroused and affirmed. No one can deny that the leader had the major role here. But what remains to be created is a republic of citizens, the replacement by a truly political society of this great audience left immobilized by the leader's performance.

Bourguibism has been defined as a course of instruction or self-improvement which has shaped its pedagogical system into a purpose and tends to perpetuate itself and become ossified. This is the area in which personification, the maker of identity, reveals its shortcomings. Its aim is to blaze a trail for the new elite, to develop the nation's cadres and set the masses in motion. But it withers and disintegrates as a defensive operation. The need to prepare for disaster is not sufficient justification for its continued existence.

But Bourguiba himself defined his creative task on March 21, 1969: "Centuries of decay and poverty, giving rise to nomadism, had left the towns and the people to molder, producing what some French press agent termed 'human dust.' It is this 'human dust' which I have started to gather up—speaking to it in its own language."

A beautiful but visionary view, which was to be tarnished by the operation mounted in 1970 by the leader against Ahmed Ben Salah.

Architect of the Tunisian economy for ten years, the former general secretary of the Tunisian National Trade Unions had given it a socialist structure by forming a constellation of cooperatives and of state-controlled units of production. The minister's authoritarianism, the brutality of the intermediaries he employed, the absence of explanation and even of any attempt to obtain popular adherence, the unbridled rhythm of collectivization, all led to the failure of that audacious enterprise. Probably no method other than state control would serve to lift Tunisia out of economic stagnation. Still, it should give that policy a human and rational character and not allow it to take on the grimacing face of sectarianism.

Habib Bourguiba had completely backed up his Minister of Economy, constantly repeating that what Ben Salah did was what he himself did. Brusquely, at the end of 1969, exactly when a cruel disease struck him and forced him to leave Tunisia for months, he decided to part company with the "boss" of the Tunisian economy and to refurbish his prestige by crushing his subordinate.

That cleansing operation did not serve his glory, for it appeared to public opinion that the abuses of "Bensalahism" had been possible and lasting only thanks to Bourguiba. The attempt at dissociation between the leader and his adjutant proved both too late and too transparent.

The campaign of accusations mounted against the minister and the trial to which he was brought were not enough to camouflage the evidence: what was on trial was not a man, but a system—a system so personified that the charismatic authority, it evidently had been thought, could be poured out over another head and taken back by the will of the leader alone. Unfortunately for Bourguiba, charisma is a personal relationship between the leader and the mass, and a nonnegotiable value, as is said of some currencies.

Bourguiba did not have the power to delegate to another or divide with another the gift of grace that history and the people had accorded him. Furthermore, it was not within his realm to recover all of what he had shared. The sad Ben Salah affair is the sign that it is time for the founder of modern Tunisia to yield the floor to that teeming mass of individuals to whose transformation into a nation he has contributed so powerfully.

Norodom Sihanouk, or the Principle of Effervescence

———⧓———

*"He is one person, becoming many, and from his
many selves he becomes once more unique."*
—*Catalogue of the Virtues of the Bikkhu*

Atop the Cambodian hillside, a gigantic face smiles in the
sky: it is one of the countless visages of the merciful Buddha
making the great Bayon (temple) at Angkor the shrine of a
benevolent art of which the European counterpart is the Angel
at Rheims and which represents the eternal symbol of Cambodia. Nearly ten centuries later, there was other laughter
echoing the Blessed One's, setting the rhythm of life for this
small nation, lending it its originality and its style.

One day toward the end of November 1961, Norodom
Sihanouk, the king who gave up his throne at the age of thirty
to enter the political arena and who thereafter bore the title
of Chief of State, was making an official visit to Kompong
Cham, third largest city in the kingdom. At that time there
was talk of nothing but the tension between Phnom-Penh
and the two neighboring capitals, Bangkok and Saigon.

Samdech Sahachivin ("my lord comrade") mounted the
rostrum. In his hand was a wire just received from a Saigon
press agency declaring that the Cambodian army, flanked by
two North Vietnamese battalions, had crossed the Thai border
and was advancing on Bangkok. He read it aloud. In any
other country it would have provoked a stinging diatribe from

the leader against this "Ems dispatch," and the crowd would
have shouted for blood.

But a volley of laughter, swelling and engulfing the crowd,
greeted the Prince's opening words. Sputters and roars of
amusement broke out. The most impassive faces melted into
broad grins directed toward the Chief of State, whose lively
wit loosed itself on Diem and his Thai colleague, Sarit. Even
the solemn bonzes flanking the Prince on the platform smiled
with their lay brothers at this mirthful tirade.

Governments come in many forms: they use the cudgel or
the law, informers, the army, or the Church. Here was government by laughter, just as effective as many others—as you can
judge for yourself by visiting present-day Cambodia. The remark is perhaps less jocular than it seems.

The chiefs of emergent states have a hard time inducing
popular participation, which is the meeting-ground of the
leader or ruling group and the masses, the interaction between
summit and base. The absence (or neglect) of intermediary
bodies, the rarity of cadres, public apathy, and the complacency
of leaders are among the factors responsible for pernicious
dislocation of the social base.

Sihanouk attempted to circumvent this problem by his
manner of reaching his people. He established a sense of
complicity between himself and his countrymen, taking them
into his confidence, "putting them in the know" in a familiar
and bantering way and in a spirit that all Cambodians understand, just as another generation of Egyptians reacted in unison
to the speeches of Nahas Pasha.

AN IMPERIAL TRADITION

The power of Prince Sihanouk, Cambodia's Chief of State,
was not simply the expression of a sparkling, dynamic, and

colorful personality—it was embedded in a monarchic, religious, national, and Asian framework.

Norodom Sihanouk, who took the Khmer throne in 1941, abdicated in his father's favor in 1955—yet the Khmers never ceased to regard him as their king. If his new status as prince and leader assured him freer action along with a different type of authority, he remained the heir to a proud dynastic lineage, and official propaganda let no one forget this. A citizen-king, a human divinity, he moved in both earthly and celestial orbits.

The proud heritage of Khmer royalty does not end with supreme power. An official pamphlet published in Phnom Penh in 1963 carried this celebrated saying as its epigram: "Jayavarman VII suffered from the ills of his people more than from his own ills; for the pain of their subjects and not their own pain is the sadness of kings."

This is the most explicit statement of what this study is attempting to trace: the theme of the incarnation and the assumption of leadership, this transference of grief and reward which is the very core of personified power. It recalls, on a sublime level of compassion, the famous line: "When Augustus drank, Poland reeled" which formulates a particular concept and a current application of power.

Jayavarman VII, whom Sihanouk acknowledged as his inspiration, had elected to establish a state religion, Buddhism, which ever afterwards left its mark on Cambodian society. And what about power? Founded upon clear understanding and calm reason, is Buddhism capable of creating a strong central authority?

In evaluating Buddhism's role in the achievement of the Khmer monarchs, Paul Mus sees the two as inextricably wedded, "just as the body is to the mind," as *rupa* (that which is visible) is to *nama* (expression of the Sacred Word). He states:

This is why the ancient Buddhist rulers chose to erect
a cosmic architecture not intended to glorify their civilization. . . . It is only a vehicle for the development of
law and the awakening of life. . . . Architecture that is
not descriptive but is normative, acting as a catharsis.
Monuments and Buddhist society, which is merely the
instinctive outgrowth of them preserved by civil power
and illumined by doctrine, together form a directional
system.[1]

And Sihanouk armed himself with that system. We can
thus grasp the significance of the legacy of Angkor, that archi-
tectural chronicle whose every stone is also an expression
of moral principles and acts. For a Buddhist following in the
footsteps of the Benevolent One, "instead of recognizing
human beings who perform *acts* and hence may try to escape
the consequences of them, Buddhism perceives only acts in
the universe it probes and illumines . . ."[2] Before Existential-
ism's day, it explained man as the sum total of his own free
acts. Solange Bernard-Thierry has said of the Khmer rulers,
"Sovereignty results from the full development of merit."
    Is Buddhism a school for action? Nordom Sihanouk believes
that it is. In speaking of his most illustrious ancestor, Jayavarman VII, he said:

This king, who did not forgo meditation and religious
retreat, ruling over a people whom others call "resigned,"
built temples and monuments that are masterpieces, as
well as thousands of miles of roads and waterways and
hundreds of hospitals. . . . Our Sangkum,[3] by "rousing"

[1] Paul Mus, *Présence du Bouddhisme* (n.p.; n.d.) pp. 195–8.
[2] Ibid.
[3] Sangkum Reastr Niyum (SRN)—"Popular Socialist Community."
(Trans.)

our people and engaging it in an intense and relentless crusade for national development, has simply returned to the sources of Buddhism and the traditions laid down by our Great Monarchs.[4]

Along the same lines, but in a different key, are the remarks of a young Cambodian intellectual, Kenn Vannsack:

The realism of the Khmers does not consist solely in translating Divinity into human terms, the sublime into the commonplace, the wondrous into the tangible. It is also a mode of conduct. Efficacy is a function not of metaphysics but of pragmatism based on a precise knowledge of existence and utility . . .[5]

Thus we find in Buddhism, more than just the well-publicized attractions of nirvana (ultimate reality as well as eternal serenity, the ideal goal to be pursued actively), a doctrine of individual responsibility, an incitement to the "task" which Sihanouk developed by extending this line of interpretation into a centripetal and dynamic movement.

The Prince of Cambodia logically related this chain of action (or, we might say, of combustion) to the traditions of the Khmer people, whose passion for building and for warfare he considers extremely significant. The tranquil Cambodia of those days, kept "alert" (this was Buddha's greatest virtue) by her spirited leader, was heir to an empire of conquest that terrorized the Thais, the Chams, the Vietnamese, and even thirteenth-century China. "When we speak of imperialism, we know what we are talking about: we practiced it too long," Shianouk told the Belgrade Conference in September 1961.

---

[4] *Kambuja* (November 1965).
[5] "Quelques aspects de la littérature khmère," cited by G. Brisse in *Europe-France-Outremer* (October 1968).

Imperialism abroad, absolutism at home: the idolatry surrounding Sihanouk's daily movements, even after he became
the comrade-prince, reflected a system of imperial power
wherein Buddhist "understanding" often bowed to the despotic practices of a tightly stratified society controlled by the
divine monarch (a harkening back to Wittfogel and his
"oriental despotism" rooted in a hydraulic-based economy—
for the Khmer state depends upon a network of canals and
dikes).

Despite Buddhist doctrine, violence has a corner of the
Khmer character, as evidenced by the Cambodian epic of the
Ramayana, which is just as bellicose as the Hindu original.

Another factor, applicable to most of Asia, tends to focus
the governing of Far Eastern peoples, from Peking to Jakarta,
and from Rangoon to Hanoi, in the hands of an extraordinary
individual. Leaving aside the influence of Confucianism,
strong as it is—and in this respect Cambodia is but a fringe—
let us look instead at a basic intellectual trait common to a
number of Asian peoples which may be described as the ability
to grasp designs more readily than concepts. For many Asians
(and let us keep in mind the Buddhist architecture as defined
by Paul Mus) form speaks louder than ideas. Chinese
characters tell us a great deal on this subject. Notwith-
standing their abstract system of writing, the Khmers are
no less sensitive to images and to faces. Sihanouk's face—just
like Sukarno's, Nehru's, Ho Chi Minh's, and Mao's—outlines
and expresses a policy and the actions behind it. The face
is a "character" that speaks and stands for law.

This explains the surprising remark made in confidence to
Paul Mus around 1950 by an elderly Vietnamese dignitary
whom he asked about the outcome of the Indochina conflict:
"Bao Dai is round. Ho Chi Minh is pointed. In time of crisis,
the pointed always wins out."

THE CHOICE OF BEING ONESELF

One close observer of the contemporary Cambodian scene, Professor Robert Garry of the University of Montreal, states that the names chosen for young Prince Norodom Sihanouk Varman marked him then and there for a special destiny.

Sihanouk means the first male lion cub, Buddha's favored one. . . . by approving the addition to the king's name of the word Varman (meaning "armor" and, by extension, the Powerful One, the Conqueror) . . . the members of the Council of the Kingdom, who had just designated the sovereign, perhaps were unconsciously thinking of the splendid days of the Angkor kings.[6]

But others, be they electors or godparents, cannot make a man great or fix his eyes on a star.

Norodom Sihanouk Varman became King at the age of eighteen in accord with a peculiar law of succession, but not until he had reigned for twelve years did his unusual personality manifest itself. In June 1953 the dimpled, pleasure-loving young King, a seemingly malleable instrument of the French protectorate,[7] opened what he called the Royal Crusade for independence.

To draw attention and to alert the French to the seriousness of his threats, he left Phnom-Penh suddenly and went to live in Bangkok (capital of the hated Thais, demonstrating that life in any free city was more tolerable than colonialist domination), and at length he was able to extort long-cherished independence from France.

The singular thing about this laudable adventure was the spontaneous personification of his act, his gift for dramatizing

---

[6] Address to the Congress of Orientalists in New Delhi, January 1964.
[7] Although he had claimed the throne as early as 1945.

it, his vivid sense of timing the psychological pressure and political exploitation. He, along with his ministers and spokesmen, saw to it that the sun should rise and set on the Royal Crusade.

Sihanouk took with him into exile his nationalist philosophy, incarnating and activating it, lending it the rumbling voice of his wrath and impatience; he struck the rock and the waters of freedom gushed forth. The rest hardly counts, neither the efforts (which were no more than sporadic) of the Cambodian governing group nor even the stepped-up pressure of the Vietminh army on the French colonial machinery in Indochina. Sihanouk alone had pulled it off. And the credit should be his.

At any rate, by choosing the moment, the means, the allies, the theme, and the style, Sihanouk had done more than anyone else for the political emancipation of Cambodia. And in so doing he had created a confusion, which was to become permanent, among the state, the nation, and himself. Personification was at work.

As the father of independence, he had to adopt a totally new and personal form of government. It was not enough to have built with his own acts the structure of freedom; he had to design an unprecedented and unique shape for his own power. The symbol signifying "the relationship between Sihanouk and his people" would emerge two years later on the heels of a bold and brilliant move: he abdicated, ceasing to reign officially in order to gain greater freedom of action.

He made his decision public on March 2, 1955. Two weeks later, he explained his act to the people: "If I continued to rule and remained shut off in my palace, I would never find out exactly what is happening to my people or what their grievances are. . . . When I was King, I saw only pomp and pageantry . . ." And he spoke of returning "all the necessary tools of power" to the people.

Depersonification, dilution, and distribution of power? Not

at all. In giving up his crown, Sihanouk revealed himself, "unmasked" and identified himself. At last he was in intimate contact with the people, no longer by virtue of a monarchic or dynastic authority sanctioned by history, legend, and habit, but by dint of his own influence, his prestige, and the services he had rendered and had yet to render.

This astounding device of theatrical disclosure was to lead to a unique relationship between the Prince and his people— over which still hovers, so they say, the awe for all that is sacred, royalty's domain—but it had already adopted a new appearance that was more natural and suitably familiar. Sihanouk went down into the arena. By-passing the ancient conflict between politics and the Crown, he set out to involve himself completely in the "public welfare."

In a letter he wrote to us on this subject,[8] the Cambodian Chief of State outlined his objectives:

> My abdication in 1955 was in no sense calculated. It became inevitable because of the intense political opposition at that time to the King's assuming responsibility for his people's future, for the unity and independence of the nation, for the welfare of the masses (the "little people," as I affectionately called them sometimes) who remained deeply attached to the King as the nation's "Father" and have steadfastly rejected the anonymous rule of parties, the majority of which were in reality no more than feuding clans.
>
> I am convinced, as are many impartial critics, that if I had not abdicated to enter politics, Cambodia today would be strife-torn, pulled to pieces by the clash of forces in our part of the world, that it would have lost its independence and certainly its territorial integrity as well.

[8] January 7, 1969.

But Sihanouk was not presumptuous enough to think that his wedding with the masses could be arranged without the help of organization. The go-between for these negotiations was the Sangkum, initially the ruling party and subsequently the only one, or, better still, the national front (in the sense that whatever is not part of it officially ceases to be "national"). But the Sangkum, owing to its incessant expansion, became only a sprawling ectoplasm, a kind of sounding board echoing the leader's message and the people's applause.

On the condition, of course, that no dissonant note marred the harmony. Sihanouk's power, like Bourguiba's, drew strength from the thrust of challenge, such as and especially the plot hatched in 1959 by his most promising, or at least most favored, supporter: Sam Sary, who incited the governor of Siem Reap, a brash fellow named Dap Chhuon, to revolt.

The plot failed despite Saigon's support of the conspirators. Sihanouk used this opportunity to personalize the crisis:

Certain powers who claim to be our friends have not given up their game. Now they hope to discover a new and unscrupulous strong man to succeed the ambitious and unlucky Dap Chhuon. And while they look for someone to replace this pawn, who is essential to their plans, we find a vicious campaign developing in the press and over the radio aimed at discrediting the monarchy, our national government, our Sangkum, and myself, who am the target of all their attacks.

"Our Sangkum and myself . . ." The phrase may bring a smile to those who claim familiarity with the Cambodian political scene. What was the Sangkum, after all, if not the projection of Sihanouk, his extended shadow, the lance that lengthened his reach? One of the cleverest inventions of this clever Prince was to have multiplied himself through such a "gathering of comrades" who existed and functioned only as echoes. In that fashion, he saw to it that his message of action carried afar over that vast loudspeaker system.

Sihanouk's relationship to the Sangkum provides an illustration of the epigraph heading this chapter (and what could be more appropriate at this hearthside of Buddhism than the *Catalogue of the Virtues of Bikkhu?*): "He is one person, becoming many, and from his many selves he becomes once more unique."

But more important, the comrade-prince's personification of power served as a response to foreign intimidation. Sihanouk has had an unparalleled record of baring his own chest to international invective, acting as the living shield of national independence, the necessary incarnation of Cambodia's identity as a safeguard against assaults upon it. That was what he spoke of in an address to the law department of the University of Paris in June 1964:

> You see before you a person who is the butt of endless controversy and whom the Western press (including the French on many occasions) usually treats unmercifully . . . a "red Prince," unpredictable and disconcerting, chameleon-like and unstable, a monarchic and progessive dictator, a satellite of the Chinese . . . and the French.

Saint Sebastian showered with arrows, each one of which reinforces his power, just as cement is reinforced by the metal ties that the builder inserts. Here was the root of this curious "herocracy," which had a disciplinary role rather than a "direct" one, and which, according to Paul Mus, could be characterized as the supremacy of structure over system.

Sihanouk represented and upheld the structure, the vital permanence, the continuity that is renewed and renewing, rather than the system (the body of state and legal instruments, the heritage of tradition and social practices). His variety of "disciplinary" leadership was constant revelation and perpetual motion. Like a bicycle-rider, he kept his balance by speed and forward motion, and also by holding fast to the historic and social principle of encouraging the growth of national roots. This was active, or rather eventful, continuity.

THE PRINCIPLE OF EFFERVESCENCE

Prince Sihanouk is the most important instrument of direct democracy in Cambodia. . . . He is a superb actor, he knows how to exploit any dramatic situation and hold his audience breathless. . . . The people call him "Samdech Euv," prince-papa. He shares his life with them. . . . He gives a Socratic character to his ties with the masses.[9]

This brief sketch of Sihanouk's style of rule came from one of the closest American observers of Khmer society, Roger Smith, and can be amplified with the remarks of two other qualified students of Cambodian life. Robert Guillain brought out what he considers to be the driving force behind Sihanouk's power, "the principle of effervescence," which "sends the Chief of State's electric words flying in every direction"; this aptly describes a type of relationship involving deployed energy as well as a potential that is hidden and more enigmatic.[1]

Simonne Lacouture, who noted that "he is distrustful of the 'Phom-Penh set,' the bureaucracy, intellectuals and politicians," pointed out that to smash this sterile screen, Sihanouk resorted to direct democracy, "which enables him to implant his auto-

[9] *Asian Survey* (June 1967).
[1] *Le Monde* (April 8 1961)

cratic power in a vital force, his popularity among the masses, and the people's deep love for him, which he returns."[2]

But where could you find a better description of Sihanouk's style and technique than in one of the weeklies he inspired?[3] Here is practically a plea for personification on the Prince's part:

> . . . Khmer politics . . . are no deep mystery. You cannot call the Prince a blunt man who makes his intentions clear; as a matter of fact, he invariably leaves a few doors ajar, giving him room to shift to the left or right, forward or backward; when necessary, he never hesitates to invoke "reasons of state" to justify a posture that at first glance may appear unorthodox. But he is certainly no Machiavelli.
>
> . . . He adopts the very style and logic of his interrogators in order to be more effective. . . . If it is true that every diplomat has something of an actor's gift for portraying the most diverse roles faithfully and convincingly, then Samdech is a master of the art—and our diplomatic friends will not deny it. . . .
>
> . . . Ambassadors have broken this down to a simple formula, which is useful nonetheless: Calculate approximately when some foreseen event may occur, taking into consideration the Prince's choice of words, or his silence, or his change of tone at some point—all this is very interesting, indeed fascinating. . . .
>
> . . . A foreign diplomat told us: "The Prince is a superb actor, but sometimes a bit too dramatic." Why not? The Khmers are a southern people who like to express their emotions, and they are lively, not sluggish; their feeling comes out. But when Samdech becomes "dramatic," he is not playing the role of thundering Jove.

---

[2] *Cambodge* (Lausanne: Éd. Rencontre; 1963), p. 138.
[3] *Réalités cambodgiennes* (February 1969).

He is the leader of a rather small nation with a moderate-sized population, no important natural resources, and an army that is courageous and loyal but poorly equipped. What else can he do to ward off the very real dangers threatening him from nations that are much stronger, and that are angry: the nearest of these because they cannot tear Cambodia to shreds, the others because they cannot reduce her to a satellite?

All that remains is the Khmer people united with its Chief of State, the will to fight and to die rather than be enslaved. To get this across to the rest of the world, Samdech has no other means but words. And he uses them to the hilt.

Sihanouk was above all a man who put language to work: to reach his people, to censure the men in power, to correspond with foreigners. His power was crammed into the words he spoke and wrote. Julien Cheverny attributed to him "the power of a tribune."[4] We must delve further into his rhetorical impact, his use of language: for all forms of expression served him as tools to influence the masses.

Speech, of course, has first place. To appreciate the range of this power of communication between the masses and the leader, you should have heard him talk to the villagers for hours on end about random subjects: history or the immortals, the future of Cambodia or of his enemies, customs among the wealthy or the needs of the poor, and always with the buoyant zest that is his trademark, as well as Fidel Castro's. Of course, he was a leader of a particular people and the son of divine kings: Samdech Euv, comrade-prince. But he functioned with greater effect because of his magnificent verbal gifts.

In Sihanouk's speeches, personification was systematic, relentless, and dramatic. The leader planted himself squarely opposite his opponent, whether foreigner or countryman,

[4] *Éloge du colonialisme* (Paris: Julliard; 1961).

rarely to batter or insult him, and more often, with his sense of irony and the ridiculous, to play up Cambodian good sense in contrast to the nonsense or stupidity of "others."

But what was most evident in Sihanouk's rhetoric was the mixture of bursting sentimentality and vibrant emotion. The scenario always involved "the people and me," "the others and me." Here is what he said to his listeners in Siem Reap in 1959: "If the people has greater love for me than for the political parties, what is to prevent it from voting for the Sangkum? To vote against the Sangkum is to vote against me . . ."

His personality emerged even more strongly during interviews. His liveliness, humor, indignation, graphic expression, all these come into play. On the eve of an official visit to Paris in June 1964, he answered questions about his relations with Peking:

> China? At the risk of sounding like a satellite or a defeatist, let me remind you that she is the most important and the largest country in Asia, and nothing decisive or lasting can be attempted without her. You know, when Callas comes onstage everyone else looks like a walk-on. China is Asia's Callas; we are aware of that. But when the performance is over, I am not one of those who remove Callas's slippers and cook her dinner. I go back to my own house for dinner, I eat home cooking, with my wife and children . . .

His wit, as we see, was focused on himself: he used imagery, the partner he mentioned was his own; China was personalized and conversed with Cambodia, personified by him. And in that same interview we hear him shift from Cambodia to himself and back again to Cambodia as he speaks of the neutralization of Vietnam:

"I am trying to promote General de Gaulle's ideas for a political solution in Vietnam—ideas which you also share. . . . And, let's be frank, which are and were from the start my own! But when one's ideas are adopted by a man of General de Gaulle's stature, common sense dictates that they should appear to come from him, while vanity demands that one applaud them louder than all others! Our small nation is ready and waiting to become a spectator or a walk-on, provided the play is good and the ending brings peace."

But speeches and interviews are the weapons of every chief of state. Norodom Sihanouk used other types of argument that are more personal: for example, articles, letters, and telegrams. Once, as a joke, he presented himself in Phnom-Penh as a correspondent for *Le Canard enchaîné.* Hardly the usual role, let's admit, for a head of state who is the descendent of divine monarchs.

On the more serious side, he was a working journalist, the director and often editorialist of three publications: *The Sangkum, Kambuja,* and *The Nationalist.* Sometimes, when he did not feel up to a job, he relied on ghost writers, but he kept his imprint on the work, providing the themes, editing, and rewriting whole paragraphs. He was an extremely practical man governing with his pen in hand. Most often it was to plead his cause, explain his actions, or rebut criticism. The power of the press was his. And, as journalism, it was intensely personal.

Further on, we quote at length from an article in *Sangkum* in which he defended his concept of power. It is full of life and first-class humor; but it also reveals his shortcomings: his self-obsession, his extreme touchiness, his tendency to personalize attacks as well as appeals.

His individuality as a letter-writer was even more pronounced. Although not on the level of Frederick II or Churchill, who corresponded with their "cousins," kings or heads of state, Sihanouk did on occasion write to Chairman Mao or to Charles de Gaulle. But most of his mail was directed to newspapers, magazines, or even private citizens.

Often one could open *The New York Times*, *Le Monde*, or *Le Canard enchaîné* and find a letter from Cambodia's chief of state methodically refuting some criticism of his country, regardless of how calmly and dispassionately it had been worded. Above all, Sihanouk could not stand the use of the word "little" to describe Cambodia. And it is the adjective that foists itself upon any foreign observer who has just arrived via China or India. A reporter guilty of such an attack was in for some acid remarks, which indicated a dangerous superiority complex. Sihanouk's rebuttal was all the sharper, for he exaggerated the personalization of what he read as well as what he said, as he always thought his own stature was the target. Unlike Alexander the Great or Louis XIV, he had no vast frontiers to blur his human measurements.

Thus, a good portion of the magazine *Sangkum* was devoted to the Prince's remarks, directed either to some commentator he considered ill-intentioned, or to a visitor who might have praised Cambodia. Even if the latter was a nobody, as a friend he was indulged with the most elegantly worded and affectionate gratitude.

But the comrade-prince established the telegram as an instrument of government, without competing with Bismarck, who used it for diplomatic maneuvering. Here is an incident that tells a great deal about the rapid and spontaneous reactions of the Khmer leader:

During a stay in Singapore, the Prince received a Cambodian newspaper in which Chau Seng, his Minister of Agriculture, took issue with the economic policy of the Phnom-Penh government. Within an hour Sihanouk sent an urgent wire to the Palace. It read as follows:

ARTICLE ENTITLED PROBLEM NUMBER ONE HAS MY AT-
TENTION STOP THIS ARTICLE CORRECTLY PICTURES
DRAMATIC SITUATION OUR COUNTRY ECONOMIC AND
FINANCIAL POINT OF VIEW STOP IT APPEARS THAT OUR
GOVERNMENT HAS NOT YET BEEN ABLE TO REORIENT
OUR POLICY AND OUR PLANS IN ORDER TO ESCAPE FROM
THIS DREADFUL TUNNEL STOP REQUEST HIGH COUNCIL
EXAMINE THIS PROBLEM WITH OUR MINISTERS STOP
OUR YOUNG *Sahachivins*[5] SEEM TO SEE SOLUTION IN
SOCIALIZATION OR BROADER STATE CONTROL STOP
KINDLY INFORM GOVERNMENT THAT I AM NOT THE LEAST
OPPOSED TO THIS AND THAT I GIVE IT A FREE HAND IN AL-
TERING THE REGIME PROVIDED PROBLEM IS SOLVED STOP
AFFECTIONATELY SIHANOUK.

Changing a social and economic structure by a telegram inspired by a newspaper article and concluding with the word "affectionately" and dispatched from a foreign capital—there is an unusual event. It is a fair illustration of Sihanouk's style, wherein his vivacity vied with his personification of problems and his emotional reactions.

But unlike many other Third World leaders Cambodia's Prince was not just a man of words. He was also a man of vigorous action. The words came first, but the action followed closely. And in conjunction with his brilliant speeches and correspondence, he rounded out this type of action with a series of popular inventions: the bed of justice, the congress, collective work projects, and sports—not to mention films.

Nothing could describe Sihanouk's power more aptly than his "popular audiences," which usually were held once a month at the royal palace. Reviving an ancient Khmer custom

---

[5] Comrades, members of the Sangkum.

established by King Ang Chan in the sixteenth century, the Prince held open court for plaintiffs to whom he offered a last appeal outside the legal system; he acted as chief justice, a personalized justice who superseded the law without jeopardizing its authority.

These proceedings were broadcast: the Prince used the microphone like a rock-and-roll star. One incident from a "popular audience" was reported by the official press agency (AKP) on December 6, 1961:

> Neang MEAS SINA, resident of the 6th District in the City of Phnom Penh and owner of a small popular restaurant, brings suit against Police Inspector HEUM SAMAN, who, out of revenge, she says, brought 7 police officers to search her house and arrest 4 of her servants. The plaintiff is suing for 50,000 *rials* in damages.
>
> After checking with the Police Department, it seems that there is no revenge involved, but that Inspector SAMAN was ordered by his superior to arrest the 4 maids, whom a detailed investigation had found guilty of prostitution.
>
> Neang MEAS SINA stood firm on the good and honorable reputation of her business and complained that these arrests by the police had driven away her customers.
>
> His Highness, who can always distinguish between serious mistakes and common human frailties, showed great lenience in dealing with the case. "Withdraw your suit," he told her, "and you have the word of the Police that your premises will not be disturbed again. But promise me that you will sell food there, and nothing else."
>
> As for the loss of her patrons, the Prince remedied that by giving free publicity over the microphone (we know these "popular audiences" are broadcast) to the plaintiff's restaurant.[6]

[6] Remember that this is the official press-agency account.

For eight hours at a stretch, Prince Sihanouk listened, examined briefs, questioned officials and magistrates, censured a minister, a brutal policeman, or a corrupt local judge. These hearings in no way deprived the regular courts of their authority or overruled them. But the Prince eased the execution of a sentence, paid a fine out of his own pocket, or amended the wording of a judgment, explaining the legal principles in each case. The screen he set up between the people and the law was the warmth and soothing assurance of his smile. This was total involvement of an individual in the public welfare: he was the leader and Providence in one, the friendly Redeemer, the benign Buddha.

But Sihanouk felt compelled to intervene still more actively in the life of his country: several times a year you would find him, with his straw hat on, breaking up a field with his pick or digging an embankment. He was doing his share of manual labor along with his ministers, his generals, his dignitaries, and a scattering of titled foreigners. So we found ourselves between a French ambassador and an American military attaché, ankle-deep in a muddy rice paddy, scooping into small native baskets the clay with which China's multitudes build her vast dam works. At the head of the row, in shorts and a T-shirt, the Chief of State had been attacking the clay with a sturdy pick-ax for three hours running, in the glaring sun that does nothing to encourage sporting ventures. And as soon as the digging was done, he was back again at the microphone, apparently tireless, making the peasants rock with laughter.

Activity or activism? When Norodom Sihanouk, son of the Kings of Angkor, played football in the palace stadium and, with his government team, won a 1–0 victory over Parliament's team (as in November 1963), was it to affirm the supremacy of the executive over the legislative arm? Or to demonstrate the nobility of physical activity? Or to set an example for Khmer youth?

He did it for all these reasons—and also to lose weight. His size appalled him. His tendency to put on weight was a torment. For years he spent three months out of every twelve taking a cure in Grasse. Then he discovered that the sports he had enjoyed all his life were a solution to the problem. After that, his ministers, high officials, deputies, and officers (and, of course, the masses) were regularly invited to football or volleyball games. With the nation's cooperation, the Prince would whittle down.

Can you push incarnation beyond the literal disembodiment of the leader? Let him reduce to the point where he swims inside his uniforms, and the nation, too, will be in the swim. Let him perspire, and we shall all be the more agile for it. But the collective limb-shaking will produce the individual slenderness, and the people will feel greater pride in itself because the leader cuts a handsome figure. Leadership becomes identification at this stage of complicity. I/we am/are the nation.

But the setting for Norodom Sihanouk's dramatic personification reached even farther. It took the most direct and technical form: cinematic incarnation. As a young king, Sihanouk delighted in staging the plays of Musset and Maurice Donnay for the palace family, and he loved to work with several types of cameras. Then he got the idea of adding to his vast power the combined magic of an Orson Welles, an Eisenstein, a Brando. And he began to make films, directing them at first, with his lovely daughter Princess Bopha Devi as featured star of the royal palace, and some prince or minister as leading man.

But why should he rely on others even if they were relatives? He himself began to act, and in a tale called *The Enchanted Forest* took the role of a kindly sprite who represented the genius of the Khmer people. That a bit of Shakespeare's *A Midsummer Night's Dream* got mixed up

with Cambodia's ancient legends did not make much difference. The Prince projected himself—full-length is the only
way to put it—upon the Khmer consciousness. He became the
image of his people's past and present history. He identified
with them and was their teacher. He appeared on the screen to
train, to coax, to demonstrate, and to express that identity.
It was a total performance.

A direct line with the masses, a system for communication
and decision-making tied in directly to the community which
he operated around the clock and which brought him the
widest credit: that was Sihanouk's apparatus of power. Direct
democracy? Perhaps we should call it direct monocracy.

The most verbal example of it was provided by the Congress of the Sangkum, the party, or rather the "community,"
which under his aegis became the mainstream of all Khmer
political currents. Twice a year, as a general rule—but in this
country everything depended on events as the Prince interpreted them, and on his decisions—all the provincial delegates
and core membership of the Sangkum met on the Men, a huge,
grassy field that flanks the royal palace and apparently was
intended for riding events and ball games.

There in the open, a permanent platform used for three
or four days at a time awaited the Prince and his closest
colleagues. A crowd of over ten thousand gathered around
them, members of the Socialist Youth of the Khmer Kingdom,
leaders, militants, and simple onlookers. The atmosphere was
one of astonishing frankness, and as the "people's" podium
was also equipped with a microphone—the primary element
of freedom in the technological era—some interesting debates
ensued. The official speakers were not always eloquent. Nor
was the climate invariably balmy, for Samdech Euv ("my lord
papa") might not be in a laughing mood. For example, in the
fall of 1963, when there was renewed tension between Phnom-
Penh and Saigon, a Khmer citizen was arrested and accused

of collaboration with the "Khmers serei," a rebel band supported by Saigon and Bangkok.

Sihanouk confronted the Congress in the role of prosecutor,
trying to wrest a confession from the suspect. But the man's
protests of innocence had a disturbing ring of truth. "Shall I
hand you over to the police?" Sihanouk shouted, angry yet
unsure, as he called for the crowd to make a path. Police?
Cambodia has no Gestapo, but the unfortunate man's fate
hung in the balance. And the Prince, not his usual buoyant
self, set up between the accused citizen, the crowd and himself,
the accusing seer, the judge eager for the public benches to
applaud his judgment, a relationship that was uncertain and
disquieting.

The people responded as a hung jury. The leader refused
to settle then and there a case that this odd proceeding had
failed to clarify. A defensive maneuver, with justice losing face
amid the general confusion. For once, Sihanouk's dialogue
with the masses was fruitless.

A POPULOUS SOLITUDE

The relationship between the Cambodian leader and his
citizen-subjects had its strong points, as we have shown. It provided for an unusual type of participation on the one hand
and the growth of authority on the other. Yet it had its faults.
Like his friend the President of the Fifth Republic, the comrade-prince was not content just to operate his direct line with
the people with spectacular virtuosity. He tended to ignore the
middle ground: the top social echelons, the intelligentsia,
technical and educational circles, the "Phnom-Penh set." He
was determined to modernize his people and was wary—often,
although not always, with good cause—of those who had
already benefited from progress.

We have quoted the astonishing telegram by which Sihanouk opened the door to socialization of the Khmer economy. Its spontaneity may have given the impression that the Prince had great confidence in those young and optimistic cadres, with their progressive ideas. Nothing could be more untrue. This outgoing man, so intent on building the future, could freeze with intense distrust at the prospect of social and political changes, not so much because their significance alarmed him, for no one was less timid than he, but because of the people who claimed the initiative for them.

His chariness had two components. The first was very simple and sprang from that tacit and indisputable monopoly of power, that direct monocracy, regardless of the form it might take from one year to the next. Any active efforts were suspect if they stemmed from a source other than himself—and efforts of this nature were likely to do so, for though he was a master politician, his store of ideological equipment was scanty. His first impulse might be approval. But, as Talleyrand warned, "Always distrust your first impulse; it is the right one."

What is more, because of a kind of inferiority complex, Prince Sihanouk had considerable misgivings about intellectual groups, with which he had occasion to work closely. He made no secret of the fact that he was called to the throne just as he was about to take his baccalaureate at the Lycée Chaseloup-Laubat in Saigon, and hence his educational gear was rather hastily assembled. He, with his exceptional intelligence, missed the cultural opportunities enjoyed by most of his co-workers. He said and even wrote[7] that he was uncultured. The new mandarins made him uncomfortable; he was more at ease with simple people.

On the whole, he had little use for the older generation of the upper crust, except for two aging and able servants

[7] *Esprit* (June 1965).

of the monarchy, Penn Nouth, who was returned many times as Prime Minister, and Son Sann, his faithful Minister of Finance or Governor of the National Bank. For most of the others, he had only contempt.

Whether or not his attitude was justified, it reinforced the populous isolation, the peopled solitude in which the Khmer prince reigned. There was one exception: the Buddhist clergy. Apart from Sihanouk, only three people in all of Cambodia were privileged to bear the title Samdech, "my lord." They were Penn Nouth, the kingdom's Nestor, and the two leading religious officials.

The Chief of State was altogether charming and deferential toward them. Not that he consulted them often. But he had constantly to call upon Theravada Buddhism—religion of the state, it has been called—to demonstrate the merits of religious practice and respect for the *bikkhus,* the monks and the dignitaries. Like all good Buddhists, he once retired to a monastery, where for several months, his head shaved, he lived off charity.

Ten years later, he revived an ancient religious rite and, behind his plow, robed in gold and wearing the headdress of his royal ancestor Ang Duong, opened the first furrow of the harvest in the rainy season—an act of humble pride and respect for traditions, which, judging by his ancestry, are not out of keeping with this legend of aristocratic progressivism. Such behavior cannot be reduced to Machiavellian logic. That would make it too simple. But it is certain that the son of the builders of Angkor was well aware of one fact: although religion is inherently neither progressive nor reactionary, no progress can be made without the endorsement and blessing of Buddhist officialdom. If the clergy were ignored or defied, Theravada's high priests could turn religion and tradition against any revolutionary effort. For the few demands the regime made on them and on the yellow-robed *bikkhus,* it could rely on their weighty influence.

. . .

Toward the end of August 1966 Norodom Sihanouk was preparing to receive a special guest, the man among men he was most anxious to entertain lavishly: General de Gaulle. Parades, royal dancers, the floodlit spectacle of Angkor—nothing was missing. There was even a surprise in store. On the third day, a concert was given in honor of the visitors. And who composed the overture that the palace orchestra played for the General? None other than Norodom Sihanouk—the same Sihanouk who two years earlier, when we were guests of his, had had us dancing to the delightful music of his own saxophone, which he played very well. Imagine it. Who else would dare that sort of thing?

His talents seemed to be endless, as did his pleasure in sharing them, not out of ostentation, but simply because he wished to show the brightest side of Cambodia's face, and as faces go, he could only see his own. Could he not have depersonalized that face, or at least kept it from multiplying? Might he not have called forth in turn the film-maker, the musician, the actor, the festival-organizer—which he is all in one? What he did for the fine architect Vann Molyvann could have been extended to other arts. But could a restrained, mediatory, withdrawn Sihanouk remain Sihanouk? He was himself only in close-up, downstage, phosphorescent.

Samdech's relations with most of his close associates were marked by the deference that was an integral part of life in the ancient kingdom rather than in modern Asia. Anyone who had known Prince Sihanouk outside his own country, in New York, Geneva or Paris, was likely to be somewhat embarrassed on meeting him again in his own capital and in his familiar surroundings. An astonishing ballet of servile motion went on around this forthright and light-hearted man: people on their knees or crouching or kissing hands.

Was this son of kings at all aware of the farce that played about him—this ritual of embalming him alive? Or did the icon react like an icon, overpowered by the odor of burning candles? In 1960, at the close of an observation tour of Cambodia, we expressed our surprise at this unshakeable servility. This seemed to upset the Prince, who immediately issued a torrent of orders for the bowing and scraping to cease.

A waste of effort. After a few months of compliance, his court and entourage resumed their slavish antics, a fact that he never seemed to notice. Or perhaps he had thought it over and decided that there was something savory, or useful, about that type of relationship with people whom he regarded as nothing more than pieces of furniture.

It was also evident that he frowned on the behavior of young intellectuals whom he had promoted to important positions and who made obvious their intention to appear before him upright as men. He liked to emphasize his consideration (i.e., concern for human dignity) by raising those who knelt to him. He was annoyed by people too unfamiliar with a certain set of relationships, too independent of him to even attempt to play the comedy of deference.

A comedy? No, the word is too harsh. For the ancestry, the personality, the talents, and the vitality of Norodom Sihanouk invited respect. The leader was entitled to it, even if he had not been the son of Angkor's builders. What seemed unwholesome was the leftover rites of servility which persisted alongside the respect due him. The personification of an innovating power, or the power of a traditional personification?

Most leaders of the Third World are rendered another type of tribute in the form of embalming: the greetings for special occasions that fill the press as paid advertising. We mentioned the messages of cheer to Habib Bourguiba while he was convalescing. Samdech Sahachivin received the same attention.

Open the issue of the weekly *Réalités Cambodgiennes* for

October 25, 1967; it celebrated the Prince's forty-seventh birthday. On page after page the country's major industries, which
had paid dearly for the privilege of prostrating themselves in
writing, assaulted the reader with their deference. Here are a
few examples:

Page 17: "The National Company of Fish Canneries (Koh
Kong) and its personnel are honored to beg Samdech Sahachivin, Chief of State, kindly to accept their respectful wishes
for his good health, long life, and happiness on the occasion of
his birthday." Warm enough, but rather restrained. More
courageous is the Khmer Phosphate Company, which "most
respectfully begs Samdech Euv, Chief of State, kindly to accept
the fervent wishes it extends for His Health, His Happiness,
and His Long Life."

Up one degree on the thermometer are greetings from the
restaurant Le Nouveau Tricotin, the management and personnel of which put their backs into "extending to Samdech
Sahachivin, Chief of State, their humble and most respectful
wishes for good health, happiness, and long life on the
occasion of his birthday." But the star defender of the cult
was the Coca-Cola factory and its personnel, who "most
humbly beg Samdech Euv, Chief of State, kindly to accept
their wishes for his health and happiness." It was very hard
to be an American in Cambodia.

Was all this humility, this groveling and begging, a sign of
healthy relations, of a society oriented toward reason and
progress? The leader might well shrug his shoulders; the style
persists. We are not altogether responsible for the spines of
our courtiers, the Prince would retort, adding with a laugh that
the fees for these ads are invested in Khmer industry.

This power, founded on the prestige of a man and of tradition, on an extraordinary talent, on a historical situation that
is scarcely commonplace, on a combination of complicitous
laughter and awesome fear, on a truly creditable record of

school and hospital construction, on diplomatic sovereignty and political stability, on the preservation of peace throughout twenty years of neighboring warfare—how could you question it? What were its defects?

The fundamental vice of the direct monocracy exercised by Sihanouk was not so much the rampant corruption, which was sniffed at like some minor spot on a fringe of the royal robe, but rather what might be termed the erosion of the political landscape. We tend to eye this brand of enlightened despotism more favorably than Nasser's or Nkrumah's, for its results are less nebulous. But was it necessary to sweep out a political society that did not lack talent and enthusiasm?

From 1940 to 1955 the country had been governed in turn by two groups of men, the leaders of the democratic party and of the National Recovery party (Rénovation Nationale): the "demos" and the "renos," as they were called. The first group was on the whole more progressive, the second more loyal to the Palace: the Whigs and the Tories. The democratic party had a good many outstanding men. There was occasional tension between them and the throne, and as Sihanouk was letting things slide around 1950, it is probable that the type of conflict which was shaping itself in Cairo at that time might have erupted, with results perhaps similar to those following the Wafd's opposition to Egypt's king. But Sihanouk was no Farouk. He had the courage to initiate and lead the struggle against colonialism, and then to take the reins of government. History will judge whether friendly competition between the king-leader and the democratic party would not have been better than seizure of absolute power by the Chief of State, for it would have drawn a number of excellent democratic leaders (and, of course, some of the "renos") into the Sangkum. Would not the preservation of political dialectics have served the public interest and the nation's stability better than this exclusive leadership? In relation to Sihanouk and the other

"demigods" of personified power, there is reason at least to
reflect on the validity of political monopoly and the mythical
incarnation of the leader.

Sihanouk was sufficiently aware of this to attempt a curious
experiment in the fall of 1946: a double government. Having
permitted (inadvertently?) a government under Ambassador
Sim Var to be formed, with a strong majority of former demo-
crats (who had come over to the Sangkum, of course), he proceeded to establish a "counter-government" closely affiliated
to himself, headed by General Lon Nol. An extremely com-
plicated situation developed. When the official premier protested this double game, Sihanouk told him sharply[8] that his
group existed only "at the pleasure of Sihanouk, who cut
short his stay at the Calmette Clinic and arrived during the
night just in time to save their necks."

And the Prince added these moving remarks: "My daily
burden—perhaps you don't realize it—is a fearfully cruel one.
I get no joy, no pleasure in facing the day's work, which drains
my life and consumes me; my only satisfaction and my only
comfort in this painful Calvary—and, believe me, it is one—
is the knowledge that I am serving most loyally my country and
my people, which are dearer to me than life."[9]

"IF THE COUNTRY TRUSTS ONLY ME . . ."

The burden of power—was it safer to share it, to distribute
it systematically? Here, again, Sihanouk believed that he
had the answer. (What did he not do, in fact? And, when
the problem was one of such direct concern to him, why
didn't he take up his pen?)

To answer an article written in 1968 by a special corre-

8 AKP (Khmer Press Agency) (November 1, 1966).
9 The Sangkum, No. 38 (September 1968).

spondent in Indochina for *Le Monde,* Sihanouk published in
the newspaper *Sangkum* the following remarkable plea *pro
domo:*

> According to this critic, I am supposed to exercise a highly
> personalized power that rules out any dialogue between
> the base and the summit and takes the form of an end-
> less monologue, which bores my listeners. . . . It is true
> that, as head of the nation, I do in fact wield extensive
> power. But at no time in my career have I sought to
> monopolize this power or even to maintain it.[1]
>
> As King, I held real power only between November
> 1953 [after France granted sovereignty to Cambodia in
> the aftermath of the "Royal Crusade" for independence]
> and April 1955, when I abdicated in my father's favor.
>
> It is important to point out that my return to power
> at the close of 1955 had no connection either with the
> King's wishes or any act of force and was entirely due
> to the will of the people itself as expressed in the general
> elections, the absolute legality of which was duly con-
> firmed by the CIC,[2] whose attitude to me at the time was
> rather lukewarm.

Sihanouk went on to point out that according to the
French journalist, he no longer had unanimous support.

> As a matter of fact, I have never had this unanimity and
> never pretended to have it. The "opposition" to Sihanouk
> in fact dates from 1941. At that time, while under French
> rule, the people did not accept me and the elite was
> hostile to me. During the Japanese period, the Thanh[3]

[1] *Sangkum,* No. 38 (September 1968).

[2] Commission Internationale de Contrôle, created by the Geneva Conference
in 1954.

[3] Son Ngoc Thanh, Prime Minister in 1945 and leader of an opposition
group in exile.

clique denounced me to the nation as a "traitor" hired by the French.

Even at my "apogee"—if I may use the word—thousands of my countrymen (who favored the democratic party or the pro-Communist "Pracheachon" party) "opposed" me during the referendum that followed the "Royal Crusade." In the general elections of 1955, nearly 20 percent of the electorate voted against the Sangkum's candidates—that is, against me. And in the 1958 elections, over 1 percent. In 1954 on the other hand, while I was directing the "Samakki" operation against the Vietminh in Battambang, the Khmer Student Union had seen fit to proclaim my "fall from the throne of Cambodia" (*sic*). So I have had to "foot the bill," if I may use the expression, to find out that I have enemies and shall always have them no matter what I do.

As for the "highly personalized power" this journalist endows me with, foreigners who have lived here for any length of time and have watched very closely what goes on in our country are well aware that I am truly burdened with too much responsibility and work. I am condemned to this "solitary" power as much by the possessive love and confidence of my supporters (monks, the military, the masses—the peasantry above all) as by what I must admit is a certain passivity and faint-heartedness on the part of our elites, who, naturally, do not hesitate to assume the responsibilities that accompany material advantages, but not those of the criticism that the exercise of "titular" power inevitably arouses.

One cannot seriously suggest, however, that I wield this power single-handed. Although the National Assembly, in periods of grave national crisis, has granted me full powers a number of times, I have always made every effort to "normalize" the situation in order to restore to Parliament its prerogatives. . . . It is not commonly known outside the country that I never attend the weekly sessions of the Council of Ministers, albeit the Constitution gives me the right to do so. Thus, members of the government are entirely free to make their own decisions.

As for Parliament, it does in fact hold legislative power. I should point out from the start that though the Sangkum has had no opposition in legislative elections since 1958 (for our Communists prefer subversion and even rebellion to open and lawful competition for the minds of the electorate), our "community" has refused to urge the people's support for candidates of the government in power.

On several occasions they have even carried motions of censure or opposition in regard to ministers or high officials—without the slightest regard for the Chief of State's feelings on these matters.

Having made these constitutional observations (which, in reality, are the least persuasive part of his plea), the Khmer leader went on to discuss his exercise of personified power:

Is there a lack of "dialogue" between the "summit" and the "base"—an "endless monologue"?

It is entirely misleading to ignore the frequent dialogues, which are spirited and utterly candid, between those who govern and the governed, and which occur through the intermediary of:

—semi-annual "national congresses," sometimes followed up by special congresses

—the popular audiences

—the "seminars" held between government officials and student representatives of the various university divisions

work sessions, most of which are broadcast, and which are always attended by the Socialist Youth of the Khmer Kingdom (JSRK) and the president of the Student Association

—my tours of the provinces, in the course of which I take up on the spot whatever problems the villagers bring me

—the Youth Assembly, a recently created organ

—the criticism and replies that appear in the daily bulletins of the "counter-government."

Certain people cannot abide my close contact with the supporters of the Sangkum and of the Monarchy as well, which include the overwhelming majority of citizens. But these citizens are glad to hear me explain often and openly the national and international problems we face, and never find my supposed "monologues" long or boring. This thirst to know, to be informed and to understand, is a part of our national character and is illustrated in a most gratifying fashion by the fact that every transistor receiver in the kingdom goes on each time the radio announces that one of my speeches or messages will be broadcast.

This same reporter adds that what I have to say is no longer accepted as "the word of the Bible." Honest observers who listen carefully to me know that I have always put the most blindly loyal of my partisans on guard against the illusion that I might be a kind of "Messiah" who could obtain Heaven's consent to make the rain fall or cease (a belief that is still common among the "elders" in our countryside). I have always stressed the fact that I am a simple mortal, that I am not infallible and have no supernatural powers.

It can be proved that every speech I have made to the people during my tours of the country follows the completion of a project of national or local interest—never precedes it. These speeches have no philosophic overtones but are altogether "earthy," so that the least educated of our citizens may understand them.

As for my "special messages," our critic has undoubtedly neglected to have his Cambodian "friends" brief him on them; otherwise he would have found nothing in them but harsh self-criticism, undiluted condemnation of our government's or our administration's errors, admission of my failures (relative), particularly in the area of erasing corruption. "Bible" in Greek means "good news"—and one can see by the preceding facts that these remarks are in no sense biblical. . . .

My allegedly "biblical words" are often none other than the painful acknowledgment of certain serious deficiencies in the regime, which I am trying to remedy. . . . I have on many occasions, and in perfect sincerity, suggested to the nation that I step down. But the fact is that my countrymen, without regard for my exhausting task and my health, insist that I remain.

This is the heavy price of trust in a single man, who is no longer the servant but becomes the slave of his people—to the point at which he has been compelled to forego trips abroad because his countrymen feel uneasy and insecure—they have told him so—when he is not on national soil . . ."

A flattering description of a situation which has a certain lustre. Let us take a second look at his last statement, not as grounds for complaint solely against the comrade-prince, but to keep in mind that when he is absent Cambodia feels lost. Whose fault is it? The leader's? Or the style of power he has imposed, a style that cannot be shared and is not likely to be bequeathed? In respect to Sihanouk as well as to Nasser and Bourguiba (of whom he reminds us most), it should be remembered that charisma rarely can be inherited, that flamboyant personification soon becomes its own end and does not appear to lead to the requisite institutionalization of founding power.

After Sihanouk, what? (Perhaps we should say "who?") The Khmer leader had a ready answer—which he gave, in fact, not so long ago—that it is not a bad record to have

brought independence to his country, given it twenty-five
years of stability, and kept it out of war. Did the miracle
still need to be systematized?

Not that Norodom Sihanouk was not interested in the
problem. This was how he spoke of it:

> If the unity of our people rests upon me alone, we must
> expect the worst for the country when, for one reason
> or another, I am no longer the basis of that unity. If
> the country trusts only me, if the Constitution is served
> by me alone, if affairs of state can be managed only with
> my help, the solidity of our regime will never be more
> than an illusion.[4]

Thirteen years later, in the letter cited earlier regarding
the future of the power he molded in his own image, he
wrote us the following:

> . . . I am forced to argue for a regime of *unity* (faced
> with a multiparty regime) with a broad-shouldered pa-
> triot at the helm whom the majority of the nation would
> accept as "leader." The return to multiparty govern-
> ment, to democracy in the "French" or "English" man-
> ner, would, in terms of my country's situation, condemn
> her to anarchy, civil war, capitulation to the powerful
> forces of imperialism, and annexation at the hands of
> our neighbors.
>
> When I am gone, the Khmer people naturally will
> have to decide its own destiny freely. According to our
> Constitution, it may choose a king or a chief of state.
> This power has been institutionalized in Cambodia since
> 1960. There is no hereditary power. Everything will de-
> pend on the will of the people.[5]

[4] *France-Asie* (June 1958).
[5] January 7, 1969.

The people's will? Was that what was expressed on March 18, 1970, when an anti-Vietnam outbreak at Phnom-Penh was stirred up by Sihanouk's leaders and transformed into a coup d'état against the leader? No, certainly not. But the fact remains that the coup was possible because of the disappearance of the will and presence of the prince-comrade.

How was it that the man whose popular triumph appeared so complete in 1968, whose ascendancy over the crowd and the political class still seemed intact, could suffer a reverse so cruel, even if temporary?

We have observed that charismatic power is made by the presence of the leader and that such direct action gives it its strength. Sihanouk had been away from Cambodia for more than two months in order to look after his health in France, leaving his responsibilities in the hands of General Lon Nol. Let us not dwell on his naïveté, which led him to trust the General—who had long been allied with other forces. Caesar is always surprised by the faces of the con-spirators.

Rather, let us speak of his Machiavellianism. If the prince-leader of the State put aside direct responsibilities for so long a period at a dangerous hour when the Vietnam conflict more and more threatened to submerge Cambodia, if he then placed his responsibilities upon Lon Nol and Sirik Matak, that was very probably because he had admitted that the presence of the Vietnamese NLF had become too big and too compromising—but did not himself want to enter a struggle with his Hanoi and Viet Cong friends.

He failed to take into consideration the General's second thoughts, the pressure of his pro-Western allies, and, we re-peat, the erosion that personal power suffers when it is not at hand.

Lon Nol, charged with the mission of dirtying his hands in order to allow the leader to keep his own hands clean and remain both the arbitrator and the maker of peace, seized the occasion and transformed the anti-Vietnam operation into one of influential men against Sihanouk, who had been humiliating them too long.

The trial that Sihanouk underwent does not suffice to condemn him or his neutralism, or his effervescent populism, but even if he should regain power, what happened nonetheless showed the limitations of even the charismatic leadership better adjusted to a diplomatic situation than to the demands for the reshaping of a traditional society.

Kwame Nkrumah and Peaceful Coexistence within One Nation

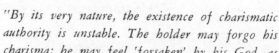

> *"By its very nature, the existence of charismatic authority is unstable. The holder may forgo his charisma; he may feel 'forsaken' by his God, as Jesus did on the Cross; he may prove to his followers that 'virtue' is gone out of him."*
> —MAX WEBER, *Essays in Sociology*

> *"The state is like an egg: if you squeeze it, it breaks; if you don't squeeze it, it falls."*
> —ASHANTI PROVERB

On October 27, 1965, Kwame Nkrumah and twenty-five other chiefs of state inaugurated the new Palace of Africa in Accra and presided over the opening conference of the Organization for African Unity—less than four months before he was overthrown by a military coup.

The benign smile of triumph no longer hovered on his lips that day, no longer lighted his face as it had in September 1960, when we heard him, dressed in his *kente* of gold cloth, lecture the United Nations on positive neutrality. The era of grand illusions is over for the Third World; the time for struggle is here. African unity is overdue, conspirators and assassins grow bolder, and the prosperous cocoa planters are in no hurry to build socialism.

But as we watched him make his way from the conference

hall, wearing one of those tightly buttoned (to conceal a bulletproof vest, it was said) military jackets that Joseph Stalin adopted as the uniform of authoritarian socialism, passing between a double file of young girls all in white and singing a hymn of praise to him which had been composed by some tribal priest of the rock-and-roll era, we had no urge to mock the man whom Accra's press referred to as the *Osagyefo,* the Giver of Victories.[1] This leader, whose life was constantly menaced, managed to radiate astonishing calm.

There was something tragic about him. But at that time nothing challenged the *Osagyefo's* authority, or the influence he exerted so openly. Yet his power was being tapped, vitiated, its force dispersed. Still, that power was so massive and so intensely experienced that even in its final moments it remained the bulwark of Ghanaian life. Power can be such that we still *see* it when it has already collapsed.

Africa adds specific traits to the general features of power which we recognize in the West or in Asia. It cannot always be defined in simple terms: from the Dogons, seen through the eyes of Griaule, to the Fangs, described by Balandier, the systems of command are just as complex and fluid as those of the Greek republics and the Rhineland principalities.

But two factors are constant: the centralized and personal nature of command that withstands the efforts of elaborate systems of control to modify it, and the religious coloration of authority, which always has some connection with prophethood or *mahdism.* At the risk of making a hasty generalization, we might say that the common form of power in Africa is likely to be, as Georges Balandier puts it, "a religious conglomerate with a temporal mission." Especially because the

---

[1] This is also the translation of "Nasser." But in the Egyptian leader's case, the word refers to God; Abdel Nasser means "Servant of the Giver of Victories."

masses cling more readily to a leader bent on taming the gluttonous local chieftains, and are thus more attached to his person and to his "performance," whether or not it reaches them only through the medium of the tribal priesthood.

The pulse of religion throbs, either internally or externally, inspiring and sustaining a power such as Félix Houphouët's and guiding that of Léopold Senghor. But this is no African version of European clericalism. In Ghana, and despite the coexistence of doctrines that normally are mutually abrasive, there is scarcely more than a trace of *Kulturkampf* or antireligious clashes over civil power, those of a Combes or a Callès.

The English sociologist Basil Davidson has brought out the dominant religious element in African tribal power.[2] In this society, whose horizons are not those of the so-called "revolutionary" governments, "religion is the expression of the reality perceived in every area of life. The exploratory function of this perception has given religion its mandate. It is the starting point for development, in one direction or another, of what may justifiably be called a science of social guidance" ("science" as Claude Lévi-Strauss applies it in *The Savage Mind* when he speaks of the "science of the concrete").

Departing from a historical fact—a certain tribe, the Kalabari, led by its founding heroes, settled in the Niger Delta—Davidson explains that this people

adapted to the demands of social development. These demands were codified in terms we call religious. And if we should wonder why Kalabari thought took a specifically religious expression, we are simply victims of our modern verbal dichotomy: science/supernatural, reality/

2 "Un mécanisme de contrôle sociale," *Diogène,* No. 63.

religion. . . . In tribal thought, this dichotomy did not
exist, for reality was perceived in global terms. This
understanding of the universe embraced not only what
was, but also what might have been.

Whether or not we would wish some Machiavelli upon
the Africans to divorce politics from religion (a role assumed
to some degree by Bourguiba in the Maghreb), the fact
remains that the principle of unity is an integral part of
African thought and, to an even greater extent, of African
political practices. And the curious fact is that the force of
unity in Africa not only amalgamates religion and politics
but also causes ordinarily antagonistic religious factions to
coalesce. It is significant that Leopold Senghor is the Christian President of a predominantly Moslem people, that
Alimadou Ahidjo is the Moslem President of a preponder-
antly Christian nation, and that Patrice Lumumba and Kwamé
Nkrumah, both Christians, have served as a common symbol
to different communities.

What counts is the consecration of power, the religious
dimension it assumes, and the traditions it evokes, not the
source, the nature, nor the specific rites of this consecration,
once it has become Africanized. God, Allah, Imana, or Karl
Marx himself may confer the requisite dimension on the power
of leadership, once Sékou Touré or Julius Nyéréré has natu-
ralized it as African. There is less concern with knowing what
source has inspired the chief than with feeling the glow of that
inspiration.

Thus the incessant evolution of the two great monotheist
religions on the Black Continent has not upset the framework
of traditional black power or generated the conflicts that it has
produced elsewhere. Africanized religion, divorced from political power in a growing number of societies, takes on this syn-

cretic function, reconciling not only Yahweh and Allah, but also God and Caesar. Almost any text dealing with the foundations of Nkrumah's power, and particularly the litanies honoring him, presents an astounding synthesis of animism, Judaism, Islam, Christianity, Marxism, and the techniques of power perfected by the inventors of totalitarianism.

These litanies are in fact the most modern expression of an African oral tradition that Jean Ziegler describes as ignorant of any separation between the religious, political, symbolic, economic, and spiritual domains.

> . . . African power exists, just as Imana exists. It is, of course, of a divine nature. It is sacred. It invades, directs, and commands all manifestations of individual and collective existence. The King is God on earth. "Umwami Uburundi-Uimana" is inscribed on the monument dedicated to Prince Ragwasore on the hill called Visiko above Bujumbura. In the mental diagram of the Barundis, the three terms (king, country, God) are synonymous. The source of power, the sole explanation for development, the basic organization of the community and of the universe, the cosmogony and the ideology of politics, the economic regime and the rules of society—all of these are "explained" by one vast, imposing and unique structure.[3]

This does not mean that African autocracy has no structural support. Custom called for the chief to consecrate the Council of Elders, a council without any formal rules governing its members which was a mystery to outsiders yet in fact represented the tribe. Once this council had anointed a Chief, he usually enjoyed unlimited power. Did he abuse it? "Democracy in the African manner" had its own system of restraints.

---

[3] "Le Pouvoir africain" (University of Geneva: unpublished essay; n.d.).

When the time came, it was up to the Council of Elders to say whether the Chief had gone too far. The Council met secretly and, if the circumstances warranted it, decided to do away with the overbearing Chief, any effort to censure him being too risky to attempt—which implies that this kind of procedure occurred very rarely and only in instances of flagrant misuse of authority. Sometimes the condemned ruler was lucky enough to reach exile; more often, he was simply erased.

But power in contemporary Africa is not distinguished by tradition alone. It is also the heritage of colonialism. The extent to which today's power bears the stamp of recent history is indicated in an as yet unpublished essay by Thomas Kanza, from which we have already quoted:

> The functions of the former colonial governor are those currently filled by the president in most new and independent African states. Only the title has changed.
>
> Colonized peoples never had any love for their colonial governor; they invariably feared, perhaps admired, and often respected him. Yet this same African community is fond of its president. All too often, however, it does not fear him, does not even admire him, and, what is worst, has little or no respect for him.
>
> The African machinery of government is in fact the machinery deliberately and painstakingly assembled by the former colonialists; they greased it regularly, and it threatened to remain indefinitely under their control. Certain African leaders have already shut down the machine and set up their own more appropriate apparatus. That is what distinguishes the so-called revolutionary African nations. Replacing the existing apparatus by another would be sheer suicide for the majority of African countries.

The formidable machinery of personal power in Africa is not simply the product of a relentless process of accumulation whereby history and religion together reinforced the sacred through politics, traditionalism through colonialism, colonialism through revolution; it is also a product of necessity, which requires in some cases resistance to neocolonialist capitalism, and in others struggle against tribalism.

Resistance to the works of neocolonialism? In a book entitled *Politics in West Africa*[4] the black economist Arthur Lewis states that it is the source of absolute power as generally practiced in Africa, which he considers harmful. His colleague Martin Kilson, a Harvard professor, agrees and attributes this surge of autocracy to an inferiority complex on the part of middle-class blacks who see foreign businessmen as more efficient, competent, and resourceful than they, and who seek to protect themselves from competition by a torrent of repressive authority.[5]

The struggle against tribalism is exemplified by those who support authoritarian power. They remind us that at the core of proliferating personal power in Africa is a confused yearning for collective strength, for national unity. The leader is the only person capable of producing a nation from a tribal jig-saw puzzle. He is the common denominator of the Treichville worker, the Baoulé shepherd, the Bamiléké peasant, and the Bassa fisherman. Thus, before incarnating power in a dramatic fashion, the leader symbolized a community that had barely awakened to its own existence.

A COMPLEX SOCIETY

If the strength of personified power can be measured chiefly in terms of the obstacles it faces, such as the ones professors

4 Oxford University Press, 1965. From 1956 to 1961 Professor Lewis was principally responsible for shaping Ghana's economy.
5 *Africa Today*, Vol. XIII, No. 4 (April 1966).

Lewis and Kilson have outlined (neocolonialist enterprise, the sense of inferiority of the black middle-classes, and the centrifugal effects of tribalism), then the Gold Coast, now Ghana, was ripe for a type of power of hurricane intensity: few African territories had such ethnic diversity or had known such a vast development of European commercial investments.

The fact that Ghana was able to throw off colonialism without the Ashanti Kingdom splitting off on its own was perhaps not owing entirely to the dramatic energy of her leader. The colonial past had lent a helping hand to the nation's founder. For more than ten years at the close of the last century, the Ashanti fiercely resisted British troops, allowing themselves to be massacred in an effort to keep the Golden Stool, a sort of Ark of the Covenant for this group, from falling into strangers' hands. In 1901, when the Golden Stool was sent to Queen Victoria, Ashanti resistance crumbled and this famed and prosperous people became the model of what Malek Bennabi harshly terms "colonizability."

But it was one thing to capitulate to the redcoats with their awesome firearms, another to join the ranks under the authority of a politician who came from one of the coastal tribes for which descendants of the Ashanti had the lowest esteem. Nkrumah appealed to the Colonial Office to arbitrate the issue of centralism (which he incarnated) versus the federalism preached by the NLM (National Liberation Movement), the Ashanti party. The Bourne Report favored centralism. But it took lengthy negotiations, from 1955 to 1957, and all the persuasive resources of the Colonial Office to induce His Majesty the Ashantchene Sir Osei Agyeman Prempeh II, ruler of the Central Kingdom, to permit his territory to be included in the new Republic of Ghana and to renounce a federation that would have turned his realm into an agricultural Katanga. For, unlike most of the major ethnic groups surviving on the Black Continent, the Ashanti are rich by standards that are not

purely historical: they produce over half of the two hundred
and fifty thousand tons of cocoa, exported annually by Ghana,
which constitute her wealth. For this reason, the apparent submission of the Ashanti was not arrived at without secret dealings and consistent efforts to discourage union.

Moreover, the Ghanaian nation has other components: the
Gold Coast Colony properly speaking, where the colonizers
resettled all those of Fanti origin, the Northern Territories,
and Trans-Volta-Togoland. To complicate the problem even
more, the two principle ethnic groups of the coastal regions,
the Ewes in the east and the Twis in the west, and in the north
the Mossis, are but the last vestiges of peoples who were pushed
beyond the frontiers by the whimsy of colonialist policy, some
into Togo, others into the Ivory Coast, the last group into
Upper Volta. The absence of a uniform language is but one
of the serious consequence of all that.

The antagonism between Christians and Moslems is said to
be less intense than that between the Coast dweller and the
Ashanti, people of the bush and the savanna, cocoa and coconut
farmers—capitalists of the soil and a work force that migrated
from the north. But a conscientious administration must weigh
the specific problems that any Moslem population poses in a
community dominated by the syncretistic traditions of Afro-
Christians.

Under British rule, this jagged mosaic had produced a relatively coherent pattern of existence. But when Governor Burns,
leaving his Accra post in 1946, called the Gold Coast a "model
colony" (and many of his French colleagues were using the
same words to describe the peoples under their tutelage), the
war intervened and overturned the precarious balance of "indirect rule": interest on war loans enriched the wealthy overnight and widespread unemployment faced returning war
veterans, so that an imminent social crisis added its weight to
the crisis of political emancipation. This recalls Egypt's situ-

ation during this same period—notably the imbalance, owing mainly to the war, between public wealth and the impoverished existence of the masses.

A period of severe unemployment began in 1947, affecting sixty thousand ex-soldiers. Petitions were followed by demonstrations, and on February 28, 1948, the returned soldiers marched on Christianborg Castle, the residence of His Majesty's governor. English troops opened fire. More than twenty persons died. The regime lived on.

Among the influential suspects the police naturally rounded up on the heels of the rioting were men who wanted only reform and peaceful development, friendly autonomy and future cooperation. Sociologist Joseph Danquah was one of them, president of the United Gold Coast Convention, an eminent and cultured commoner, and the "inventor" of Ghana both as a myth and as a principle of development. Even though he, like Lenin, had lost a brother on the gallows for a political "crime" (and, what was worse, the condemned man's executioners were advised of his pardon just minutes after he died), he was the ideal spokesman.

The enormous revenues from cocoa farming[6] enabled the British to institute a system of higher education. With the cadres so educated and with this money, they laid the groundwork for a black middle-class that was intended at the proper time to supplant the outworn colonial regime: from "indirect rule" to "indirect influence."

But, as it happened, this relay force (which, moreover, was given the opportunity to experience prison life from the inside) found itself outclassed by a handful of dynamic men trained under an exceptional leader. The sociocultural "elites" did not even have time to offer their services, for a "madman" had already stepped forward as the future leader. A man from

6 The Marketing Board sold the cocoa on the world market for twice the purchase price set for Ghana's farmers.

the common herd, a Coast dweller of humble birth, he obscured the appointed heirs forever.

Kwamé Nkrumah, arrested along with Danquah and four other nationalist leaders, already had a history. But he was relatively unknown in the Gold Coast. He came from Nkroful, a coastal village in the territory of the Nzima (a branch of the Twi people, itself related to the Fantis), and his family was Catholic and poor. His father was an ironworker, a trade that instills both fear and respect in those who practice it. Under the name of Francis, the child studied with priests. He became a school teacher and was widely known in the Twi villages for his love of debate, his curiosity, and his eagerness to persuade. He soon made his mark as a local leader.

At the age of twenty-four he set out for Liverpool, and from there went on to the United States with a scholarship to study at Lincoln University, a black institution in Pennsylvania. He received a B.A. in philosophy there and founded the Association of Colored Students. He read some Marx and even more of Marcus Garvey, to whom the Black Power concept may be traced. He returned to England in 1945 and worked with George Padmore, the Antillean who was Pan-Africanism's theoretician and was then on the verge of breaking with Britain's Communist Party, yet who would remain its constant inspiration.

Under the guidance of Dr. DuBois they organized the Manchester Pan-African Congress, which marked an important stage in Nkrumah's career, for it focused the attention of Accra's nationalists on the expatriate. During a stay in Paris he met Félix Houphouët, who like himself was active at that time in communist circles. On his return to London, he found a wire from Joseph Danquah, leader of the United Gold Coast Convention (UGCC), who was fighting for autonomy (as Bourguiba was in that period): it offered him the post of secretary general of the organization at a salary of twenty

pounds a month. Other students had refused the job. But
not he.[7]

In Accra, he increased the schedule of party meetings. Under
his guidance, the UGCC ceased to be a club of bourgeois
nationalists and became a type of revolutionary movement
(bringing to mind Bourguiba's take-over of the Destour in
order to forge it into a weapon of combat). In less than three
months he had created a situation culminating in the events
of February–March 1948: Danquah and Nkrumah were
thrown into prison, where their relations (again like those of
Bourguiba and his aides) grew embittered. The British court
of inquiry brought three major charges against him, involving
his inciting speeches on the eve of the riots, an unsigned Communist Party membership card that was found in his room,
and his affiliation with a secret organization known as The
Circle, which aroused even greater anxiety in the British in-
vestigators because a touch of African illuminism (the members had commingled their blood, each from his own wound)
sparked its Leninist methods.

He defended himself so ably before the investigating committee that he was allowed to go free. He broke with Danquah, founded his own newspaper, the *Accra Evening News,*
which was to write his legend, and built his own party, the
Convention People's Party (CPP), to which most of Danquah's supporters flocked.[8]

Thus began the most dazzling phase of Kwamé Nkrumah's
love affair with the people of a country he chose to call Ghana,
following the example of Joseph Danquah, in commemoration
of one of the great empires of medieval Africa, located farther
north along the edge of the Sahara. But this fable-tinged name

[7] Charles-Henri Favrod, *Le Poids de l'Afrique* (Paris: Éd. du Seuil; 1958),
p. 130.
[8] He chose to retain the word *Convention,* for he felt that "the people
have linked this word to my name and would not accept the party."

attracted him even more because it had been the king's title
before it served to designate the nation.[9] In any event, from
1949 to 1957 the CPP's founder was in the fullest sense the
embodiment of a society in search of a leader, status, and
national identity.

Later the corruptions of power, day-to-day struggles, vested
interests, repression, and the schemes and enticements of influential persons alienated a segment of Nkrumah's supporters.
But in the process of achieving independence for the country
and popular dictatorship for its leader, what he exercised was
charismatic authority. We shall see that it lacked permanence,
but its establishment was phenomenal.

Thus Nkrumah, who roused and led the masses, is unique.
The techniques of subversion and propaganda, the evocation
of traditional African magic, and subtle shifts from revolutionary nonviolence, which he called "positive action," to negotiation, which he called "tactical action": all these combined
to make him a successful demagogue and an exceptionally
effective party leader.

His chosen watchword, "Self-government now," had the
edge on Danquah's "Self-government as soon as possible." He
regrouped his followers and broadened his base of support—
originally the "verandah boys" in Accra, homeless boys
who slept under the porch roofs of the rich—to include the
urban proletariat, the petty bourgeoisie of clerks, and the
youth of "Ghana schools," which were founded by him and
amounted to nationalist centers.

He made inroads in Ashanti country thanks to two of his
comrades who came from there, Kojo Botsio and Krobo
Edusei. He began winning over students at the University of
Legon despite their predilection for English standards. He
revived the wearing of the kente, the traditional bright-colored

9 He makes no bones about identifying the nation with himself; his autobiography is entitled Ghana.

toga with its eloquent symbols, yet he was shrewd enough to know that he must combat feudalism as well as colonialism: "The tribal chiefs will take to their heels," he said, "leaving their sandals behind."

On January 13, 1950, he was rearrested and taken to James Fort. Thirteen months later the first legislative elections gave him a triumphant 90 percent of the Accra vote. The prisoner became premier. His release represented an extraordinary plebiscite.

Here is the description of those moments in his autobiography:

> It was a day of triumph for me, and those people were my fighting men. No general could have been prouder of his army. . . . In the amphitheater, which is the cradle of my party, the customary rite of expiation was deemed appropriate: a lamb was sacrificed and I plunged my bare foot into its blood seven times to purify myself of prison . . .[1]

What made Nkrumah a charismatic leader (before he became no more than the holder of a power that was all the more vividly personified when its charisma was gone) was his creation of the relationship and the symbol, and his possession of the ability.

The relationship he established with the Ghanaian people had greater warmth and intimacy than simple popularity; the pattern of symbols he developed was that which gives rise to social and national institutions; and the structure of power he laid, though not perfect, marks him nonetheless as a founder of the state.

If charismatic authority can exist during the process of creating a double system of relations (between the chief and his

[1] *Ghana* (New York: Nelson; 1957).

disciples, between the disciples and the masses), a system of meanings, a style of power, a normative authority, a dynamic social and cultural transformation, then it must be attributed to the Kwamé Nkrumah of the years 1949–54. His promotion of populism and nomadism as creative forces, his profound resourcefulness in using tradition as a model for reshaping the future, his highly persuasive demagogy: all of these characterized Nkrumah in the 1950's as well as they did his exact contemporary, Bourguiba. Of the two, the Ghanaian leader had bolder vision, but he was the weaker culturally and creatively.

> He was the man of the hour for every group. The English considered him less dangerous than he might have been. The Party membership, the youth and the poor saw their chance. . . . Idle passersby were his spies, schoolmasters his agents, taxi drivers his communication network, and the English his staff. His organization did not constitute a legal and formal power—it was a catch-all, but it worked. His charisma became a vessel upon which authority floated . . .[2]

Nkrumah's "gift of grace" in the period before independence was his ability to draw together the various cultural sectors, even the interest groups, so as to create the new man, the responsible African. All too soon the Promethean scope of his endeavor exhausted him. The crusade of the 1950's, based upon a Marxist-inspired populism and a vaguely Pan-African nationalism, resolved itself around 1954 into a legalized opportunism that gradually became self-sublimating.

1954? That was the year when, according to Dennis Austin, in the most detailed history of modern Ghana,[3] Nkrumah's

[2] David Apter, "Nkrumah, Charisma and the Coup, *Daedalus* (Summer 1968), p. 779.

[3] *Politics in Ghana: 1946–1960* (New York: Oxford University Press; 1964).

power underwent a fundamental change. It was then that he bartered dynamic heroism for the responsibilities of conventional politics. The showman became an heir and began paying close attention to transitions, to equilibrium, and to formulae.

He spent three years wooing London after having won the heart of his own people. For indeed it was the British who held the key to the Ashanti territory. Macmillan helped him to swallow up the cocoa kingdom. Yet it was not in London but in Ghana that he made history. If he had been more skillful in manipulating the ambitious rural bourgeoisie, which he had forced into conflict with Ashanti power through a reform of the inheritance system,[4] he might have forgone its support, the loss of which was costly in the long run. In any event, even before Ghana's day of independence, the magic spell binding him to the people had worn off.

His vigorous influence over the crowd still persisted, as did his abilities and his impulsiveness. But now he had to resort to the love-potions of the power-makers. To palliate the decline of his charismatic authority, he was obliged to dramatize his person. So off he went in quest of what might be called political aphrodisiacs. It suggests the heavy makeup of an actress in classic roles, or the tricks of an aging actor. From 1947 to 1951 his expanding authority opened the way to power. From 1954 onward his declining authority reduced his power to absolutism, his absolutism to comedy. But neither his power nor his comedy was second-rate.

Kwamé Nkrumah was a born actor. With his handsome build, his deep, velvety voice and winning smile, his imperious brow, excellent memory, and gift for repartee, he had the full wardrobe of a showman, which is what appealed to the Accra crowds.

Here is a vivid portrait of the leader from the pen of Conor

4 P. Kouprianov, "La Différenciation sociale parmi les producteurs de cacao ghanéens," *Moscow* (1967).

Cruise O'Brien, a former vice-chancellor of the University of
Accra, which appeared in *The Observer* on February 27, 1966,
just after Nkrumah's fall:

> Kwame Nkrumah was a splendid actor, which made it
> difficult to talk to him because he tended to "overact,"
> as if his expression—be it amusement, indignation or
> anguish—had to be vehement enough to reach a vast
> audience. After being with him, I invariably went away
> with a sort of mental crick in the neck as if I had watched
> a film from the second row of the orchestra. . . . I had
> several opportunities to admire his performance on the
> stage of Parliament, with his private herald chanting his
> praises in the corridors and his eight spokesmen with
> their gold-headed halberd. . . . The audience warmed to
> him, the way it does in the theatre, not at a political rally.
> It made me think of those Italian soldiers who responded
> to the sword-waving exhortations of their commander,
> not budging from the trenches, with a chorus of "Bravo!
> bravissimo!"
>
> On three occasions in three years, I heard Nkrumah
> demand that any ministers who had deposited funds in
> foreign banks return them—adding that if this were done
> promptly the guilty persons would not be punished. And
> each time the entire Parliament burst out laughing at this
> quaint suggestion . . .

The struggle for independence did, however, lend a measure
of gravity and pathos to his performances. Was the leader
testing his spell? His autobiography is studded with accounts
of his success in this area. He seemed to have perfected control
of this technique without making it an end in itself. Once he
had attained his first goal, independence, and African unity
appeared as a substitute goal, less action-oriented, he returned
to "his warriors" with an offer of new conquests; and began
building the myth.

In stressing the leader's tactics and strategy, we are not losing sight of the essential nobility of his purpose. African unity and the liberation of the entire Black Continent from imperialism are not minor goals. Nkrumah's downfall may be traced to the fact that he was greater as a pioneer than as a statesman, greater as visionary than as catalyst. Yet he was all things to all men: "radical in the eyes of radicals, Afro-American for the Americans, Anglo-African for the British, African-Socialist for the nationalists and Socialist-African for the Marxists."[5]

Kwamé Nkrumah was able to integrate the many facets of the personality he had painstakingly composed. The mask he wore, which provided a unique and fascinating rallying-sign for all of Ghana (and eventually, he hoped, the whole of Africa), can be reduced to its principle components

Five features characterize the figure of Nkrumah as a popular leader and chief of state: the aim of creating and formulating a political doctrine; the conviction that only the exercise of unlimited authority can change the course of history; the absence of racism in daily life; the treatment of customs and religious beliefs as revolutionary values; and, finally, boundless pragmatism.

Nkrumah saw himself as a philosopher in the image of the amazing Anthony William Amo, a native of his own province who had caught the public eye in Jena and Wittenberg around 1740.[6] And to make his intentions perfectly clear, he decided to shift from "Nkrumaism," the regime's official doctrine until 1964[7] whose name might have seemed like a simple and opportunistic formula for his political strategy, to "consciencism."

5 David Apter, p. 781.

6 Cf. W. E. Abraham, *The Mind of Africa* (Chicago: University of Chicago Press; 1963).

7 *The Spark,* an ideological weekly, had its "Studies in Nkrumaism" in each issue.

His ideological efforts met with great success. What is consciencism? As he expressed it in the preface to his book, it is
"a philosophy and a doctrine of decolonization and development, with particular reference to the African revolution."

So from 1964 onward the Kwamé Nkrumah Ideological Institute at Winneba taught consciencism, the basic doctrine of
the regime. Somehow they managed to find (it took a lot of
searching, was the tongue-in-cheek reaction of the orthodox
Marxists who were the backbone of the Institute) an instructor
sufficiently subtle to teach consciencism, the title of the book[8]
that was handed around not so very long ago in Accra like the
Bible in a Salvation Army hostel. What we learn from that
book—and it is not easy reading—is that Dr. Nkrumah condemns idealism, despite the idealism seemingly implied in the
name of his philosophy, and that he is committed to dialectical materialism.

But the obvious purpose of this ambiguous volume was to
prove to African readers that the adoption of Marxism as a
fundamental doctrine did not imply the denial of a religious
system of metaphysics. "The moral principle of this philosophy," he maintained, "is to regard each human being as an
end in himself and not as a mere tool." And he went on:
"Consciencism is the sum total, in intellectual terms, of the
organization of forces which will permit African society to
assimilate the Western, the Moslem and the Euro-Christian
elements present in Africa and to incorporate them in the
African personality."

This would scarcely differ from the approach of ideologues
such as Sékou Touré who seek "not to Marxize Africa, but to
Africanize Marxism," if the leader-philosopher did not give
the most astounding twists to his theories of revolution and
decolonization. Nkrumah, a remote disciple of the Fabian

[8] *Présence Africaine* published a French translation in 1965.

Socialists, those famous jugglers of algebraic formulas, expressed his central idea in the following equation: "Given that S = socialism, M = materialism, C = consciencism, U = unification, Gi = a liberated territory: $S = M + C + C + UGi$." This is the simplest of all his formulas; although Nkrumah's behavior at times is rather unpredictable, at least he tries to stick to the rules in his philosophic pursuits.

Ideologues tend to develop muscle along with ideas, as if a lofty objective justified whatever measures are needed to realize it. Nkrumah was no exception. Had he been hesitant, the moving appeal of Richard Wright's open letter to him in *Black Power* would have reinforced his own view:

> Be merciful by being stern! If I lived under your regime, I'd ask for this hardness, this coldness. Make no mis take, Kwamé, they are going to come at you with words about democracy; you are going to be pinned to the wall and warned about decency; plump-faced men will mumble academic phrases about "sound" development; gentlemen of the cloth will speak unctuously of values and standards. . . . But you know as well as I that the logic of your actions is being determined by the conditions of the lives of your people. If, for one minute, you take your eyes off that fact, you'll soon be just another African in a cloth on the streets of Accra! You've got to find your OWN paths, your OWN values. . . . YOU MUST BE HARD! . . ."[9]

It is significant that Nkrumah used this passage as an epigraph to the book he wrote in his Guinean exile after his downfall. But in fact the leader never was reluctant to bear down. Several competent observers of African politics (Rupert Emerson and Jane Rouch) quote phrases of his such as "only

[9] Richard Wright, *Black Power* (New York: Harper & Row; 1954), p. 347.

totalitarian measures can preserve liberty." Moreover, Emerson points out that "in any Ghanaian tongue, the word 'opponent' has no other meaning than 'enemy'."[1]

There is treason the minute you have disagreement, for the chief-incarnate is infallible and the people know it. During the summer of 1961 the *Osagyefo* had a visit from an important international official. A few days earlier he had hurled a stinging rebuff at President Tubman of Liberia for having organized a conference that most of the French-speaking African states elected to attend. Nkrumah had accused these heads of state of having "sold themselves to America." When his visitor grew alarmed at such vehemence, the *Osagyefo* retorted: "All Africans know that I represent Africa and that I speak in her name. Therefore no African can have an opinion that differs from mine. If one of them acts against my better judgment, he must be doing it not because he wants to but because he has been paid."[2]

This is the source of the torrent of purges that struck first at the opposition—at Joseph Danquah, the old statesman, who died in prison in the spring of 1965, Joe Appiah and K. A. Busia, who were exiled in turn—and next at those who were the "first lieutenants." The apostles' treason is part of the epic, a painful but exalting episode. Courage was in the air, and the closer the traitor was to the master's person, the greater his punishment must be. The harshest sentence, banishment from the Chief's presence, was imposed when so-called treason (on the parts of Botsio, Gbedemah, Adjei, and Adamafio) was proved.

Although he was a merciless purifier, Nkrumah cannot be accused of racism. He had already experienced it in the American South. The white colonialists had been his enemies; the

<hr>

[1] *From Empire to Nation*, (Cambridge: Harvard University Press; 1960), p. 284.
[2] Interview with the author, January 1969.

regimes of Salisbury, Pretoria, and Bissau were his major targets. But his Pan-Africanism had no racist roots, and in choosing his co-workers and friends he paid no attention to whether they were Europeans or Africans. One might even point out that Ghanaians were the last to gain his trust—which inevitably contributed to his overthrow.

Kwamé Nkrumah chose to be a revolutionary and to change men. But, unlike the promoters of the cultural revolution, he never rejected traditional values or religious beliefs. And what is even more unusual, he did not create an ideology solely from his own African heritage of beliefs and customs but also sought in Islam and in Western Christianity principles to support his consciencism. Never wary of syncretism, he always called himself a Catholic Marxist. And until February 24, 1966, prayers were offered in every house of worship throughout the country "for the triumph of Kwamé Nkrumah over his spiritual and temporal enemies."

Nevertheless, Africa provided him with the bulk of his religious or mystical raw material. His autobiography is veined with sacred and supernatural lore. He proudly recounts that one of his faithful women followers, after choosing to call herself Ama Nkrumah, slashed her face with a sword and painted her body with the blood to serve as an example to the CPP militants. He was seen washing himself in animal blood to erase the taint of prison after his release. In Ashanti, on another occasion, he delivered a speech only after having first bathed his feet in the blood of a sacrificed ram. And in the spring of 1961, when he was scheduled to make a public announcement of socialization policy, he took to the airwaves at dawn in the image of the Akan sovereigns whose glory was believed to reflect that of the rising sun.

The power of magic had a compelling effect on this Marxist-Catholic which is best illustrated by an incident reported by an eyewitness. At the close of a visit to Abidjan in March 1957,

soon after Ghana became independent, Nkrumah arranged to
go to the tomb of Fanta Madi in Guinea, the famous miracle-
worker who had recently died after predicting a great destiny
for the leader's mother; Nkrumah hoped that this pilgrimage
would assure him protection "against the mounting perils"
that beset him.

The diviner's son pointed out that because the leader was
a Christian, he could not benefit from the anticipated blessing.
Then he got an idea. It was to be an unprecedented ritual:
tablets inscribed with verses of the Koran were immersed in
water that was then sprinkled on the leader and a few mouth-
fuls of it swallowed by him. Having thus imbibed the faith
of the thaumaturge, he was fit to receive the blessing indirectly,
and he went away with an easy mind. Let him who has never
taken part in a sacred rite for the sake of expediency have the
first laugh.

Another incident is to the same point. In 1961 the mammoth
statue of the leader which he had erected outside "Parliament
House" was attacked. An explosion blew off one leg, which
was subsequently restored. Afterwards, an enormous white
robe was placed over the *Osagyefo's* figure and his forehead
was bound with a white bandage: a two-fold symbol of victory in the Ashanti tradition which was intended to inform
the regime's enemies that the "father of the nation" had triumphed over his adversaries.[3]

The story of his marriage is even more unsettling. One
morning the President was announced to the Israeli Ambassador, his close friend Mr. Avriel, along with a fair-skinned
young woman who spoke no English. Nkrumah informed the
wide-eyed Ambassador that there was an ancient legend promising the African Empire to the first son born of a black African man and a white African woman. He also said that he

[3] *Le Monde* (April 3, 1962).

had secretly sent two of his confidants to Egypt to find a white woman. This had absolutely nothing to do with his relations with Nasser, he hastened to assure the Israeli. And anyway, the chosen woman was not a Moslem but a Copt and came from a family that had opposed the regime and gone into exile; this Egyptian woman had just arrived in Accra, the marriage would take place shortly, and Africa would soon learn of the birth of its future Emperor. In the meanwhile, Nkrumah had wanted to explain the meaning of his act to the Israeli.

This "materialist" is susceptible to all varieties of religious appeals, from the noblest sort down to those of hazy origin. One of his close followers told us how amazed he was to see the leader ecstatically listening to the Christmas carols sung by a group of children. At the height of his struggle against the Anglican clergy, he repeatedly urged the reading of the Scriptures. And in December 1965, seven weeks before the coup d'état, the Ghanaian government spent fifty thousand pounds for a half million Bibles in English and in the various dialects.

Should one view this effort to encourage religion (mingled with strains of the supernatural) alongside "scientific socialism" as an ulterior motive on the part of a leader avid for glory and for worship? Or is it simply a stratagem?[4] In any event, religion lends a helping hand to absolutism, and the demigods fare better where no idols have yet been torn down.

This coupling of materialism and spiritualism is only one aspect of the startling eclecticism that greatly contributed to the success, and perhaps also the downfall, of Ghana's leader. This perpetual juggling and incessant compromise, this ex-

[4] In his *Idéologie des Indépendances africaines* (Paris: Maspéro; 1969), Yves Benot quotes a very revealing passage on this subject from Peter Abraham's novel *A Wreath for Udomo* (New York: Knopf; 1956), in which the hero, a pan-African leader strongly resembling Nkrumah, describes this short-term reliance on magic as a means of loosening the grip of the past.

hausting attempt to conciliate East and West, socialism and capitalism, God and Caesar, autocracy and collective freedom, violence and nonviolence, specificity and universalism, is what made a nightmare of Nehru's political career as well as Nasser's and Sukarno's, while Kwamé Nkrumah went on his way with utter self-assurance.

Here is what one of his opponents[5] had to say about the leader's ability to assimilate the African past:

> "Oath-taking? Libation-pouring? The purpose of all that is to bind the masses to the CPP. Tribal life is religious through and through. . . . These practices . . . insure, with rough authority, that the masses will follow and accept the leadership. The leaders of the CPP use tribal methods to enforce their ends."
> "I take it that you wouldn't use such methods?"
> "I? I'm a Westerner."

When it came to taking power and assimilating tradition, Nkrumah's self-possession was more admirable than laughable. André Blanchet described the ceremonies lasting from June 30 to July 4, 1960, which marked the proclamation of the Republic of Ghana:

> The same guests, in the same hall, were treated on Thursday to the traditional spectacle of Westminster and, on the following Monday, to an African version of this same ceremony. Despite the rustling and the gold of kentes (the national toga) in front of the throne modeled after the traditional stool of the tribal chiefs, despite the libation poured upon the threshhold while a trumpet wailed, it was still an English parliament that the Ghanaian Republic had adopted; gone were the powdered

[5] K. A. Busia, conversation with Richard Wright, in Wright's *Black Power*, p. 228.

wigs of yesteryear and the sea of arms that clanged to attention, yet the design of the chamber and the ceremony persistently evoked the House of Commons rather than a gathering of black dignitaries . . ."[6]

Nothing was simpler or more rewarding to him than reconciling the irreconcilable. He was a master of that art. And he was also a victim of it, branded a madman by the conservatists and the feudalists, accused of folklorish moderatism by the revolutionary sector.

As we have seen, the mythification of Kwamé Nkrumah does not date from 1961–2, the period of greatest threat to the regime, when conspiracy and outright violence forced him to exorcise the demons by invoking the archangel of the pan-African revolution. The semideification of Nkrumah in fact began in 1949–50, when his charismatic authority was so potent that it did not require those trappings. But in this instance personification should not be regarded as an artificial substitute for waning charisma.

Here is a description of an electoral assembly in the north, over which Nkrumah presided in March 1949:

Then Kwamé Nkrumah made his appearance in elaborate tribal dress, borne on the shoulders of six red-turbaned bodyguards. . . . He stated: "We have nothing to fear but fear itself.[7] We have no arms, but we have a great national soul. With the aid of self-government, we shall turn this country into a paradise inside of ten years. Let us seek the political kingdom and all the rest will come to us as a matter of course."[8]

6 *Le Monde Diplomatique* (August 1960).
7 The Franklin D. Roosevelt quote used as the title of Aneurin Bevan's book, which appeared at that time.
8 *Ashanti Pioneer* (March 5, 1949).

Reporting on the 1951 elections, which resulted in Nkrumah's triumph and his passage from prison directly to government office, a *Daily Telegraph* commentator wrote on January 16, 1951, "He has been virtually deified by the people which attributes to him the virtue and transcendence of an ancestral spirit. . . . His name is substituted for Christ's in the hymns they sing."

During the 1956 elections the campaign mood rose to giddier heights. Witness this portion of the leaflet circulated on the eve of the voting:

> Why should you vote for Nkrumah? Because he is a man of the common people. Because he is honest, hard-working, and vigilant. Because it is he who asked the youth of Ghana to make this country into a paradise so that when Peter opens the gates of Heaven we may all sit there, watching our children pilot their own planes and command their own armies; because in Africa the sun no longer rises in the East, but in the West, through the person of Kwamé Nkrumah . . . [9]

Others have built their image and drawn their "mask" without giving special attention to the clothes they wore. With Nkrumah, there is a symbolic universe of dress, the importance of which may be judged from the fact that the signs woven into the *kente* or traditional toga constitute a language.

In 1957, on the night of independence, he and his companions—Ako Adjei, Krobo Edusei, Kofi Baako, Botsio, and Gbedmah—all wore convicts' uniforms, which none of them had ever had on in English prisons: they were unfurling the flag of liberation. For three or four years afterwards, the leader wore Western clothes: he was embodying modernism. During the next period, around 1960, he dressed only in the magnifi-

[9] *Accra Evening News* (July 13, 1956). See also Dennis Austin, p. 334.

cent Ghanaian toga: to honor Africa. The loose-fitting pilgrim's robe, vaguely reminiscent of Tolstoy's, was his subsequent choice: he was marching for peace and for liberation. Finally, there was the age of the military tunic, styled at first after the Indian model, long and pinched at the waist, then after the severe Mao style.

Thus the leader filled out his image in stages, to draw attention, to manifest the symbol, to say that history is on the march. One after another, he adopted the visible signs of prison and of liberation, of modernism and of cultural authenticity, of peace and of pan-Africanism, of austerity, of the revolution, and of internationalism. He was both man and spectacle, man and symbol.

Already the gigantic statue nearly forty feet high was going up outside the entrance of the Kwamé Nkrumah Ideological Institute at Winneba; already the cult of semidivinity, not of personality, was being spun out. It is adequately summarized by the following three documents: on a minor note, the list of titles and honors that Nkrumah himself compiled for *Ghana's Year Book* in 1965; on a major note, the series of honorary titles conferred on him by his followers; on a note of sheer delirium, the recitations of the "Young Pioneers" of Nkrumaism.

First, this sober notice:

> Instructor (1931–41); history instructor at the University of Pennsylvania (1944); Secretary General of the Association for West Africa (1945–47), then of the United Gold Coast Convention (UGCC); imprisoned in February 1948; founded CPP in 1949, demanded immediate autonomy; campaigned for "positive action" and was reimprisoned; delegate to the National Assembly (1951); Prime Minister of the Gold Coast (1952), then of Ghana (1957). Chancellor of the universities of

Ghana. Thirty-six decorations. Queen's Privy Councilor
(1961). Lenin Peace Prize. Published "Consciencism"
(1964). Hobby: writing books.

This cool self-assurance, with its all too visible undercurrent
of arrogance, was not the attitude of his close associates. Who
then was the brains behind the sparkling cluster of epithets
that ringed his haloed head? Who provided the dramatic
crescendo to the myth of Kwamé Nkrumah, raising it to the
heights of a mystical ascension?

The pressrooms of the *Accra Evening News,* the newspaper
he founded in 1949, had an active hand in brewing this lyrical
concoction: "The greatest African of our generation," *Kata-
mento* (he who never forswears himself), *Oyea Dieyie* (the
renewer of all things), *Kokodurni* (brave warrior), *Kasapreko*
(he who speaks once and for all), and, in a nutshell, "the
Messiah."

But the members of Accra's Parliament were no more spar-
ing of encomia than the press. Here is what some members
said during the debate that took place in May 1961 over the
question of making into a national museum the house in which
Nkrumah had been born. He was "a man the likes of whom
does not appear more than once in a generation." They spoke
of the *Osagyefo* in one breath with Confucius, Mohammed,
Shakespeare, Napoleon, and St. Francis of Assisi. His words
ranked with those of Buddha and of the Sermon on the
Mount. And the outcome was that Nkroful, his birthplace,
was to "serve as a Mecca for Africa's statesmen." At this, one
of his disciples cried out: "Kwamé, we shall bring you one of
the golden shields of the Emperors of Ghana!"

Philippe Decraene, a special correspondent of *Le Monde*
in Ghana, was less reverential in reporting on the welcoming
ceremony given to the Republic of Mauritania's President at
Accra's airport:

Before the Osagyefo's Rolls-Royce had come out on the landing strip, preceded by his fifty-two man motorcycle escort, the "stocking-knitters" of the party's female sections, wearing pagnes as Nkrumah did, had been hopping around for a solid hour, singing "Lead us, kindly Light" and "Osagyefo [thrice repeated], I want to see you, Kwamé Nkrumah." In the stands, hundreds of militants intoned slogans behind a wall of diplomats who appeared deaf and indifferent. An extraordinary figure wearing a jockey cap and an indescribable costume in which white, green, and red predominated—the colors of the Convention People's Party (CPP)—cut through the crowd at a run chanting a froth of syllables addressed to the "father of the country."[1]

But the chorus of journalists, officials, and courtiers is far outsung by the Young Pioneers (who were from eight to sixteen years old, after which they become Nkrumah Pioneers), who are the soul of dedication to the *Osagyefo*. Jane Rouch tells of her visit to the "Chinese Pavilion" at Accra:

With their right hands raised, fingers pressed tightly together symbolizing African unity and the absence of discrimination, they greet me and the litany begins:

Group leader: "Nkrumah is infalible."
Pioneers: "Nkrumah is our leader."
Group leader: "Nkrumah is our Messiah."
Pioneers: "Nkrumah is immortal."

Then the children intone: "If you follow him, he will make you fishermen of men's souls. Become his beloved disciples . . ."

And Jane Rouch (who takes a favorable view of the African revolution) adds a remark made by the national director of the

[1] *Le Monde* (April 3, 1962).

Pioneers: "Yes, our slogans are targets of criticism, especially 'Nkrumah is immortal.' All we mean is that his soul, his spirit, is eternal."[2]

Can these flights of fancy be explained simply by the fact that his subjects were wholly in the grip of a delirious servility? That became doubtful once you heard the claques that trailed the *Osagyefo* wherever he went, from Addis Ababa to Léopoldville or Cairo, their clamor obliterating any shouts of opposition, their chorus of thunderclaps punctuating the leader's oratory. Nor could you believe it once you had seen Accra's central square alight with signs worthy of Times Square: in enormous flaming letters: KWAMÉ! Further on: KWAMÉ NKRUMAH! And finally: KWAMÉ NKRUMAH CIRCLE! Then total darkness, as if the name of Ghana's leader alone could provide light.

Nkrumah was not merely the deep-throated hero of this prodigious mystical opera: he was its inventor and director, its orchestra leader and manager as well. *Persona*—a mask for the theater. Personification—the act of incarnating a person. As Jane Rouch has put it, "The effect is to consecrate through his person the political transformation that has taken place." The phrase is apt. But what must be included in this strategy of incarnation for the sake of revolution is a touch of Nero's arrogance. And perhaps the revolution could have borne its fruit without this added baggage. Where do you draw the line between mystique and mystification?

VOICES IN THE DESERT

On February 24, 1965, while the *Osagyefo*'s plane was approaching Peking, where he was to be a guest of the Chinese

---

[2] *Ghana*, p. 71.

government, a group of army officers under the command of Major Afrifa[3] and Colonel Kotoko announced the overthrow of the regime and, after battling Nkrumah's guard for several hours at Flagstaff House, installed the "National Council of the Liberation," thereby making military dress de rigueur in government circles. The first statement issued by this Council echoed the group that had unseated Ben Bella eight months earlier (except for the last accusation, which no Moslem would ever think of making to another Moslem) :

> To Kwamé Nkrumah, Ghana's independence meant his personal freedom to act according to his fancy. . . . He had made religion an instrument of his power. . . . He had deliberately fostered the cult of personality. He was omnipotent. He came to believe he was God. He was a god.

Nkrumah was not a man to take things lying down. You don't build a forty-foot statue like his and not believe in yourself. Bitter defeat, desertion by most of his companions, and six violent attempts on his life had in no way weakened his confidence in himself or in his role as builder of a socialist Ghana, an African socialism, a united Africa. The prophet complex goes hand in hand with the martyr complex and leads inevitably to the redeemer. And when he had to choose between exile in Cairo and exile in Conakry, he opted for Sékou Touré's country: he would be closer to Ghana for the day of his return.

During his exile in Guinea, the *Osagyefo*[4] had time to brood on his misfortunes. He turned out a flood of pamphlets and, under the title *Dark Days in Ghana*,[5] sent his London publisher a detailed rebuttal of the accusations brought against

[3] He became President of Ghana in April 1969.
[4] He invariably uses this title in his letters to loyal followers.
[5] Panaf Books: London; 1968.

him by the National Council of the Liberation. Is this at all
surprising? Kwamé Nkrumah wasted little time over the
charge of self-deification and chose to deal at length instead
with those of autocracy, megalomania, malversation, and corruption, which offered more grist for his mill.

His defense gave him the chance to point out his enemies.
"The intellectuals and professionals had always opposed my
regime, judging it a threat to their privileged position. . . .
Lawyers and clergymen thus aligned themselves with criminals
at large . . ."[6]

It is apparent that the educated sector he condemns is a
middle-class intelligentsia. But from the moment a regime
angers the feudalists, confuses the peasantry, dismays the rest
of the world, and antagonizes the religious quarter, where can
it turn in time of need after it has alienated the intelligentsia?
The University of Legon made no effort to conceal its distrust
of him. It even managed to voice this on occasion: "setting
itself up as sole judge of right and wrong, as in the Middle
Ages" was the bitter comment of Geoffrey Bing, the former
Labour deputy who was one of the *Osagyefo*'s closest colleagues.[7]

Nkrumah certainly had won the support of the industrial
proletariat. But it was only a marginal element in a country
just entering its industrial stage. The Takoradi longshoremen
(after the period of violent, retaliatory strikes in 1961), the
workmen who built the splendid complex at Téma and those
who were just completing the huge Akosombo Dam on the
Volta (one of the great achievements of the regime that came
in with the coup) remained basically loyal to the leader until
1962, through the agency of the CPP unions and their chief,
John Tettegah. Still, as we shall see, this loyalty did not wear
very well under stress.

[6] Ibid., p. 29.
[7] *Reap the Whirlwind* (London: MacGibbon & Kee, 1968), p. 365.

The final scenes took place in Accra itself. There, the working class manifested something of the uneasiness and instability, the shaky moral fibre common to poorly integrated social groups and revealed when in contact with easy money and cosmopolitanism. Prices had risen more than 20 percent during the last months of his rule and cost Nkrumah the support of those awesome, stocking-knitting "mammies," the revolution's "middlewomen" who had borne him triumphantly on their sturdy shoulders in 1952 but who, after February 24, 1966, were only too happy to lavish upon his effigy their most exuberant execrations.

Could he at least rely on the backing of a handful of important militants? Their support was doubtful. The guiding lights of the Ideological Institute at Winneba, the editorialists of the *Evening News* and *The Spark,* the heads of the Bureau of African Affairs, the rank-and-file leaders of the "Freedom Fighters," the spokesmen for Ghanaian socialism and for pan-Africanism joined in a chorus of mounting criticism of the *Osagyefo.*

Some attacked the cult of personality, the principle of which was currently under fire in Peking as well as in Moscow; others found fault with the ideological maneuvers and pseudo-philosophic syncretism of this so-called Catholic Marxist; still others were angered by his relentless and often humiliating efforts to conciliate the notables, the feudalists, a bourgeoisie, and a cosmopolitan "establishment" whose hostility, if not contempt, he was forever hopelessly seeking to overcome—that sense of being parvenu which he could not put down by a Hapsburg marriage or Wehrmacht victories. The rampant personification of Nkrumaist power was popularly thought to be the result of a conspiracy on the part of the privileged class to bind and immobilize him in the chains of a demeaning adoration.

Those of Accra's Marxists who had not resigned themselves to equating socialism and Nkrumaism, consciencism and Leninism, lost no chance to expose the bald ambiguity of certain statements issued either by the leader or by his less adroit or less inspired lieutenants. "In a Nkrumaist-socialist state," wrote Kofi Baako, "the peasant will not lose his farm; the land-owner will not lose his property—but he will be prevented from exploiting the farm worker. . . . No property honestly acquired and utilized will be called into question . . ."[8] And the least enlightened of the *Osagyefo*'s spokesmen, that dull-witted fellow Krobo Edusei, stated that "socialism is a system whereby those who have a lot of money can keep it . . ."[9]

We should point out that this dictatorship permitted some extremely heated and curious debates to take place. The afore-mentioned pronouncements from the high priests of the regime were savagely exploited by avant-garde organs, par-ticularly *The Spark*. Yves Benot[1] quotes from an article by Julius Sago published on December 11, 1963, in that staunchly Nkrumaist weekly, which was in fact under the management of prominent Marxists: "The antisocialist factions of the CPP wield their influence through certain state organs. . . . The battle for socialism rages in the ranks of the CPP. . . . This is a struggle between the power of the state and the supremacy of the party . . ."

When the chips were down, Kwamé Nkrumah found his last stronghold of support among the committed revolution-aries. His friends were all on the Left. But unfortunately for this patriot, most of them seemed to be non-Ghanaians: Geof-frey Bing, Heymann, Damz, and William Smith were to re-main his staunch allies.

The final act took place in that political and social climate. He could not have left himself more isolated, having alien-

8 *West Africa* (May 13, 1961), p. 505.
9 *Monthly Review* (July–August 1968), p. 112.
1 Yves Benot, pp. 231–2.

ated all political support. In the spring of 1961 he had approved a decree establishing arrest and five years in prison (without trial, of course) as the fate of anyone he considered dangerous to the state. In August 1962 he had finally allowed himself to be "talked into" a life term as president. In June 1965 another twist was given to the screw. According to the Accra press, the scheduled elections were to provide "a model of democratic procedure in the framework of single-party government." But no one dared run against the candidates of power, all of whom were elected to office.

As soon as the election results became known, thousands of militants swarmed into local party offices, singing party hymns, shouting the leader's name, and gathering all the party workers into a massive street parade.

And the *Ghanaian Times* observed in its editorial:

This was truly a glorious day in the history of Ghana. It marked the unshakeable confidence of the people in the dynamic national party and its leader, the Osagyefo Dr. Kwamé Nkrumah. The Party's supremacy has once more been demonstrated. The spontaneous mass support of the Party was greatly strengthened by the results of the nominations, which prove beyond a doubt that there are no longer any lone voices crying out in the wilderness. For us, there is indeed a chosen path and the assurance of success despite any and all misfortune, a path that is paved with faith, honesty, integrity, and overflowing confidence in the ideals given to the nation by the source of its honor, the Osagyefo Dr. Kwamé Nkrumah.

When the relationship between the leader and the masses reaches the point where it silences the "voices in the wilderness," that does not mean that the dissidents have been won over; it means that the system has annihilated opposition. At that stage, the denial of any political dialectic leads to ataxia of the social organism, which thenceforth can react only spastically.

David Apter has said, "The charisma of Nkrumah was the source of a populist movement that introduced a parliamentary system, which in turn put an end to charisma itself."[2] Here is the vicious circle of this type of power, which, under the pretense of creating institutions, becomes self-perpetuating and rules out the very institutions it was intended to create. In order to gild his own image, the hero makes a desert of the political landscape and obliterates it.

Nkrumah will perhaps remain the prototype of those solar and solitary political prophets destined to wander from one desert to another. His ideological emptiness inevitably led him onto barren soil.

This type of man is the product of colonialist alienation or of prison, of defeat or exile; he lives, constructs a world, develops ideas, and simmers in disgust and righteous anger. Suddenly the future looms, the lightning path from obscurity to renown, and overnight he is hurled upward to the summit and must shoulder the burden of power. Still stunned by his own success, he begins to act. The potency of all the theories he had worked out during long and lonely years of reflection, his sudden appearance in the midst of crisis, and the sense of relief his natural authority brings—all these things promise him an impressive career.

The structures that did not exist before his coming (in Nkrumah's case) or that were destroyed when he arrived (in Nasser's case) are either built or rebuilt around his person, at his own pace. Once an exile or a prisoner, he has become the heart of a nation and a system. He is smothered by attention and flattery. Yesterday he was a nobody; now he

2 "Nkrumah, Charisma and the Coup," *Daedalus* (Summer 1968), p. 788.

is adulated and glorified, especially by the representatives of foreign powers, who rush to clasp hands with the new master. Reality itself, seen through his entourage and the ceremonies that envelop him, seems to take the shape of whatever crosses the master's mind. He has no reason to question his success. And as his self-confidence grows, his scorn for the rest of mankind develops.

Then we have what appears to be a split personality. Perhaps there is an element of humility in it: the man, the poor man, Kwamé, slowly slips away from the hero, Africa's leader, the Chosen One, Nkrumah, the person with whom all Africans identify, the one whom God—or History—lovingly created to fill the role of liberator.

Kwamé, the man, admires and respects this giant, Nkrumah. He offers himself as a sacrifice so that Nkrumah shall be exalted. He risks his insignificant mortal life so that the symbol may triumph; each attempt to assassinate him becomes a sacrament. He trains himself not to notice the fraud, the petty maneuvering, or the farce around him so that the Other may grow, so that the Hero may be strengthened, made invulnerable, deified. And his success is so overpowering that Kwamé is finally convinced of it. Because it is written that the son of the Other shall be emperor, and the people believe that this emperor shall be born of two Africans, one of whom is white, Kwamé will find a woman for the Other and marry her.

But this split, this gap between the man and the sublime or divine leader—is it not simply the distance that has grown between the person and the function, between leadership as an end in itself and the people who were to be liberated?

As a matter of fact, Kwamé Nkrumah had no right to count on the support of the masses whose spokesman he claimed to be. The tensions that came to light, particularly during the great Tanoradi strike in September 1961, and those which followed soon after, were brought out quite clearly in an article entitled "Ghana: End of an Illusion"[3] in a special issue of the American Marxist *Monthly Review* six months after the *Osagyefo*'s fall.

The authors of that unvarnished analysis, having first exposed the petty bourgeois roots of Nkrumah and his staff, as well as the reformist nature of his shifty tactics vis-à-vis the colonialists and the local bourgeoisie, define his enterprise by a formula borrowed from Marx: "partial political revolution." They emphasize the paternalistic character of Nkrumah's system: "It is the CPP that guides the workers, keeps them informed about the program and protects them from themselves. Thus the workers are exhorted to become Stakhanovites of a revolution that has not really begun."[4] They conclude:

> . . . In the period that followed their common struggle for independence, the political elite and the working class collided. . . . To combat the mounting dissatisfaction of the proletariat and the urban sub-proletariat, the political elite was forced to turn to mystification as a source of legitimacy. The cult of the leader was born— not of the national hero's hunger for flattery but of the fact, as Fanon has observed, that "the leader becomes all the more essential as the party loses ground."

However, it is hard to see how the cult of personality, or what we would call the delirious personification of power, is a concomitant of "partial political revolution," a few examples of which we have already examined. There is nothing less partial than the cultural revolution that opened in Peking in 1966—and nothing more universal than the cult that was established thereafter.

[3] By Bob Fitch and Mary Oppenheimer (July–August 1966).
[4] Ibid., pp. 104–5.

What seems more pertinent to the situation than a "partial political revolution" is the idea of "peaceful coexistence within one country," a phrase borrowed from the authors of "Ghana: End of an Illusion." This apt definition of Nkrumaist ambiguity is extremely revealing. It provides the key to this somewhat mystifying "populism" which mitigates class conflicts and places the enemies of revolution outside the country: imperialism alone.

In this fashion the hero, a glutton for unanimity, claims to speak for the people as a whole and to gather within the folds of his striking toga the proletariat and the bourgeoisie, the intelligentsia, and the peasantry. And thus the delirious personification of power, which declares itself the founder of nations and the creator of institutions, confuses the ends and the means, the exploiters and the exploited, the weight of tradition and the forces of progress.

"Nine out of ten citizens hate me? No matter, so long as the tenth one alone is armed."[5] The phrase is Cromwell's. Ghana's leader has been compared to the Lord-Protector, who controlled with only one brake: the question of reinstituting the monarchy. The parallel does not hold here, however. Kwamé Nkrumah is no ordinary man. But what he destroyed—the collective desire to build freedom, implying independence—will perhaps never reappear.

Just as "socialism in a single country" leads to Stalinism, which by denying social and political interaction brands every opponent "a spy of Hitler's," so the embalming of the leader results in silencing genuine debate and establishing the pernicious religion of unanimity.

[5] Quoted by Maurice Duverger in the epigraph to his book *De la Dictature* (Paris: Julliard; 1961).

Personified power is not only a threat to the hero's integrity and mental and emotional balance: it also condemns the masses to an impotent state of lethargy. We have already reconstructed the positive and fruitful side of the love affair between leader and people. But once you have seen what Algiers was like in early July, then August, and then November 1962, you can no longer be cynical or indifferent toward the dangers. And the same is true for the return of Mohammed V to his throne, Habib Bourguiba to Tunis, Gamal Abdel Nasser from Bandung, Ho Chi Minh addressing the people of Hanoi in 1946, or Sékou Touré crossing the terrace at Conakry, his residence, to meet General de Gaulle. These are events that demonstrate that power and legitimacy are products of mass participation. Leadership draws its strength from the crowd. Leader and people are one.

But the prolonged ectasy becomes ritual, then habit and even boredom. The delegation of authority to the hero develops into acceptance; the exchange into hierarchy. And the masses have no other function than that of admiring and obedient spectators. They are in danger of being anesthetized. Irresponsibility takes hold, and soon they find themselves in the grip of alienation. Not the same alienation they knew under colonialism. (Habib Bourguiba once remarked jestingly that the difference was in the fact that the policeman pushing you around was no longer an alien but one of your countrymen. Of course, at that time the policeman was his.) In any event, the concentration of responsibility in the hands of the personified leader and of his invisible administrators is not a system very conducive to the modernization of a society—to the institutionalization of authority, citizen participation, and the gradual elimination of social, ethnic, and economic inequities.

Once the masses are relegated to the sidelines ("We are working for the people, but do they realize this?" the leader says) and parliamentary government comes to be regarded as nothing more than warmed-over colonialism or an instrument of neocolonialism, where are the checks and balances of power? To oversimplify the matter by contrasting representative government to autocracy would be a mistake. Public criticism takes many forms, and even in a Marxist-oriented party a complex system of democratic controls can operate.

Something of this sort seemed to be developing within the Sudanese Union, Mali's single party, as well as in the Neo-Destour party (conceived along totally different lines and on different foundations). Yet we know what befell Modibo Keita's leadership in November 1968. What leader is willing to allow give-and-take within "his" party? Houari Boumediène posed the question very explicitly in a speech he gave in March 1966. But three years have passed and he has not yet given an equally clear answer.

What the leader usually organizes is a basic system for communicating themes and slogans and for mounting propaganda campaigns. The party echoes them. When does it provide ideas? When does it exert control? What role did the Neo-Destour party play in the Bizerte crisis, if not to furnish the brave men who died on the outskirts of this base? And what was the role of Guinea's people's party in the dispatch of Sékou Touré's wire to François Mitterand, which ruined any chance of a détente with France at the end of 1965? The leader seeks complete personal autonomy, pulling up his own anchors, which could provide contact with the modest desires of the people through the intermediary of national organizations. For the services he has rendered, he claims the right to go adventuring, and the nation must bear the consequences.

There is no doubt that the noblest motives inspire the majority of these leaders and that they have long given proof of their concern for the public welfare. But the start of a successful enterprise too often turns out to be the first step toward disaster. The people have no better claim to foresight than the hero. But the instruments he controls, if he were to use (or even retain) them, would serve as screening devices for restraining some elements of his adventurism.

The value and performance of personalized power should not be gauged solely in the areas of leadership and the control of authority. The educational field, in which it claims to excel, should also be examined. We have stressed the role of identity, its contribution to unity: leader-symbol, leader-axis. It also has a driving force. But each of these assets is linked to a particular period in the emergence of the state which is difficult to isolate in terms of the calendar.

This infancy stage of the nation under the aegis of its leader-tutor might be said to cover the period of history which sees a generation of students agitating against colonial power become the governors of an independent nation.

Between the time when young members of student-worker committees joined forces with commandos led by army officers and Moslem Brothers to harry British bases along the Suez Canal (in November 1951) and the time when the survivors became the *maamour* of Denderah or Aboukir, there is a critical interval: the transition from colonialist rationality to irrationality and back to nationalist rationality. There is no disputing the fact that this historical period favors the development of personal power, even demands its presence. The question is whether the ensuing modernization of society is compatible with the protraction of such power.

When there are ferment, uncertainty, and disorder, heroic leadership has an educational function, although it may not be aware of this. Fortunate or unfortunate, each of Nasser's undertakings in 1956 taught the Egyptians about themselves. His campaigns to unite the Nile Valley, to remove the British from the Canal Zone, to appropriate the Canal, and to promote "positive neutrality"—all these, together with the naïveté, the audacity, and even the delusions that sustained them, helped to instill Egyptian identity. The whole of Egypt was forcibly enrolled in a history course; it was an educational experience regardless of whether or not the lessons stuck. The same is true of the various rungs on the ladder of Bourguibist policy which the "Supreme Commander" obliged his people to climb, from his attempts at cooperation in 1936 to the crisis of 1958.

But once the new state has found its bearings and set its course, once its borders are calm again, once individual and collective identity is established, then the relationship between the people and power enters a new phase. Of course, this is a simplified picture. Perhaps the word "people" is ill-chosen for a divided society, half of whose members live by a different system of exchange and production and whose access to information has little in common with that available to members of the advanced sector. Yet it points up the problem at hand.

The leader willingly takes on the role of instructor. Bourguiba excels in this role, just as Saad Zaghlul did; Hassan II and Sékou Touré have attempted it with less success. The masses are treated as if they were ignorant— and indeed they are, of their own interest perhaps more than of their culture. "It is essential to make them aware of their rights as well as of their responsibilities," was Bourguiba's comment to us in Le Kef in December 1962. Rights? They are easier to define under colonialism than during its aftermath. What an opposition leader says is not always supported by what he does once he becomes the executive. But in the realm of leadship, even Harold Wilson is more consistent than Kwamé Nkrumah. Once the hero has seen the last of imperialism's prisons, he must concentrate on orienting the rights of his people; traditional privilege can lead only to abuse. Thus, once education ceases to be liberating, it becomes remedial and coercive.

But the content of these lessons is not as important as the relationship they establish between the leader and the people. As Harold Lasswell put it, there is no integration, just "allocation"; no exchange, just distribution; no information (which implies movement in two directions), just projection. There is only one source of light: overhead.

Of course, a certain degree of familiarity between the hero and the masses (the Harun-al-Rashid streak in all these leaders) makes the learning process somewhat reciprocal: not Nasser nor Senghor nor Ben Bella brings his message to flocks on a hillside; each is aware that he is addressing a human community that stirs his interest, his sympathy, and his compassion. This relationship has no element of scorn. But there is a sense of hierarchy, a mixture of paternal and fraternal feelings which ties the tongues of the people— their only, communal expression is their applause.

The benevolent instructor stoops a bit in addressing the infant-people and explaining the policy made in its name. Is this a school for citizens or for truants? Again, it was Bourguiba who told us, in December 1962, that "these people need to be taught from A to Z. . . . I have to keep a steady rein on them and not let them 'cut a class.' "

This application of "modernizing" power, which is essentially didactic and authoritarian, helps to produce solidarity and to channel emotions and energy. But there is the risk that this energy will dissipate itself in the endless learning process. A people whose involvement is limited to the role of listener, disciple, or observer cannot develop. If it is true that outside aid, even under ideal conditions, does no more for a society than colonization did, and that the only fruitful development is that which evolves inside a community as a result of internal forces, it is also true that only participation can bring lasting social change. Carrying out a program dictated from above causes only a slight stir. After the tidal wave of activity generated by the Kemal regime came the ebb tide under Menderes.

If the leader has not prepared the way for progress and participation "in depth"—and leaders such as Zaghlul, Nehru, and Mohammed V, despite their eminence and ability, fall into this category—what can be expected when they are gone? One is tempted to say that the likelihood of resolving the problems of succession is in inverse proportion to the concentration of power and the personification of authority. There are examples of hereditary charisma, of course, the most interesting of which is Indira Ghandi. In her case, the growth of authority was aided by leaders of Congress and the instrument of representative government. But what will become of Nasser's power, of Houphouët-Boigny's, Bourguiba's, Nyéréré's?

Reduced to the role of followers (whose complex relations with the hero have been exhaustively analyzed by Max Weber), each of the lieutenants is so perfectly adjusted to his subordinate position, and at the same time so eager to recover his personality, that the combination of timidity and exaltation can lead to bitter conflict and repudiation: the "heirs" of Mustapha Kemal and Ben Bella's "victors" provide examples of this. Personal power does not prescribe the end of the story, but leaves it hanging. The predominant trait of this seemingly muscular power is its fragility.

Another minor point: one might expect that the various "molds" of colonialism would have produced some fundamentally different concepts of postcolonial power, but that is scarcely the case. English pragmatism and French rationalism gave rise to very similar forms of liberating leadership. One is not apt to confuse Nkrumah and Sékou Touré, Ben Bella and Nasser, Kenyatta and Bourguiba, Hassan and Hussein, Nyéréré and Houphouët-Boigny, or Nehru and Sihanouk. Yet is there a clear line between English- and French-speaking heroes?

Perhaps we might say, as Chamfort has suggested, that the former are more eager to establish respect for law, and the latter, respect for authority. The principles of power outlined by Hobbes and Laski are not so different from those of Rousseau and Jean Rous. In neither case does law constrain a leader. In both cases his personal impact is the source of law and of authority.

Considering the failings of personalized power, is "democracy" the best alternative? The ideologues of the Third World have no illusions about the implications of the word as it applies overseas. They, along with the Marxists, are all too ready to condemn what they call "formal democracy." And they have every reason to confuse representative government with capitalism, for in their view, capitalist power is in a position of sufficient strength within the political society it creates to permit a code of innocuous civil liberties to operate. Although they admit that Western liberalism may have its points, they insist that once its inherent illusions and contradictions function within a national framework, such tolerance is not in the public interest in countries where capitalist pressure is exerted from the outside and, when given free rein, induces a two-tier alienation: of the masses from the holders of "real" power, of the nation from foreign interests.

As we have seen, personified power can serve as a transmitter for such pressures. In a country like Morocco foreign capitalism operates through the agency of the authoritarian leader, not through the elected Assembly; brief as the existence of the Assembly was (1963–5), it was scarcely receptive to that type of influence. On the whole, however, improvised parliamentary regimes in newly independent countries have been more vulnerable to foreign pressure than have their leaders. Egypt is an exception, for there personified power has improved this situation to some degree, but neither Ghana nor Iran is. (But it should be added that the oil interests have greater latitude in dealing with a headless regime, such as Libya's, than with a zaïm such as Abdulkerim Kassem.)

The desire to preserve national integrity and the need to awaken drowsy and ill-fed societies have produced strangely similar manifestations of power, from one continent to another, from Perón to Sihanouk, and all of them can be called national populism.

It has three components: the charismatic authority of the leader whose person incarnates, unites, and mobilizes the people; the resistance to intermediary bodies and classic procedures of debate, the leader maintaining direct contact with the masses and relegating the various elites to the background; and the persistent lack of distinction between social and national objectives, between improving the standard of living and expanding the military potential, goals that are the core of friction between Right and Left in most modern states. Hence the stubborn insistence (on the part of the leadership, at any rate) that there is no Right-Left cleavage in the nations of the Third World because the doctrine of national populism automatically rules out this type of conflict.

Such a system has its virtues, or at least its usefulness, if it is developed and operated by a leader who is also a statesman—Nasser, Bourguiba, Nyéréré. But to magnify one individual and place total responsibility in his hands is to risk perverting the leader, habituating the masses to irresponsibility, forcing the majority of the technical cadres into purely executive work (if not out of the government entirely), and leaving the regime in perilous balance, dependent on one man's existence and the outcome of the inevitable struggle to succeed him.

This type of regime, whether or not it has a doctrine to justify it, is capable of creating both nation and state. But it cannot make them endure. It offers no real solution to the fundamental problem of replacing a society that has been divided by feudalism, tribalism, or colonialism with a political society based on participation and responsibility.

The holders of power may well maintain that this absence of a "political society" is precisely what makes them indispensable, and that their exercise of unlimited power is intended to usher in the development of such a society. One answer to this is that proliferating power is like a tropical tree whose shade stunts all the surrounding growth.

The effects of the abusive personification of power are given (along with a certain amount of cant) in the statement issued on June 19, 1965, by the "Revolutionary Council" established in Algiers upon the ashes of Ben Bella's power:

> However important his mission may be, no single person can claim to incarnate Algeria. Whatever form the concentration of power may assume, it cannot allow the

country and its affairs to be handled as if they were one individual's private and personal property. . . .

* * *

If the tyrant we have now neutralized permitted himself to believe that the masses were fast asleep, events have now taught him that whenever the idols created by necessity have turned away or proved disloyal, their punishment will have been proportionate to the confidence and faith the people placed in them. . . .

* * *

Under a regime of personal power, all national and local institutions of the party and the state are at the mercy of a single man who meets responsibilities in his own fashion, with his own confused and improvised tactics, delegating authority according to impulse, whim, or his own pleasure.

In passing, it is interesting to note the curious phrase "the idols created by necessity," a concession Brutus reluctantly makes just before striking with his dagger, and which suggests both how complex the problem is and the good judgment needed to deal with it.

What is a political society? It is one that functions not by means of the vitality and prestige of a single individual— god, man, or tyrant—but by cooperation, concentrated effort, and responsibility. It tends to put an end to the alienation, discontinuity, and irresponsibility that characterize tribal societies. What must be created is a sense of community, of continuity and responsibility—a state of mind proper to citizens. Whether one speaks of development, secularization, or modernization, the effect is always to break down clannish structures, to replace tribes, castes, and sectors of outmoded development with a community pervaded by the belief that in a given framework development will be a cooperative and not a divisive effort.

The personification of power is not basically opposed to these aims. But once it has adopted them and set itself up as both teacher and activator, there is a risk that after a promising start it may cause the machine to shift into reverse and back itself into a new wall of alienation. There is also a risk, even in the initial stages of this process, that heroic leadership may offer itself as an alibi and a reprieve for collective responsibility. A spur, an instrument for creating identity and unity, personified power threatens to change its face at the end: the hero becomes a substitute for yesterday's gods.

Having dealt with the strong tendency of personalized power to magnify itself into divine authority, we should look for the antidote to it or the means of checking it. There are a number of possibilities. No matter what strength power may attain, or how efficiently it may appear to operate (in Egypt, Tunisia, and Cambodia, for example), in order to secure its future and allow for a certain amount of social and political dialectic it must place restraints upon itself. The universities, the trade unions, and the courts can provide such restraints.

A revolutionary "founding" regime can certainly get along without a parliament traditionally elected by universal suffrage; it can do without a free press, in the Western sense— under existing conditions, press control is a minor evil; it can also exist without a system of intergovernmental debate elaborately defined, as in the developed nations.

But it will inevitably extinguish itself if it does not allow some measure of criticism from the people responsible for economic growth; if it does not encourage a spirit of inquiry, of intellectual freedom within the university framework; and above all, if it interferes directly in the legal system. The three-fold tendency of all these regimes is to bridle the unions, silence the students, and control the courts.

If they succeed in doing this, they will end up with a hostile work force, paralyzed elites, and a citizenry that distrusts government. If the society is not given that much room to breathe in, discipline and indifference finally will drain the energies of both state and nation. What good is it to spur a people toward development while withholding the components of development: participation, initiative, and responsibility?

The whole problem of national growth lies in the balance between forward motion and cooperative effort, between authority and the individual conscience, between education and the sense of responsibility. There is no balance in the long-term personification of power. The strength or weakness of the sociopolitical fabric of new nations can be determined by the relations that evolve between driving force at the summit, which is indispensable in time of crisis, and participation at the base, the consciousness of responsibility.

If such a relationship has not been established, or has been falsified, this consciousness will take the form of rebellion. This will not mean that the new nation has chosen to destroy itself, but that it has chosen to resist confiscation and respond to leadership's spur towards development.

Conclusion

More facts than explanations have emerged from this study, more descriptions than theories, more "hows" than "whys." Recourse to Weberian analyses, admirable as they may be, enables us to examine the functions but not to see the reasons for the constantly recurring phenomenon of the personification of power.

A better clue to the motivations rather than the operations involved in the personification of power may perhaps be found in a certain Marxist, or Marxian, line of thought. Antonio Gramsci, following the reasoning of Karl Marx in *The 18th Brumaire of Louis-Napoleon Bonaparte*, maintains that Caesarism, or Bonapartism, or fascism had its origin in an immobilized condition of society resulting from a particular balance between political and economic forces. When the financial oligarchy and the working masses have reached a certain equilibrium of power, neither one able to prevail over to the other, the Man of Destiny comes forth, in 1851 as in 1920, to decide a struggle between contenders so nearly equal in strength as to have brought about a state of social paralysis.

This thesis, however, does not seem to cover adequately all the situations we have examined. Gramsci is dealing with kinds of immobilization affecting European political societies. Yet no type of society is more fluid and open, hence less immobilized, than that which in the mid-twentieth century has given rise to the powers here described. Egypt in 1952, Ghana in 1957, the Congo in 1960: all are fluidity and elusiveness, all spontaneity and freshness.

But if the rise of the flamboyant leader is not owing to a state of social paralysis, does it, on the other hand, tend to cause that state? The complaisance of a great variety of forces surrounding him suggests that what we might call the Gramsci Theorem is applicable a posteriori.

We mentioned this idea in connection with Nkrumah. Let us look at it more closely. The hero and his more or less mythified image were projected and taken up by the masses in the course of the struggle for independence. But that image and that personality could not survive, be perpetuated, and evolve without some minimal complicity on the part of the forces heir to colonialism, forces that have retained the powers of organization and of propaganda not only in Egypt or Tunisia or Ghana, but even in liberated Algeria.

Why do these forces intervene toward consolidating and promoting the extravagant image of the hero?

Why are their efforts and those of the masses bent on making the liberation leader into a permanent demigod? Because they hope, through his person, to halt the revolution. By investing total power and total authority in one man, they try to freeze the social dialectic, to block the unpredictable course of a movement by means of his name, his face, and his legend. The cult of the hero serves the aims of a social class whose interests it would appear to threaten and many of whose privileges it has already destroyed, simply because that group relies on the leader to surmount the class struggle. This man will become the revolution incarnate.

Any individual placed in that position cannot help playing a conservative role in one way or another. In his own person he carries out and therefore achieves the revolution. He is its objective, he sets its limits. Incarnating it, he centralizes it, bridles it, simplifies it. Nothing is more striking in the speeches and interviews of these liberators and founders than this leitmotif: We have advanced beyond the concepts of right and left; there is no longer any class struggle; the revolution is fulfilled in me.

And so the ruling classes, or those which formerly ruled, have in a sense won out. Certainly the leader is costing them enough: Nasser's socialist legislation of 1961, the Ghanaian revolution's flirtation with Marx in the 1962–65 period, and even the quasisocialist phase of the Bourguiba regime between 1964 and 1969. We can say that the bourgeoisie attempts to minimize its losses by puffing up the leader. It cuts off some of its own flesh and feeds it to the hero to fatten him up, blow him up, lull him to sleep. Soon enough the deified leader will proclaim the revolution fulfilled in him and the class struggle resolved in him.

But this working hypothesis cannot and does not account fully for all the forms of power touched on in these pages, and accounts even less for all of those known to exist nowadays in the Third World: it hardly applies in Ben Bella's case, and even less in Fidel Castro's. We must in some way also take into account psychosociology, social pathology, even the sociology of the theater, in order to describe and then explain the varieties of political behavior which Marxism (especially where it has become less Marx than Marxist practice) fails to encompass.

But before selecting one or another hypothesis that will lead to the constants involved in the personification of power, we should look beyond them and consider the current perspectives of personified power.

There is every indication that we are presently emerging from what might be called the Golden Age of Personification. The historical boundaries are traceable: from 1955 to 1965, from the Bandung Conference, which made Nasser into a popular hero, to the failure of the second Afro-Asian Conference in Algeria, closely preceded by the elimination of Ben Bella and soon followed by the political demise of both

Sukarno and Nkrumah. During that decade, from Nasser's personification of power to the downfall of the Ghanaian leader, charismatic power reached its apogee. Not that this type of power has not survived the crises of 1965–66, but that nearly all the structural changes in the countries under consideration evidently have taken place to the detriment of this type of leader, and that where feudalism has been overthrown (as in Libya, for example) the Sukarnos and Nkrumahs have not benefited.

Why this twilight of personification? Is it because the hero as teacher foresees his own end and postulates it, as colonization itself does? Is it because the leader has played out his role as a checkrein on revolution, the role he was licensed by conservatism to play until it could quietly resume its leadership in his place, as in the case of Nkrumah? Or, on the contrary, is it precisely because he failed to play that role and allowed the revolutionary forces to gain ground that he was ultimately rejected, like Sukarno? Or because populism appears strongly suspect to those in power, who prefer technocracy? Or because authentic new forces are gathering which reject the mediator, the Man of Destiny, and take matters into their own hands?

The era of bureaucracies—whether civilian or military— is with us, so it seems. What is happening, or is about to happen, from Cairo to Accra, from Djakarta to Tunis, if not at Phnom-Penh in March 1970, appears to be moving in that direction. The hero is not seeking fulfillment in a context of democracy. He calls in that counteragent, or rather that negation of the democratic idea: the bureaucrat.

Bibliography

Books Cited

Abdel-Malek, Anouar: *Egypt: Military Society.* New York: Random House; 1968.

Abraham, William Emmanuel: *The Mind of Africa.* Chicago: University of Chicago Press; 1963.

Abrahams, Peter: *A Wreath for Udomo.* New York: Alfred A. Knopf; 1956.

Amer, Abdel: *La Faillite du système constitutionnel égyptien.* Paris: Doctoral dissertation; 1955.

Apter, David: *The Gold Coast in Transition.* Princeton: Princeton University Press; 1955.

Austin, Dennis: *Politics in Ghana: 1946–1960.* London and New York: Oxford University Press, 1964.

Balandier, Georges: *Anthropologie politique.* Paris: PUF; 1967.

——: *Daily Life in the Kingdom of the Kongo.* New York: Pantheon; 1966.

Banfield, Edward C., and Banfield, L. F.: *The Moral Basis of a Backward Society.* New York: Glencoe Free Press; 1967.

Bendix, Reinhard: *Max Weber, an Intellectual Portrait.* New York: Doubleday Anchor; 1960.

Benot, Yves: *Les Idéologies des Independances africaines.* Paris: Maspéro; 1969.

Berque, Jacques: *Le Maghreb entre deux guerres.* Paris: Éd. du Seuil; 1962.

——: *Structures sociales du Haut-Atlas.* Paris: PUF; 1955.

Bing, Geoffrey: *Reap the Whirlwind.* London: MacGibbon & Kee; 1968.

Boudhiba, Abdel Wahed: "La Formation de la nation tunisienne," address delivered at the Conference on Sociology. Royamont, 1965.

Bourguiba, Habib: *Cinq hommes et la France.* Paris: Éd. du Seuil; 1961.

——: *La Tunisie et la France.* Paris: Julliard; 1954.

——: *La Voix du Tunisien.* N.p., February 1931.

Burdeau, Georges: *Le Pouvoir politique de l'État.* Paris: Librairie générale de droit et de jurisprudence; 1942.

Camau, Michel: *La Notion de démocratie dans la pensée des· dirigeants maghrébiens.* Aix-en-Provence: Doctoral dissertation; 1969.

Charnay, Jean-Paul: "Temps social en Islam." Institut de Sociologie de Rabat, May 1967.

Cheverny, Julien: *Éloge du colonialisme.* Paris: Julliard; 1961.

Debbasch, Charles: *La République tunisienne.* Paris: Librairie de droit et de jurisprudence; 1962.

De Jouvenel, Bertrand: *On Power.* Boston: Beacon Press; n.d.

Duverger, Maurice: *De la Dictature.* Paris: Julliard; 1961.

Ellul, Jacques: *Propaganda.* New York: Alfred A. Knopf; 1965.

Emerson, Rupert: *From Empire to Nation.* Cambridge: Harvard University Press; 1960.

Estier, Claude: *L'Égypte en révolution.* Paris: Julliard; 1965.

Evans-Pritchard, Edward E.: *The Sanusi of Cyrenaica.* London: Oxford University Press; 1949.

Fanon, Frantz: *The Wretched of the Earth.* New York: Grove Press; 1965.

Fath, Ahmed Abul: *L'Affaire Nasser.* Paris: n.p.; 1958.

Favrod, Charles-Henri: *Le Poids de l'Afrique.* Paris: Éd. du Seuil; 1958.

Frazer, Sir James George: *The Magical Origin of Kings.* New York: Barnes & Noble; 1968.

Friedrich, Carl J.: *Man and His Government: An Empirical Theory of Politics.* New York: McGraw-Hill; 1963.

Guiart, Jean; *Structure de la chefferie en Mélanésie du Sud.* Paris: Institut d'Ethnologie; 1963.

Halpern, Manfred: *The Politics of Social Change in the Middle East and North Africa.* Princeton: Princeton University Press; 1963.

Lacoste, Yves: *Ibn Khaldoun, naissance de l'histoire, passé du Tiers-Monde.* Paris: Maspéro; 1966.

Lacouture, Jean, and Simonne Lacouture: *Egypt in Transition.* New York: Criterion; n.d.

Lacouture, Simonne: *Cambodge.* Lausanne: Éd. Rencontre; 1963.

Lenin, V. I.: *A Propos a Profession of Faith.* N.p., 1899.

———: *Left-Wing Communism: An Infantile Disorder.* San Francisco: China Books and Periodicals; 1965.

———: *State and Revolution.* San Francisco: China Books and Periodicals; 1965.

Lévi-Strauss, Claude: *The Savage Mind.* Chicago: University of Chicago Press; 1966.

Lewis, Arthur: *Politics in West Africa.* London: Oxford University Press; 1965.

Linton, Ralph: *Nativist Movement.* N.p., n.d.

Lipset, Seymour Martin: *The First New Nation.* New York: Basic Books; 1963.

Malek, Anouar Abdel: *Egypt, Military Society.* New York: Random House; 1968.

Merleau-Ponty, Maurice: *Humanism and Terror.* Boston: Beacon Press; 1969.

Mills, C. Wright, and Gerth, H. H.: *From Max Weber: Essays in Sociology*. New York: Harcourt, Brace & World; 1946.

Moore, Clement H.: *Tunisia Since Independence*. Berkeley: University of California Press; 1965.

Mülhmann, W. E.: *Messianismes révolutionnaires du Tiers-Monde*. Paris: Gallimard; 1968.

Mus, Paul: *Présence du Bouddhisme*. N.p., n.d.

Nasser, Gamal Abdel: *La Philosophie de la Révolution*. Cairo: n.p.; 1954.

Nkrumah, Kwamé: *Le Consciencisme*. Paris: Payot; 1964.

————: *Dark Days in Ghana*. New York: International Publishers; 1969.

————: *Ghana*. New York: Nelson; 1957.

Rossi, Pierre: *La Tunisie de Bourguiba*. Tunis: Éd. Kahia; 1967.

Rouch, Jane: *Ghana*. Lausanne: Éd. Rencontre; 1964.

Rouleau, Éric, et al.: *Israël et les Arabes, le troisième combat*. Paris: Éd. du Seuil; 1967.

Russell, Bertrand: *Power*. New York: W. W. Norton; 1969.

Safran, Nadav: *Egypt in Search of Political Community*. Cambridge: Harvard University Press; 1961.

Touraine, Alain: *Le Mouvement de mai ou le Communisme utopique*. Paris: Éd. du Seuil; 1968.

Vatikiokis, P. J.: *The Egyptian Army in Politics*. Bloomington: Indiana University Press; 1969.

Weber, Max: *The Theory of Social and Economic Organization*. New York: Glencoe Free Press; 1957.

Wittfogel, Karl A.: *Oriental Despotism: A Comparative Study of Total Power*. New Haven: Yale University Press; 1957.

Wright, Richard: *Black Power*. New York: Harper & Row; 1954.

Ziegler, Jean: "Le Pouvoir africain." University of Geneva: Unpublished essay; n.d.

Articles

Abdallah, Ridah: "Le Néo-Destour depuis l'indépendance," *Revue politique et juridique d'Outre Mer*. October–December 1963.

Apter, David: "Nkrumah, Charisma and the Coup," *Daedalus*. Summer 1968.

Baako, Kofi: in *West Africa*. May 13, 1961.

Balandier, Georges: "Messianisme et nationalisme en Afrique Noire," *Cahiers Internationaux de Sociologie*. XIV (1953).

————: in *Le Monde Diplomatique*. April 1966.

Berque, Jacques: "Valeurs de la décolonisation," *Revue de Métaphysique et de Morale*. 1963.

Blanchet, André: in *Le Monde Diplomatique*. August 1960.

Courrières, Yves: in *France-Soir*. December 14, 1968.

Debbasch, Charles: in *Jeune Afrique*. May 5, 1963.
Davidson, Basil: "Un mécanisme de contrôle sociale," *Diogène*. No. 63.
Decraene, Philippe: in *Le Monde*. April 3, 1962.
Edusei, Krobo: in *Monthly Review*. July–August 1968.
Erikson, Erik H.: "In Search of Gandhi," *Daedalus*. Summer 1968.
———: "The Leader as a Child," *The American Scholar*. Autumn 1968.
Fairbank, John: "How To Deal with China," *The New York Review of Books*. February 17, 1966.
Faust, Jean-Jacques: in *Études Méditerranées*. June 1957.
Fitch, Bob, and Oppenheimer, Mary: "Ghana: End of an Illusion," *New York Monthly Review*. July–August 1966.
Friedrich, Carl: "The Pathology of Politics," *Political Quarterly*. January–March 1966.
Gellner, Ernest: "Tribalism and Social Change in North Africa," *The Listener*. July 1964.
Gaudemet, Jean: "Esquisse d'une sociologie historique du pouovir," *Politique revue internationale des doctrines et des institutions*. July–December 1962.
Huntington, Samuel P.: "Political Development and Political Decay," *World Politics*. 1966.
———: "Political Modernization: American vs Europe," *World Politics*. April 1966.
Jaafar, Moncef: in *L'Action*. March 19, 1967.
Kilson, Martin: in *Africa Today*. Vol. XIII, No. 4 (April 1966).
Kouprianov, P.: "La Différenciation sociale parmi les producteurs de cacao ghanéens," *Moscow*. 1967.
Lenin, V. I.: "On the Stalin Question," *Remnin Rinsao*. China: September 13, 1963.
———: in *Izvestia*. April 28, 1918.
Michel, Hubert: "Le FLN et la personnalisation du pouvoir," *Revue française d'étude africaine*. April 1968.
Mabileau, Albert: in *La Revue française de Science politique*. March 1960.
Mus, Paul: "Présence du Bouddhisme," *France-Asie*. 1955.
Perlmutter, Amos: "Seminar on Political Development," Harvard–M.I.T. March 1966.
Pothekin, I.: "Problèmes méthodologiques pour l'étude de la formation des nations au sud Sahara," *Présence africaine*. January 1968.
Shils, Edward: "The Concentration and Dispersion of Charisma," *World Politics*. October 1958.
Tucker, Robert C.: "The Theory of Charismatic Leadership," *Daedalus*. Summer 1968.
Vannsack, Kurt: "Quelques aspects de la littérature khmère," cited by G. Brisse in *Europe-France-Outremer*. October 1968.
Weber, Max: "The Three Types of Legitimate Rule," *Berkeley Publications in Society and Institutions*. Summer 1958.

Willner, Anne-Ruth, and Willner, Dorothy: "Rise and Role of Charismatic Leaders," *Annals of the American Academy of Political and Social Science.* March 1965.

Colloquia

Berque, Jacques, J. P. Charnay, et al.: *De l'impérialisme à la décolonisation.* Paris: Éd. de Minuit; 1965.

Chevallier, J. J., et al.: *Le Pouvoir,* Vols. I and II. Paris: PUF; 1956–7.

Hamon, Léo, Albert Mabileau, et al.: *La Personnalisation de pouvoir.* Dijon: PUF; 1964.

Rémond, René, et al.: *La Démocratie à refaire.* Colloque France-Forum, 1963.

Conférence de Rhodes: *La Démocratie dans les nouveaux États.* 1959.

Berlin Seminar on heroic leadership. 1960.

Tuxedo Seminar on charismatic power. 1967.

General References

Ardant, Gabriel: *La Tunisie d'aujourd'hui et de demain.* Paris: Calmann-Lévy; 1961.

Arendt, Hannah: *The Orginis of Totalitarianism.* New York: Harcourt, Brace & World; 1968.

Aron, Raymond: *L'Homme contre les tyrans.* Paris: Gallimard; 1946

————: *Introduction to the Philosophy of History.* Boston: Beacon Press; 1961.

————: *Main Currents of Sociological Thought.* Boston: Beacon Press; 1965–9.

Balandier, Georges: *Ambiguous Africa: Cultures in Collision.* New York: Pantheon; 1965.

Bankole, Timothy: *Kwamé Nkrumah.* London: Allen & Unwin; 1955.

Berque, Jacques: *The Arabs: Their History and Future.* New York: Praeger; 1964.

————: *Despossession du Monde.* Paris: Éd. du Seuil; 1964.

————: *L'Égypte, impérialisme et révolution.* Paris: Gallimard; 1967.

Burdeau, Georges: *La Démocratie.* Paris: Éd. du Seuil; 1966.

Duverger, Maurice: *La Démocratie sans le peuple.* Paris: Éd. du Seuil; 1968.

————: *Les Régimes politiques.* Paris: Presses universitaires de France; 1960.

Duvignaud, Jean: *Tunisie.* Lausanne: Éd. Rencontre; 1964.

Erikson, Erik H.: *Young Man Luther.* New York: W. W. Norton; 1958.

Freund, Julien: *L'Essence du politique.* Paris: Éd. Sirey; 1965.

Hauriou, André: *Droit constitutionnel étranger.* Paris: n.p.; 1962.

Julien, Charles-André: *L'Afrique du Nord en marche.* Paris: Julliard; 1952.

Kauffman, Robert: *Millénarisme et acculturation.* Brussels: n.p.; 1954.

Lanternari, Vittorio: *Religions of the Oppressed: A Study of Modern Messianic Cults.* New York: Alfred A. Knopf; 1963.

Little, Tom: *Modern Egypt.* New York: Praeger; 1967.

Mendé, Tibor: *Conversations avec Nehru.* Paris: Le Seuil; 1956.

Micaud, Charles, et al.: *Tunisia: The Politics of Modernization.* New York: Praeger; 1964.

Ortega y Gasset, José: *The Revolt of the Masses.* New York: W. W. Norton; 1967.

Raymond, André: *Tunisie.* Paris: PUF; 1961.

Scheler, Max: *Ressentiment.* New York: Glencoe Free Press; 1961.

Schumpeter, Joseph: *Capitalism, Socialism, and Democracy.* New York: Harper and Row; 1950.

Schweinitz, Karl de: *Industrialization and Democracy.* New York: Glencoe Free Press; 1964.

Schafer, Boyd C.: *Nationalism: Myth and Reality.* New York: Harcourt, Brace & World; 1955.

Sorel, Georges: *Reflections on Violence.* New York: MacMillian; 1961.

Talmon, J. L.: *Political Messianism: The Romantic Phase.* London: n.p.; 1960.

Van Mook, H. J.: *The Stakes of Democracy in South East Africa.* New York: W. W. Norton; 1950.

Weber, Max: *Max Weber on Charisma and Institution Building.* Chicago: University of Chicago Press; 1968.

Weil, Eric: *Hegel et l'état.* Paris: Librairie philosophique Vrin; 1950.

Index

INDEX

v

National Union, the, 117
nationalism, 53, 68, 97, 108, 138,
139, 140, 141, 142, 147, 150, 156,
157, 204–5, 208, 209, 261, 281;
Egyptian, 84; revolutionary, 109
nationalization, 109, 110, 111, 112,
149
"nativism," 48–9; see also Linton,
Ralph; Mülhmann, W. E.
neocolonialism, 14, 51, 52
Néo-Destour party, 59, 118, 137, 140,
142, 143, 144, 145, 146, 147, 148,
149, 151, 156, 158, 162, 164, 166,
173, 183, 187, 194, 247, 280
Nigeria, 28, 34, 58, 61
Nkrumah, Kwamé, 20, 21, 23, 25, 27,
30, 40, 42, 53, 58, 60, 61, 66, 70,
119, 120, 126, 127, 236–75, 283,
285, 292, 294; philosophy of, 236,
253–5
Nyéréré, Julius, 25, 43, 67, 239, 284,
287

operational concentration, 6, 9,
12–13, 27, 30, 32, 41–2, 56, 57,
59, 81, 82, 83, 85, 98, 103, 106,
107, 113, 114, 126, 132, 237, 239,
279, 284; definition, 9–10;
Jouvenal on, 9; Rousseau on, 10
Organization for African Unity, 236
Otto, Rudolph, 15, 16, 17

Palestine War, the, 88
pandemia, 32–47
party systems, 12, 17, 19, 26, 27, 59,
60, 63, 105, 106, 117, 118, 144,
145, 172, 207, 270, 271
Passeron, Jean-Claude, 4
paternalism, 69, 274
peasantry, 268, 270, 275
personification, 14, 22, 23, 24, 25,
26, 32–47, 56–63, 81, 86, 99, 113,
125, 127, 128, 129–35, 150–51,
153, 162–70, 173, 174, 181, 188,
194, 196, 197, 200, 204–5, 208,
210, 211–12, 215, 224, 226, 227,
228–32, 242, 249, 262–66, 269,

273–5, 279, 284–6, 287–9, 290,
291–2, 293, 294; in the West, 3;
in the Third World, 3; Jouvenal
on, 6; Hassan II on, 7; Touré on,
7; in Arab societies, 11; as
incarnation, 13–31; and identity,
30–1, 32, 39, 42–3, 46; see also
hero-leader; leader
politics: dramatization of, 13, 30–1;
art of, 98
power: theatrical display of, 3, 11,
20–1, 30–1, 42–3, 53, 123–4, 181,
204, 206, 209–20, 223, 238, 242,
251, 253, 293; definition of, 4;
symbols of, 4, 25, 140–50, 191–2,
205, 249; absence of, 4, 5;
crystallization of, 6; Jouvenal on,
6; absolute, 9, 33–4, 38, 81, 137,
242, 251, 287; symbolization of,
10; mechanisms of, 12, 19, 26–7;
Friedrich on, 14; Moore on, 14;
and charisma, 14–16;
secularization of, 21, 58;
"personalized," 24–5, 30, 46, 53,
57–8, 60–1, 64–6, 69, 92, 123, 147,
169, 171, 172, 173, 174, 175, 194,
199–200, 207, 228, 229, 234, 241,
279, 281–2, 284–5, 288, 289, 292,
294; individualization of, 30;
impulse to, 34; dynastic, 35; postcolonial, 36–7, 39, 40;
simplification of, 43; centralized,
45; rites of, 54; misuse of, 57; and
decision-making, 67; dilution of,
73; and the masses, 119;
community of, 127; transition to,
148; structure and style of, 150–62,
249; "creative," 153; solidification,
162; instruments of, 170;
monopoly of, 221; see also
counterpower; operational
concentration; personification
power, mythical incarnation of: see
mythical incarnation
proletariat, 45–7, 268, 275

raïs, 11, 24, 29, 43, 70, 74, 103, 113,